Also by Kenneth C. Davis

Don't Know Much About History

Don't Know Much About Geography

Don't Know Much About the Civil War

Don't Know Much About the Bible

Don't Know Much About the Universe

Don't Know Much About Mythology

Don't Know Much About Anything

Two-Bit Culture: The Paperbacking of America

Smithsonian Books

Collins
An Imprint of HarperCollinsPublishers

America's Hidden History

❦

*Untold Tales of the First
Pilgrims, Fighting Women,
and Forgotten Founders Who
Shaped a Nation*

❧

Kenneth C. Davis

Designed by Nicola Ferguson

ISBN 978-0-06-111818-0

BOOK CLUB EDITION

In grateful memory of my father, Richard McShane Davis, for those childhood camping trips to Lake Champlain, Valley Forge, and Gettysburg that sparked my abiding passion for history.

Contents

Introduction

If you are of a certain age, the name Flip Wilson may mean something to you. After all, comedian Flip Wilson made history. During the early 1970s, the late comic became one of the first African American stars to host a hit television series. With his prime-time variety hour, Wilson helped put some of the color in color TV. But Flip Wilson might not be the first name you would expect to find in a book about America's beginnings.

Here it is, though, because one of his signature routines was a sketch in which Wilson, bewigged, bejeweled, and fabulously bedecked in elaborate drag, played Spain's Queen Isabella. The queen is pondering whether to give Columbus what he wants when the Italian sailor whispers something into the regal ear. Sashaying across the stage, Wilson's Isabella exults in a triumphant falsetto, "Chris gonna find Ray Charles!"

And that, my friends, is what Columbus was really looking for when he sailed from Spain in 1492.

I relate this story because my historical sensibilities have admittedly been shaped by bits from Flip Wilson, *Laugh-In*, Mr. Peabody's Wayback Machine, and *Mad* magazine, alongside such masterly historians as William Manchester, David McCullough, Doris Kearns Goodwin, and Thomas Fleming—and because I have always believed that history should be much more fun than most Americans believe it is. But fun doesn't have to mean frivolous.

Take "Isabella's Pigs," the opening chapter of this book. If it were a movie, Johnny Depp might get the lead. If it were a video game, parents wouldn't let their kids play. Spotlighting the Spanish conquest of Florida long before Jamestown and Plymouth were settled, it includes pirates, shipwrecks, lost treasure, cannibalism, torture, and numerous massacres, all topped off by feuding monarchs who put the current crop of royals to shame. And pigs.

It was, after all, the real Isabella who told Columbus to pack some pigs on his second voyage. Those pigs kept Spain's conquistadors alive as they laid waste to the Americas—and the pigs also possibly introduced some of the diseases that wiped out whole native nations. So Isabella's pigs may have played a leading role in the accidental discovery and conquest of the Americas and the decimation of millions of people—certainly one of history's great unintended consequences.

Another of those world-changing accidents came when a brash, untrained young militia officer in colonial America led his men on a murderous raid that set off the first "world war" in history. That ambitious twentysomething was George Washington, and his first brush with battle was nearly his last. Young Washington's deadly miscalculation not only altered history but also clearly helped forge the man who led America through the Revolution and became its first president.

It is those unintended consequences, particularly the ones that were overlooked or sanitized in gilding America's great national myth—Columbus as intrepid discoverer, Pilgrims and Indians at a joyous feast, the Continental Congress as a colonial-era Kiwanis club—that lie at the heart of this book. The stories that unfold in these six chapters, which span a period from the Spanish arrival in America to George Washington's inauguration in 1789, were selected because each plays a central part in shaping the nation's destiny and character and each, in some way, belies that American myth.

For the most part, these are tales that the textbooks left out. The picture they present is largely at odds with the safe, sterile version still provided by schoolbooks, teachers, and Hollywood. Those tidy tableaus are the ones preferred by politicians, preachers, and pundits who cling to the simple, whitewashed portrait of America's past. If any of the harsher realities found their way into our schoolbooks, they were boiled down to a single bloodless line of text, or worse, to a monotonous list of dates and documents. In these stories, I've tried to flesh out that picture and set the record straight by unearthing some of the buried pieces of America's "hidden history."

Some of these episodes were chosen because they reveal unfamiliar details about familiar events, such as the battles of Lexington and Concord. And some uncover the unknown side of very well-known people, as in the rise and fall of a young American hero whose ego and greed wreaked havoc, turning him into America's greatest villain: Benedict Arnold. Others were chosen because they include "fulcrum moments" in which America's future was tipped in a new direction. Such a shift came when a British assassination plot aimed at a trio of Boston's leading patriots went awry. Had the plan—detailed in "Warren's Toga"—succeeded, the course of the Revolution might have been completely altered.

These stories also highlight what novelist Graham Greene called "the human factor." Textbook writers rarely explore such human motivations as ambition and avarice, loyalty and betrayal, duty and honor, courage and cowardice. They prefer to leave pride and prejudice to the novelists. But these stories fascinate because they plumb the flesh and blood behind the marble statues or the faces on our currency. The three Puritan women depicted in "Hannah's Escape" never made it onto any of our money. But the courage and resilience they displayed speaks loudly of a harsh colonial environment far removed from the traditional Thanksgiving Day idyll.

Most importantly, all of these stories continue to reverberate in our world. And that is the real point of telling them—and of teaching history—in the first place. We have been conditioned, by television and now the Internet, to look at history in short bursts. These disjointed bits and pieces rarely seem to have much connection to the present. But of course they do; as Shakespeare put it, "The past is prologue."

The great conflict engulfing the Western world and elements of Islam is the most immediate and pressing example of history's long, slow ripples. It returns us to Isabella's triumphant "Chris gonna find Ray Charles." To most Americans, 1492 means only one thing: "Columbus sailed the ocean blue." But that is only one part of the story of that year. A dynamic, extraordinary woman in a man's world, Queen Isabella also set in motion two other events in 1492 that remain fulcrum moments for our times: the forced conversion or exile of Spain's Jews and the culmination of *la reconquista*—the Reconquest—in which Spanish armies defeated the last remnant of the Moors, the North African Muslims who had invaded and then occupied the Iberian peninsula for centuries.

So why does that matter? The bombers who struck Madrid's commuter railroads with murderous force on March 11, 2004, saw their attack as long-deferred vengeance for 1492. Their hope for an Islamic Reconquest of Spain was not some radical religious fantasy but has a long, bitter history. It animates their jihad. And yes, some people's historical memories are much longer than others.

History's ripples also wash over current American political debates. At a time when Hispanic Americans constitute the fastest-growing demographic group in America, the country found itself in the midst of a white-hot controversy that mushroomed over "broken borders," immigration reform, and establishing English as America's "official language." In fact, Spanish has been spoken in a good part of America far longer than English has. No, that is not an argument for or against any official language in America. It is simply a historical reality, much overlooked.

The proverbial eight-hundred-pound gorilla sitting squarely in the center of this story is religion, or more precisely, centuries of blood shed over beliefs. The degree to which religious conflict has driven America's history is a central theme threading through this book. Several of its stories illuminate one of history's most fundamental lessons: people fear what they don't understand—or what is different. That fear moves in tandem with the arrogant superiority that comes from the notion of possessing the exclusive "truth." This volatile mixture of fearful ignorance and righteous certitude allows one group to demonize and dehumanize another. And once you have accomplished that, it is much easier to hang people as heretics, burn them at the stake—or in ovens—and fly jetliners into their buildings. Could any story be more relevant to our times?

What ultimately ties all of these stories together is one of history's pivotal themes—getting and keeping power. Whether it is the power of faith or force, the power of ideas or ideology, the power of propaganda or persuasion, these stories reveal how power has changed hands in American history. And all too often, this American history, to quote Thomas Hobbes from a slightly different context, is a tale of "continual fear and danger of violent death."

This hidden history of America's beginnings reveals a drama that is often appalling and far from noble or tidy, but also consistently remarkable. Like actual childbirth, the birth of America was messy, bloody, painful, and sometimes tragic. Yet it remains rather miraculous. As this book tracks America's sometimes tortured development, it also recognizes the halting steps made toward the dawn of a new era in human history—an era predicated on that remarkable and radical concept that each of us is entitled to "life, liberty and the pursuit of happiness."

And maybe Ray Charles too.

—Kenneth C. Davis
Dorset, Vermont
September 2007

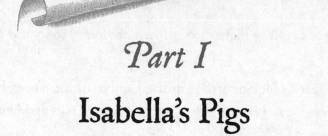

Part I
Isabella's Pigs

1469   Isabella of Castile and Ferdinand of Aragon are married.

1492   The Reconquest (*la reconquista*) forces the last Moors out of Spain.

As part of a revived Inquisition, all Jews are forced to convert or leave Spain.

Christopher Columbus arrives in the Caribbean; he names Hispaniola (modern-day Haiti and the Dominican Republic) and founds the settlement of La Navidad.

1497   John Cabot, an Italian sailing for England, sights North America, probably around Newfoundland, and claims the territory for England.

1501   Amerigo Vespucci, sailing for Portugal, reaches the South American coast. Upon his return, he writes to his patron, Lorenzo de' Medici, that he has voyaged to a "new world." A mapmaker attaches Amerigo's name to the New World.

1509   Henry VIII is crowned king of England and marries Catherine of Aragon, daughter of Ferdinand and Isabella.

1516   King Ferdinand dies; Charles I, grandson of Ferdinand and Isabella, inherits the Spanish throne.

1528   Pánfilo de Narváez, accompanied by Cabeza de Vaca, leads a Spanish attempt to conquer Florida.

1531   King Henry VIII divorces Catherine of Aragon to marry Anne Boleyn. In 1534, the Act of Supremacy declares the king to be the head of the Church of England, completing the break with Rome.

1536   John Calvin's *Institutes of the Christian Religion* is published, expanding the Protestant Reformation.

1539-1543   Hernando de Soto leads a Spanish army through the Southeast; de Soto dies on the banks of the Mississippi on May 21, 1542.

1553   Mary I, daughter of Henry VIII and his first wife, Catherine of Aragon, becomes queen of England. In 1554, she marries Philip II, the future king of Spain, but dies childless in 1558.

1556   Philip II becomes king of Spain.

1558   Queen Elizabeth I succeeds her half sister Queen Mary.

1564   French Huguenots establish Fort Caroline near the St. Johns River in Florida.

1565   St. Augustine, Florida, founded.

Fort Caroline massacre.

1588   The Spanish Armada is defeated by a smaller British fleet.

I have established warm friendship with the king of that land, so much so that he was proud to call me and treat me as a brother. But even should he change his attitude and attack the men of La Navidad, he and his people know nothing about arms and go naked, as I have already said; they are the most timorous people in the world.

—Christopher Columbus,
letter written as he returned to Spain (1493)

Upon seeing the disaster we had suffered, our misery and distress, the Indians sat down with us and all began to weep out of compassion for our misfortune, and for more than half an hour they wept so loud and so sincerely that it could be heard far away.

—Alvar Núñez Cabeza de Vaca (1555)

The pigs De Soto brought from Cuba may have been descendants of the pigs Queen Isabella enjoined Columbus to take with him on his second voyage.

—Charles Hudson,
Knights of Spain, Warriors of the Sun (1997)

St. Augustine, Florida—September 1565

I T WAS A STORM-DARK NIGHT in late summer as Admiral Pedro Menéndez pressed his army of five hundred infantrymen up Florida's Atlantic Coast with a Crusader's fervor. Lashed by hurricane winds and sheets of driving rain, these sixteenth-century Spanish shock troops slogged through the tropical downpour in their heavy armor, carrying pikes, broadswords, and harquebuses, primitive, front-loading muskets that had been used with devastating effect by the conquistador armies of Cortés and Pizarro in Mexico and Peru. Each man also carried a twelve-pound sack of bread and a bottle of wine.

Guided by local Timucuan tribesmen, the Spanish assault force had spent two difficult days negotiating the treacherous thirty-eight-mile trek from St. Augustine, their recently established settlement further down the coast. Slowed by knee-deep muck that sucked at their boots, they had been forced to cross rain-swollen rivers, home to the man-eating monsters and flying fish of legend. Wet, tired, and miserable, they were far from home in a land that had completely swallowed two previous Spanish armies—conquistadors who themselves had been conquered by tropical diseases, starvation, and hostile native warriors.

But Admiral Menéndez was undeterred. Far more at home at sea than leading infantry, Admiral Menéndez drove his men with such ferocity because he was gambling—throwing the dice that he could reach the enemy before they struck him. His objective was the French settlement of Fort Caroline, France's first foothold in the Americas, located near present-day Jacksonville, on what the French called the River of May. On this pitch-black night, the small, triangular, wood-palisaded fort was occupied by a few hundred men, women, and children. They were France's first colonists in the New World—and the true first pilgrims in America.

Attacking before dawn on September 20, 1565, with the frenzy of holy warriors, the Spanish easily overwhelmed Fort Caroline. With information provided by a French turncoat, the battle-tested Spanish soldiers used ladders to quickly mount the fort's wooden walls. Inside the settlement, the sleeping Frenchmen—most of them farmers or laborers rather than soldiers—were caught off guard, convinced that no attack could possibly come in the midst of such a terrible storm. But they had fatally miscalculated. The veteran Spanish harquebusiers swept in on the nightshirt-clad or naked Frenchmen, who leapt from their beds and grabbed futilely for weapons. Their attempts to mount any real defense were hopeless. The battle lasted less than an hour.

Although some of the French defenders managed to escape the carnage, 132 soldiers and civilians were killed in the fighting in the small fort. The Spanish suffered no losses and only a single man was wounded. The forty or so French survivors fortunate enough to reach the safety of some boats anchored nearby watched helplessly as Spanish soldiers flicked the eyeballs of the French dead with the points of their daggers.[1] The shaken survivors then scuttled one of their boats and sailed the other two back to France.

The handful of Fort Caroline's defenders who were not lucky enough to escape were quickly rounded up by the Spanish. About fifty women and children were also taken captive, later to be shipped to Puerto Rico. The men were hanged without hesitation. Above the dead men, the victorious Admiral Menéndez placed a sign reading, "I do this, not as to Frenchmen, but as to Lutherans." Renaming the captured French settlement San Mateo (St. Matthew) and its river San Juan (St. John), Menéndez later reported to Spain's King Philip II that he had taken care of the "evil Lutheran sect."

A priest who accompanied the Spanish army as chaplain took special pleasure in recording the large number of "Lutheran" Bibles they had captured and destroyed, adding, "The greatest victory which I feel for this event is the victory which Our Lord has given us so that his Holy Gospel may be planted and preached in these parts." Of Admiral Menéndez, the chaplain wrote, "The fire and desire he has to serve Our Lord in throwing down and destroying this Lutheran sect, enemy of our Holy Catholic Faith, does not allow him to feel weary in his work."

Victims of the political and religious wars raging across Europe, the ill-fated inhabitants of Fort Caroline were not "Lutherans" at all. For the most part, they were Huguenots, French Protestants who followed the teachings of John Calvin, the French-born Protestant theologian. Having built and settled Fort Caroline more than a year earlier, these French colonists had been left all but defenseless by the questionable decision of one of their leaders, Jean Ribault. An experienced sea captain, Ribault had sailed off from Fort Caroline a few days earlier with between five hundred and six hundred men aboard his flagship, the *Trinité*, and three other galleons. Against the advice of René de Laudonnière, his fellow commander at Fort Caroline, Ribault planned to strike the new Spanish settlement before the recently arrived Spanish could establish their defenses. Unfortunately for Ribault and his shipmates, as well as those left behind at Fort Caroline, the hurricane that slowed Admiral Menéndez and his army also ripped into the small French flotilla, scattering and grounding most of the ships, sending hundreds of men to their deaths. According to René de Laudonnière, it was "the worst weather ever seen on this coast."[2]

Unaware that Fort Caroline had fallen, groups of French survivors of the storm-savaged fleet came ashore near present-day Daytona Beach and Cape Canaveral. Trudging north, they were spotted by Indians, who alerted Menéndez. The bedraggled Frenchmen were met and captured by Spanish troops at a coastal inlet about seventeen miles south of St. Augustine on September 29, 1565.

Expecting to be imprisoned or perhaps ransomed, the exhausted and hungry Frenchmen surrendered without a fight. They were ferried across the inlet to a group of dunes, where they were fed what proved to be a last meal. At the admiral's orders, between 111 and 200 of the French captives—documents differ on the exact number—were put to death. In his own report to King Philip, Admiral Menéndez wrote matter-of-factly, if not proudly, "I caused their hands to be tied behind them, and put them to the knife."[3] Sixteen of the company were allowed to live—self-professed Catholics who were spared at the behest of the priest, who reported, "All the rest died for being Lutherans and against our Holy Catholic Faith."

Twelve days later, on October 11, the remaining French survivors, including Captain Jean Ribault, whose *Trinité* had been beached further south, straggled north to the same inlet. Met by Menéndez and ignorant of their countrymen's fate, they too surrendered to the Spanish. A handful escaped in the night, but on the next morning, 134 more French captives were ferried across the same inlet and executed; once again, approximately a dozen were spared. Those who escaped death had either professed to be Catholic, hastily agreed to convert, or possessed some skills that Admiral Menéndez thought might be useful in settling St. Augustine—the first permanent European set-tlement in the future United States, born and baptized in a religious bloodbath.

Although Jean Ribault offered Menéndez a large ransom to secure his safe return to France, the Spanish admiral refused. Ribault suf-fered the same fate as his men. Following Ribault's execution, the French leader's beard and a piece of his skin were sent to King Philip II. His head was cut into four parts, set on pikes, and displayed in St. Augustine.[4] Reporting back to King Philip II, Admiral Menéndez wrote, "I think it great good fortune that this man be dead, for the King of France could accomplish more with him and fifty thousand ducats than with other men and five hundred thousand ducats; and he could do more in one year, than another in ten."[5]

JUST SOUTH OF modern St. Augustine, hidden off the well-worn tourist path of T-shirt stands, sprawling condos, and beachfront hotels, stands a rather inconspicuous national monument called Fort Matan-zas. Accessible by a short ferry ride across a small river, it was built by the Spanish in 1742 to protect St. Augustine from surprise attack. Fort Matanzas is more a large guardhouse than full-fledged fort. The modest structure, about fifty feet long on each side, was constructed of coquina, a local stone formed from clamshells and quarried from a nearby island. Tourists who come across the simple tower certainly find it far less impressive than the formidable Castillo de San Marco, the star-shaped citadel that dominates St. Augustine's historic down-town.

Unlike other Spanish sites in Florida named for Catholic saints or holy days, the fort's name comes from the Spanish word *matanzas,* meaning "killings" or "slaughters." Fort Matanzas stands near the site of the grim massacre of the few hundred luckless French soldiers in an undeclared war of religious animosity. This largely unremarked atrocity from America's distant past was one small piece of the much larger struggle for the future of North America among contending European powers.

The notion of Spaniards fighting Frenchmen in Florida four decades before England established its first permanent settlement in America, and half a century before the Pilgrims sailed, is an unexpected notion to those accustomed to the familiar legends of Jamestown and Plymouth. The fact that these first settlers were Huguenots dispatched to establish a colony in America in 1564, motivated by having suffered the same sort of religious persecution that later drove the Pilgrims from England, may be equally surprising. That the mass execution of hundreds of French Protestants by Spanish Catholics could be mostly overlooked may be more surprising still. But this salient story speaks volumes about the rapacious quest for new territory and brutal religious warfare that characterized the European arrival in the future America.

That history begins with the Spanish. It commences not with Columbus sailing in 1492 but in 1469, the year in which the teenage cousins Ferdinand of Aragon and Isabella of Castile were married. Isabella and Ferdinand were a remarkable couple whose successes in uniting several fractious small kingdoms into a nation, eliminating the last vestiges of Islamic power in Iberia, revving up the Inquisition, and setting Spain on a path of world domination were extraordinary by any measure. Far from bit players in the American drama, they changed the course of history with their vision of a united, Christian Spain with a vast overseas empire. In chronicling the rise of that empire, Hugh

Thomas wrote, "The work of Isabel in the first ten years of her time as both heiress and Queen of Castile was . . . remarkable by any standard. *No woman in history has exceeded her achievement.*"[6]

Born in April 1451, Isabella was the daughter of Castile's King Juan. She came of age in a Europe that had one foot in the medieval age of knights and castles and one in the blooming Renaissance. Gutenberg's first books were printed two years after Isabella's birth, and his first Bible was produced in 1456. Constantinople had fallen to the Islamic Ottoman Turks in 1453, sending many Greek scholars fleeing to Italy, where the classics were rediscovered, accelerating the rise of the Renaissance. The loss of Constantinople, a key crossroads in the Silk Road trade between Europe and Asia, forced Europeans to look for sea routes to the East, as the Ottomans imposed stiff tariffs on the Asian caravans bound for Europe.

The modern nation called Spain did not yet exist at Isabella's birth. Instead, several small, warring kingdoms dominated the Iberian peninsula, with Castile among the most powerful of these. Isabella's adolescence came during a time of tremendous intrigue and infighting, both within Castile and among the other Spanish kingdoms, as well as the emerging nations of Europe. These struggles were set, in turn, against the backdrop of the Moorish occupation of Granada, the southernmost region of Spain and the last bastion of Islamic power on the Iberian peninsula. Beginning in 711, the Moors—Arab and African Muslims from North Africa—had dominated Iberia, creating a culture rich in art, architecture, literature, and learning. For more than seven hundred years, the Moors had lived through shifting periods of coexistence and conflict with Christian Spain. With the rise of the Ottoman Empire threatening Europe from the east, the great conflict with Islam and the desire to recapture Jerusalem only grew more intense. In Isabella's century, there was only one goal, one holy quest—*la reconquista* and the removal of the "heathens."

Following her father's death, the convent-educated Isabella was brought to the court of her older half brother, King Enrique IV, a notorious fop whose open homosexuality was noted by the court scribes. His inability to produce any offspring had inspired the derisive nickname "Enrique el Impotente." Civil war among competing groups of nobles who questioned Enrique's legitimacy as king and the likely poisoning of Isabella's younger brother Alfonso by Enrique's allies engulfed Castile in deadly intrigues. Striking a compromise, Isabella and her supporters acknowledged that Enrique was indeed the rightful king, and she was named heir to Castile's throne. Enrique attempted to arrange a marriage for her. But the remarkably strong-willed teenager fended off the suitors presented by her half brother, including the future Richard III of England. Casting about for a husband herself, Isabella settled on a match with her second cousin Ferdinand, heir to the throne of Aragon, one of Spain's other chief kingdoms.

Although not as well educated as his intended, Ferdinand was said to possess the quality that inspires devotion. One report to Isabella said: "He has so singular a grace that everyone who talks to him wants to serve him." Younger than Isabella by a year, the prince had already led his father's troops in combat. But the battlefield was not the only scene of his conquests. Before the marriage agreement with Isabella was concluded, he had fathered children with two different women; in modern tabloid parlance, he'd be headlined a "hunk." In fact, the pair would have been *People* magazine's dream royals. The tall, blue-eyed beauty Isabella and the muscular Ferdinand would have dwarfed most contemporary celebrity couples.

In 1469, the eighteen-year-old Isabella wed seventeen-year-old Ferdinand, with an assist from a papal dispensation that allowed the marriage despite their close blood ties. Among those officiating was Spain's cardinal, Rodrigo Borgia, the most infamous of that notorious family. It was Rodrigo Borgia who had arranged for the bull of dispensation that enabled the cousins to marry, and he was rewarded with a dukedom for his eldest son. Father of Lucrezia Borgia, Rodrigo Borgia was elevated as Pope Alexander VI in fateful 1492 and later bestowed upon Ferdinand and Isabella the title *los Reyes Católicos*, the "Catholic monarchs" of Spain, in 1496.

Theirs was a remarkable marriage of political convenience that became a richly successful partnership as well as a torrid love match. In his will, Ferdinand directed that he be buried with his queen: "We were united by marriage and by a unique love in life. Let us not be parted in death." The two monarchs kept their individual crowns, but each was named consort of the other's kingdom. As part of their unprecedented prenuptial agreement, Isabella held equal authority—an astonishing role for a woman in those times. Their shared power was expressed in an official motto, *Tanto monta, monta tanto—Isabel como Fernando* ("It comes to the same thing—Isabel is the same as Fernando").

Supported by Spain's powerful clerics, Ferdinand and Isabella aimed to unite Spain and took the field—both of them literally went off to battle—with Isabella proving her mettle as both a military organizer and strategist. When an enemy was defeated, she personally rode out to accept the surrender. Having subdued Spain's contentious nobles, Ferdinand and Isabella moved on to their crowning accomplishment. In 1491, with an army that bridged the medieval world of armored knights and lancers with the new era's first artillery weapons, they surrounded Granada, Islam's last Iberian bastion. A force of some eighty thousand men, including ten thousand knights, began the siege that would complete *la reconquista.*

But ridding Spain of the Moors was only part of their holy war. In their quest for a kingdom free of heathens and heresy, the *Reyes Católicos* viewed Jews and other "unbelievers" as another threat. They brought the Inquisition—known as the Holy Office—back to Spain in 1478 and saw it rise to new heights of power and cruelty. Isabella and Fernando were urged on by prominent clerics who claimed that many of the Spanish Jews who had converted—conversos—secretly continued practicing their religion, which in the Church's view posed a grave threat to Christianity. The notorious court that imprisoned, tortured, or killed those suspected of heresy was led by Tomás de Torquemada, whose name became synonymous with the Spanish Inquisition's worst excesses. A descendant of a converso himself, Torquemada joined the Dominicans and acquired a reputation for zealously wearing the penitent's hair shirt and sleeping on rough planks. After Isabella took the throne, Torquemada served as her confessor and made her pledge to devote herself to "the liquidation of heresy."

During the next few years, some thirteen thousand people were found guilty of carrying out secret Jewish practices, often making their confessions after torture. During this time, at least two thousand people were executed for heresy by the Inquisition. Thousands of others were imprisoned or had their property confiscated. In 1492, Torquemada wrote the royal edict that ordered the Jews from Spain unless they were baptized. The number of Jews expelled from Spain is uncertain, and old estimates ranged from two hundred thousand to as many as eight hundred thousand. However, contemporary historians such as Henry Kamen argue convincingly that such numbers were exaggerated by centuries of English propaganda aimed at Spain and

Roman Catholicism—the so-called Black Legend—and he suggests a much lower number, perhaps forty thousand of the approximately eighty thousand Jews in Spain at the time.[7] Some of those expelled Jews found a welcome, although an expensive one, in Rome, where Pope Alexander VI willingly received them as long as they could meet his price for sanctioning their conversions.

To Isabella, the Inquisition was a useful political tool as well, consolidating the power of the Catholic monarchs. As James Reston Jr. wrote in *Dogs of God,* "Of particular interest to Ferdinand was the provision in the pope's bull which authorized the crown to fine the culprits and confiscate their holdings, and to deposit the sizable proceeds into the hard-pressed royal treasury."[8] In other words, the Spanish Inquisition financed the war against the Moors. It would also help underwrite the Age of Exploration and Spain's New World empire.

Late in 1491, the Moorish leader, Boabdil, agreed at last to terms of surrender of the besieged Granada. On January 1, 1492, the last Muslim city in western Europe surrendered, and five days later, the triumphant monarchs entered the city. Throughout Europe, the Spanish victory over the Muslims in Spain was celebrated. In Rome, Cardinal Borgia staged a bullfight—a novelty to Romans—and Pope Innocent celebrated an outdoor mass to honor the conquest of the Moors.

This epochal triumph also opened the door for Columbus. Convinced that the risks were small and the potential returns great, Isabella approved the Columbus expedition. And what about the legendary pawning of her jewels to pay for the trip? Already in debt to finance the war against the Muslims, Isabella did offer to pledge some of her royal jewels to fund the undertaking, which actually cost less than the wedding of Isabella's daughter Catherine to the prince of England. But with some of her necklaces and crowns already in one bank to secure an earlier loan, there was no need. Her bankers saw a wise investment as well, and put up most of the cash. On April 17, 1492, the Spanish monarchs agreed to terms with the Genoese sailor. The document named Columbus "Admiral of the Ocean Sea" and said he would be governor-general of all territory he discovered. He would be named a don—a title with certain privileges. Columbus would also have a right to 10 percent of *everything* he found—gold, jewels, spices, land—in the new territories.

Columbus sailed out of Palos, Spain, in August 1492. The rest—as they say—is history.

> These islands are richer than I yet know or can say. . . . In this island of Hispaniola, I have taken possession of a large town which is most conveniently situated for the goldfields and the communications with the mainland both here, and there in the territories of the Grand Khan, with which there will be a very profitable trade. I have named this town Villa de Navidad and have built a fort there. Its fortifications will by now be finished and I have left sufficient men to complete them. They have arms, artillery and provisions for more than a year. . . .
>
> In fact, the men that I have left there would be enough to destroy the whole land, and the island holds no dangers for them so long as they maintain discipline.[9]
>
> —CHRISTOPHER COLUMBUS,
> *letter written as he returned to Spain (1493)*

For his second voyage, begun in June 1493, the admiral was provided with many more ships, as well as some fifteen hundred settlers, including a full complement of priests, royal accountants, and an unspecified number of women. Queen Isabella also made a very significant suggestion. Understanding the old adage that an army "fights on its stomach," Isabella is credited as the one who encouraged Columbus to take some pigs aboard ship, along with dogs and horses.

Once introduced to the New World, Isabella's pigs became one of the staples of Spanish armies and colonists. Able to forage for themselves and remarkably fertile, the pigs provided a valuable source of easily transported and self-perpetuating protein. For the conquistador on the move, the pigs offered many advantages, according to historian Charles Hudson: "Pigs are the most efficient food producers that can be herded. . . . A pig's carcass yields 65 percent to 80 percent dressed meat. . . . A four-ounce serving of pork yields 402 calories. . . . Pigs are unusually fecund. A female as young as nine months may become pregnant, and she can give birth to as many as twelve in a litter. . . . Thus a herd of pigs can increase prodigiously within a few years."

Along with the side benefit of producing fertilizer in the form of manure, these pigs offered one other very estimable advantage to Spanish Christians, as Hudson points out. "They ate pork not only for sustenance but also to remove any suspicion that they were Jews."[10]

Perhaps the greatest unintended consequence of this mobile mess hall may have been the waves of disease that are credited with wiping out so much of the native American populace the Spanish encountered. In 1491, Charles C. Mann fingers the pigs, the "ambulatory meat locker," as the possible culprit behind the deadly epidemics that swept the New World's original inhabitants. "Swine, mainstays of European agriculture, transmit anthrax, brucellosis, leptospirosis, trichinosis, and tuberculosis. Pigs breed exuberantly and can pass disease to deer and turkeys, which then can infect people. . . . Only a few . . . pigs would have to wander off to contaminate the forest."[11]

The Spanish ships plying the routes to the New World carried something else. A generation of battle-tested Spanish soldiers, many with little hope of inheriting wealth or titles, had seen that there was a new path to power in Isabella and Ferdinand's Spain. Glory, gold, titles, and property flowed from service to crown and Church. Armed with the latest weapons of war and the conviction that heathens could be converted or killed, the new breed of Spanish warriors were no longer the courtly knights of medieval romances. They became the conquistadors who laid waste to the Caribbean islands and Americas.

Following Columbus' four voyages, Old World knowledge of the New World exploded in the dazzling Age of Discovery. As Spanish ships brought back news of this New World and its riches, what more proof did anyone need of the righteousness of Isabella and Ferdinand's quest to defend the faith? In ridding Spain of the Jews, defeating the Moors, and purifying the faithful through the Inquisition, the Catholic monarchs had done God's work. And they'd found a whole new world of heathens to convert! The fact that so many of the natives were falling to dreadful epidemics seemed only to offer further proof that those pagan gods were false and their Christian God was taking no prisoners.

This is how the world must have appeared to Spain's King Charles I, successor to Ferdinand in 1516. On his father's side, Charles was a member of the royal Hapsburg family and through that association was also named Holy Roman Emperor Charles V in 1519. The future king of Spain was raised in Brussels and did not learn to speak Spanish until after he succeeded to the throne. But he clearly understood the language of conquest. In 1521, he ordered the governor of Cuba, Diego Velázquez, to send an expedition to explore Mexico. Velázquez in turn handed the job to Hernan Cortés. What Cortés discovered and conquered surely confirmed the belief that Spain was favored by

God, as conquistador Bernal Díaz recorded in a subjective account, written some fifty years after the Spanish arrival in Mexico:

> And when we entered the city . . . the sight of the palaces in which they lodged us! They were very spacious and well built, of magnificent stone, cedar wood, and the wood of other sweet-smelling trees, with great rooms and courts, which were a wonderful sight, and all covered with awnings of woven cotton.
>
> When we had a good look at all this, we went to the orchards and gardens, which was a marvelous place both to see and walk in. . . . The Caciques of that town . . . brought us a present of gold worth more than two thousand pesos; and Cortés thanked them heartily for it . . . telling them through our interpreter something about our holy faith, and declaring to them the great power of our lord the Emperor.
>
> —BERNAL DÍAZ,
> *The Conquest of New Spain* (1568)

After subduing Mexico and commencing to strip its riches, the Spanish began to look elsewhere in this marvelous New World for empires to conquer and heathens to convert. Among these was Florida, where men with grandiose visions of another Aztec city of gold would meet a different end. Florida had first been sighted and named by Spanish explorer Juan Ponce de León of "Fountain of Youth" fame on Easter Sunday 1513. He called the territory "La Pascua Florida," the name of a Spanish Eastertime festival, and the Spanish later called it simply "La Florida"; in time, plain Florida is what stuck. The Spanish probably should have taken a cue about their prospects in Florida from Ponce de León's fate. Returning to Florida in 1521 to establish a colony, Ponce de León was wounded by a poisoned arrow when Indians attacked during the landing near present-day Fort Myers. Transported back to Cuba, Florida's "discoverer" died an agonizing death in July 1521, one of many conquistadors done in by the New World.

But the Spanish pressed on. Several years later, another expedition sailed for Florida. Commissioned by King Charles, this group of explorers held out great hopes of uncovering new lands and more gold. Following its departure from Cuba for Florida in 1528, however, the expedition vanished in Florida's swamps. Its fate would remain a mystery for nearly eight years.

And then the silence was unexpectedly broken an entire continent away from Florida. Late in the winter or early spring of 1536, a nearly naked man covered in tattoos emerged from the wilderness near what is now Mexico's Pacific coast. Accompanied by a dozen or so Indians and a black man, he called out to a group of Spanish slave hunters looking for Indian captives. At first, the soldiers who saw this wild man must have thought he was one of the Indians. But then, to their amazement, the man addressed them in Spanish. As he later recounted the meeting, "Next morning, I overtook four mounted Christians, who were thunderstruck to see me so strangely dressed and in the company of Indians. They went on staring at me for long space of time, so astonished that they could neither speak to me nor manage to ask me anything. I told them to take me to their captain."[12]

Emaciated and half naked, this strange apparition might as well have been a ghost; his name was that of a man long thought dead. A trusted courtier of Spain's King Charles I, Alvar Núñez Cabeza de Vaca had disappeared along with more than four hundred other Spaniards not long after they left Cuba for Florida in the spring of 1528. Cabeza de Vaca was a member of the Spanish army that had come to conquer Florida and perhaps discover another magnificent New World empire. But the riches dreamed of in Florida were a myth—fool's gold. This ill-fated army encountered little but hunger, disaster, and misery before disappearing from view.

Cabeza de Vaca's extraordinary odyssey had begun in 1527, when conquistador Pánfilo de Narváez was commissioned to try again where Ponce de León had failed. Narváez had earned his stripes with Diego Velázquez and Cortés in the brutal 1512 campaign to subjugate Cuba, described as "the laboratory of the destruction of the New World: slavery, mining, forced conversions, extermination."[13] In 1520, Narváez had been dispatched by Velázquez with orders to arrest an insubordinate Cortés, then beginning his conquest of Mexico. Alerted to the plot against him, Cortés struck first against his fellow Spaniard. The battle left Narváez wounded, broken, half blind, and festering in a sweltering, mosquito-infested Mexican cell. Cortés went on to conquer Mexico, becoming wealthy beyond dreams and inspiring a generation of conquistadors.

Eventually released from prison, Narváez recovered from his wounds and humiliation, but he still dreamed of finding a civilization the equal of Mexico. Now in his fifties, he left Spain in 1527 with five ships, approximately six hundred men, and a handful of women to serve as cooks and servants. Also on board was Alvar Núñez Cabeza de Vaca, who acted as "treasurer and chief officer of justice." The expedition sailed first for Cuba, where Narváez hoped to add fresh provisions, horses, and additional recruits. If the priests who accompanied the expedition had asked for good weather, their prayers went unanswered. Events in Cuba might have served as a harbinger of what was to come, as a powerful hurricane—a word the Spanish had borrowed from the name of the Mayan storm god, Huracan—struck the fleet, sinking two ships, killing more than fifty men, and convincing many others to remain in Cuba.

Narváez pressed on with a single-mindedness that is the hallmark of many successful adventurers. But in his case, it proved to be the foolhardiness of a man so desperate for gold and glory that all caution was abandoned. Led by ship's pilots who talked a good game about knowing the waters off Florida but seemed as lost as anyone, the expedition, now numbering some four hundred, finally arrived in Florida's Gulf waters on April 14, 1528, reaching the vicinity of what is now Tampa Bay.

From the outset of the expedition, Alvar Núñez Cabeza de Vaca did not find Narváez an especially judicious leader. And Narváez viewed this fussy "accountant" as a royal spy. In his forties, Cabeza de Vaca was an educated courtier whose family was reasonably well-to-do. His name, which literally means "head of the cow," was an honorific title bestowed, according to family legend, by a grateful king upon an ancestor who, in 1212, had helped the king by marking a secret mountain pass with a cow's skull, allowing a Christian army to surprise a Moorish enemy. One of his relatives had been a tutor to King Charles I, and Cabeza de Vaca had pulled court strings to secure his appointment. In Cabeza de Vaca's memoir of the expedition—which must be read with a jaundiced eye, as it is clearly the self-aggrandizing work of a man with an agenda—Narváez is consistently depicted as making poor decisions and ignoring good advice, usually dispensed by Cabeza de Vaca himself. At one point, annoyed at Cabeza de Vaca's repeated cautions, Narváez suggested that Cabeza de Vaca turn back. The courtier balked at the suggestion that his wariness was cowardice.

Their first significant dispute came when Narváez divided his forces, again ignoring Cabeza de Vaca's counsel. Disembarking with about three hundred men and some women, Narváez left the other hundred men on the three ships, with orders to sail along the coast of Florida to an eventual rendezvous with the army—although where this rendezvous would actually take place was never established. Lacking experienced pilots, the men on the ships soon became hopelessly disoriented and headed back to "New Spain" (Mexico), giving up Narváez and his army for lost.

Narváez *was* lost. He was leading his troops inland, moving north, roughly parallel to Florida's Gulf coast. Their horses and heavy armor were poor choices for negotiating swamps filled with alligators, poisonous snakes, and mosquitoes in Florida's tropical heat and humidity. Relentless in the hope of finding an empire of gold, they recklessly hacked through the wilderness without competent guides or a sense of direction. The Indian encampments they discovered were often empty of both people and maize, as the natives had the good sense to disappear at the first sight of Europeans. Still, Narváez pressed on, spurred by the fact that the few Indians they captured all told tales of bigger villages with more food and the gold that the Spaniards seemed to care for more than anything. "Apalachee" is what the Spaniards thought the Indians called this kingdom. All of these desperate, hungry, and sick conquistadors must have had visions of another gold-encrusted city like Tenochtitlán. But they had fallen for a common trick. Telling the Spanish that the grass was greener in the next neighborhood was an excellent tactic that few Spaniards ever figured out.

After months of debilitating tropical illnesses and constant skirmishes with Indians, and completely demoralized by their failure to find gold or food, the expedition reached the sea at what is now Pensacola Bay. With no sign of the three ships that were supposed to rendezvous with them, the survivors of this disastrous foray made a desperate decision. They would build boats and sail to Mexico by hugging the shoreline of the Gulf of Mexico.

With incredible ingenuity, they melted down stirrups and nails, scrounged bits of leather and deerskin, and wove strands of palmetto fiber to create five flimsy boats, tarred with some pine pitch and rigged with sails improvised from their shirts. Holding nearly fifty men each and hardly seaworthy, this patchwork flotilla set sail in late September—"with none among us having any knowledge of the art of navigation," Cabeza de Vaca noted in supreme understatement. Caught in bad weather and buffeted by the powerful currents produced where the Mississippi River enters the Gulf of Mexico, the overloaded boats were quickly separated. Narváez and most of his men were never seen again. Fewer than a hundred survivors washed up on the shore of an island that Cabeza de Vaca called the Isle of Misfortune—most likely Galveston Island, off the coast of Texas. It was here that Cabeza de Vaca spent the winter, and the band of survivors was soon reduced to fifteen, some of them resorting to cannibalism to survive. Finally, Cabeza de Vaca found himself alone, except for the natives who eked out a harsh life on the coast.

After years of wandering as a self-described trader in shells and itinerant medicine man, Cabeza de Vaca learned of three other "Christians," including the Moroccan Estevanico. Together, they set out for New Spain (Mexico). When Cabeza de Vaca and his three companions emerged from the mountains on Mexico's Pacific coast after eight years, much had changed in Spain's American empire. Another great civilization had been discovered and devastated in Peru. Led by Pizarro in a conquest stunning in its cruelty, the men who swept into the land of the Inca captured cities and found mines filled with vast wealth, and Spanish galleons were soon sailing for Spain laden with gold and silver. Among Pizarro's lieutenants was conquistador Hernando de Soto. When Cabeza de Vaca finally reached Spain, hoping that he might be given leave to explore Florida, he was disappointed to learn that de Soto had already been named governor of Cuba and granted the right to conquer Florida.

Before leaving Spain, de Soto briefly met with Cabeza de Vaca. But if de Soto had gleaned anything useful from Cabeza de Vaca, he did not put the intelligence to good use. Well schooled in the conquistador's most brutal techniques, de Soto employed them in a scorched-earth march through Florida and other parts of the American southeast. Starting in 1539, de Soto's disastrous campaign replayed all of Narváez's worst mistakes, tragically for both his men and the Indians they encountered. Utterly blinded by the hope of uncovering another Aztec or Incan empire, de Soto led a forced march that was little more than a reign of terror.

These were the things they brought: crossbows; the harquebus; horses, not seen in the Americas before Cortés; and many war dogs. Long used in Europe, these fearsome, armored mastiffs and wolf-hounds were trained to attack and rip humans to pieces. The Spanish employed them with horrible effect against people who had never seen horses or guns, had no steel, and fought their highly ritualized battles with obsidian knives, wearing cotton armor. "Dogs were as standard as horses in the Spanish invasion," as Paul Schneider described their grim value. "Cortés took them to Mexico, Ponce de León took them to Puerto Rico. In Panama, Balboa used dogs not just in battle but to enforce good Christian sexual mores and dress codes: 'The (native) king's brother and a number of other courtiers were dressed as women, and according to the accounts of the neighbors shared the same passion. . . . Vasco ordered forty of them to be torn to pieces by dogs.'"[14]

Now de Soto put them to deadly use in Florida, setting them on Indian villagers to break any resistance. But in vain. With his army

wandering aimlessly, bested by tribes who had learned from their earlier encounters with the Spanish, de Soto's campaign ended in misery.
Sickened by disease, he died on the banks of the Mississippi on May
21, 1542. The remnants of his army limped back to Mexico a year
later.

꒳

WITH THESE AND other mounting, costly disappointments, King
Philip II, who had succeeded to the throne in 1556, put an end to Spanish attempts to settle Florida in 1561. But when word of the French
settlement at Fort Caroline reached Philip in 1562, all that changed.
Philip II decided to remove the French Protestant menace there. This
was no small matter. French "privateers" had been preying on Spanish
treasure ships for nearly thirty years, and during an undeclared war in
the 1550s they had cut in half the Spanish crown's take in gold and
silver from the Americas.

Philip selected his ablest naval commander, convicted smuggler
Admiral Pedro Menéndez de Avilés, also a dutifully loyal Catholic,
and directed him "to burn and hang the Lutheran French." *Luteranos*
was the Spanish term for all Protestants, despite the fact that these
French Protestants, or Huguenots, were more accurately Calvinists.
Like his father, Charles I, Philip II was sworn to stamp out the her-
esies of the renegade German priest Martin Luther and his growing
ranks of followers.

In October 1517, Luther had written his "Ninety-five Theses" (formally, *Disputation of Doctor Martin Luther on the Power and Efficacy of
Indulgences*), a stinging rebuke of church practices, and supposedly
nailed it to the door of Castle Church in Wittenberg, Germany. The
Wittenberg church possessed one of Europe's largest collections of

Christian relics, which included purported vials of the Virgin Mary's milk and straw from Jesus' manger. By making a donation to preserve these sacred items, visitors to the Wittenberg church received an "indulgence" that effectively reduced their time in purgatory by more than five thousand years. Challenging such indulgences, and ultimately the authority of the Pope, Luther wrote, "It is certain that when the penny jingles into the money-box, gain and avarice can be increased, but the result of the intercession of the Church is in the power of God alone."

Dismissed by Pope Leo X as the work of a "drunken German," Luther's ideas quickly spread through Europe with the help of Gutenberg's printing press. Excommunicated in January 1521, Luther was called to a civil hearing before Holy Roman Emperor Charles V (King Charles I of Spain) at the Diet of Worms on April 17, 1521. Urged to retract his teachings, Luther refused, famously declaring: "Unless I am convinced by the testimony of the Scriptures or by clear reason (for I do not trust either in the pope or in councils alone, since it is well known that they have often erred and contradicted themselves) . . . I cannot and I will not retract anything, since it is neither safe nor right to go against conscience."

Unmoved, Holy Roman Emperor Charles V declared Luther a "notorious heretic" and an outlaw, banning his literature. Luther's words and actions—he altered the communion sacrament and later married—did not set off a polite debate over how to say one's prayers. He had put the match to a powder keg of religious politics that exploded in sectarian wars across Europe. The Reformation and the holy wars it inspired transformed Western history and dominated European, and later American, statecraft for centuries, at enormous cost in lives and treasure.

IT WAS TO protect his nation's treasure, as well as stamp out the heretical French *luteranos,* that Philip II had dispatched Menéndez, commander of the Caribbean fleet, to Florida. Arriving at the site of a marshy coastal Timucuan Indian village on September 8, 1565, Menéndez established St. Augustine, the settlement he named in honor of the early church father whose name day is celebrated on August 28, the day that Menéndez had sighted Florida.

In present-day St. Augustine, the Mission of Nombre de Dios, with its 208-foot-tall stainless-steel cross and a small shrine to the Virgin Mary (Nuestra Señora de la Leche y Buen Parto, "Our Lady of the Milk and Happy Delivery"), marks the approximate spot where Admiral Menéndez landed and ordered the celebration of what is acclaimed by local boosters as "the first parish mass in the future United States." Another fact generally left out of the glowing arrival narrative in tourist brochures is that Menéndez also brought along Africans as "laborers," which should properly give Spain—not the English in Jamestown in 1619—the distinction of introducing African slaves to what would become the United States.

Within days of the Spanish landing, the French captain Jean Ribault fatefully and foolishly sailed from Fort Caroline with his five hundred men, intent on destroying the Spanish before they could erect proper defenses. He left behind a mere twenty soldiers to guard the French settlement and its settlers.

This was not Ribault's first disastrous decision in America. He had led the first French attempt to settle North America. Landing on Florida's east coast on May 1, 1562, Ribault sailed up a river he named the River of May. Constructing a stone column there, he claimed the territory for France. He sailed further north and left thirty men at a settlement called Charlesfort, on what is now Parris Island, South Carolina. Then Ribault sailed back for France, expecting to return with supplies and more colonists. With France engulfed in another religious war, Ribault was forced to England instead, where a suspicious Elizabeth had the Frenchman thrown in the Tower of London.

The men Ribault left behind at Charlesfort fared miserably. When the expected relief ships failed to arrive, their situation became desperate. Building an improvised boat, they set sail for France, but their meager food supplies ran out. Forced to eat shoe leather and dried animal skins and to drink their urine, the men were ultimately reduced to that most unthinkable act of desperation. "Finally it was suggested that it would be wiser that one die rather than all of them. The lot fell on . . . Larcher. He was killed and his flesh was equally divided among them. Then they drank his warm blood."[15]

Undeterred by this disaster, French Huguenot leader Gaspard de Coligny won royal permission for a return to America. With Ribault languishing in an English prison, the new expedition was led by René de Laudonnière, Ribault's second in command during the earlier voyage. With some three hundred colonists, men and women, aboard three ships, this was a large, well-organized venture, carrying livestock, seeds, and agricultural supplies. Also aboard was a force of soldiers, cannons, and other weapons to arm a fort. Landing in June 1564, the Huguenot colonists settled on the banks of the river where Ribault had left his stone marker. After assembling to give thanks to God— in essence, the true first American "Thanksgiving"—they set about constructing a wooden fort they called Fort Caroline, in honor of King Charles.

Initially far better equipped than the later English settlers would be, these Huguenot pilgrims added storehouses and wood-frame living quarters, along with a flour mill, bakery, and blacksmith. And in true Gallic fashion, they found some local grapes and made twenty barrels of wine. Relations with the Timucuans were reasonably good at first, and several French colonists took Indian women as wives. The settlers also learned the local Indian practice of smoking a local herb, and tobacco was soon very popular.

The Indians they encountered were eastern Timucuans, part of a larger grouping of at least fifteen different tribes scattered across what is now northern Florida and southern Georgia. Living inside palisaded circular towns with thatched-roof houses, the coastal-dwelling eastern Timucuans fished, hunted, and farmed, growing corn and beans as staples. The tribe near Fort Caroline was led by a chief named Utina, who enlisted the French in a series of attacks on a neighboring tribe, the Potano. Forging an alliance pitting one local tribe against another repeated the strategy that Cortés had successfully used in Mexico and would be employed by the English in Massachusetts as well.

Expecting resupply ships from France, the French quickly went through their food stores. Many of the colonists had been lured to America by visions of finding the earth littered with gold. Instead of planting crops, they spent far more time looking for gold and silver. The friendly trade relations between the French and natives soured as the Indians began to experience the disastrous epidemics introduced by Europeans. When the supply of desirable French trade goods dwindled and the Indians jacked up prices on the desperate settlers, the French commander ordered the chief Utina taken hostage, leading to a brief standoff.[16]

With the Timucuans unwilling to feed the French, tensions grew and discontent among the settlers spilled into outright mutiny. One group of colonists commandeered a boat and sailed off to attack a Spanish outpost in Cuba, bringing swift Spanish retaliation. A second contingent did the same and was quickly captured. Since treasure ships bound for Spain had to sail past the Florida coast as they caught the Gulf Stream, these French attacks on Spanish shipping set the stage for King Philip's order to Admiral Menéndez.

When the expected relief failed to appear, the dwindling French colonists contemplated a return home and set about building a ship. Like good Calvinists, they probably prayed for deliverance, which unexpectedly arrived in the form of an English slave-trading pirate. In August 1565, several English ships under the command of Captain Sir John Hawkins put into the River of May seeking fresh water. Later to achieve fame as one of Queen Elizabeth's "sea dogs," John Hawkins had started out in the African slave trade. But he, like the French, had learned that there was far more profit to be gained from stealing Spanish gold. Hawkins and other famed English sailors, including Francis Drake and Walter Raleigh, enriched themselves and Queen Elizabeth's royal treasury by looting Spain's treasure galleons.

Besides taking on supplies, Hawkins was willing to barter a seaworthy ship for some of the cannons and powder that protected Fort Caroline. With the English ship, Laudonnière and the remaining colonists prepared to return to France. But as they readied to sail, Captain Ribault and the promised relief from France arrived. Following his release from English prison, Ribault had returned and taken command of the fleet that arrived in late August 1565 with supplies and reinforcements. When he learned the Spaniards had arrived, Ribault set off on the fateful mission that cost his life and hundreds of others.

❧ Aftermath ❧

Three years after the Fort Caroline massacre, the French exacted a measure of vengeance. A French naval force led by sea captain Dominique de Gourgues attacked the Spanish garrison at San Mateo in 1568 with the assistance of the Timucuans, who were now eager to turn on their Spanish conquerors. On the very spot where Admiral Menéndez had once hanged the Frenchmen, Gourgues did the same with his Spanish prisoners. Above these men, the sign read, "This is done, not as unto Spaniards, but as unto liars, thieves, and murderers."

But it did not end there. On August 23, 1572, nearly seven years after the Fort Caroline massacres, an assassin attempted to kill Admiral Coligny, the moving spirit behind the Fort Caroline expedition. On the next day—St. Bartholomew's Day—a coordinated attack on Protestants swept over France. Admiral Coligny was murdered in his bed, his corpse thrown from a window. In Paris and soon across the country, a paroxysm of one-sided sectarian violence exploded.

The precise number of Huguenots massacred during this anti-Protestant pogrom is uncertain. An estimated two thousand Protestants were killed in Paris, and as many as ten thousand died across France. Contemporary accounts describe bodies floating in French rivers for months afterward. In Rome, a jubilant Pope Gregory XIII ordered all the city's bells to ring in a day of thanksgiving. It was also reported that the normally taciturn King Philip II actually smiled at the news.

The slaughter of Fort Caroline's colonists and the St. Bartholomew's Day Massacre resolved one of King Philip's chief problems. The Protestant threat in France had been crushed. But another danger loomed with a troublesome distant relative, England's Queen Elizabeth. Unlike her predecessor, her half sister Queen Mary—a descendant of Isabella and a devout Catholic who purged Protestants, earned the nickname "Bloody Mary," and then married Philip—Elizabeth was a Protestant. The daughter of Henry VIII and Anne Boleyn, Elizabeth had provided support to the Huguenots and sent troops to aid the Protestant rebels in the Netherlands, even though Spain and England were officially at peace. She also encouraged Francis Drake and others to raid Spanish ships and towns. During his voyage around the world in 1579, Drake had sailed into San Francisco Bay, claiming the region for Elizabeth and England, and freely attacked Spanish ships carrying gold from Peru as he completed the circumnavigation.

After Queen Mary's death, Philip considered marriage to Elizabeth as the solution to his "Protestant problem." But as ruler of an increasingly Protestant country, Elizabeth realized that such a prospect was impossible. Since Philip could not marry her, he concluded, why not kill her?

A series of Spanish-inspired plots to undermine and then assassinate Elizabeth all failed. Philip conspired with English Catholics to kill Elizabeth and place her Catholic cousin—Mary Stuart, Queen of Scots—on the throne. When that plot backfired, Mary was executed in February 1587. By then, Philip was already planning the "Enterprise of England," an invasion of England intended to put an end to English piracy and restore Catholicism to England. Mary, Queen of Scots' execution provided the catalyst for the launching of the enterprise.

Construction of the Spanish Armada had begun in earnest in January 1586. Consisting of some 130 ships and carrying more than twenty-nine thousand men, the armada was brought together at Lisbon in

May 1588. England had meanwhile armed many of its merchant vessels and added to its fleet of warships. When it sailed out to meet the Armada, Elizabeth's navy had about two hundred ships and nearly sixteen thousand men, most of them experienced sailors, with squadrons commanded by such accomplished privateers as John Hawkins, Francis Drake, and Martin Frobisher.

Early on August 8, the English sent "fireships," filled with gunpowder and set ablaze, toward the armada. The Spanish ships sailed out to sea to escape the flames. Later that morning, about sixty English ships attacked an equal number of Spanish ships off the French port of Gravelines, with the English sinking two Spanish ships and damaging scores of others. Crippled, the remnants of the armada attempted to return to Spain by sailing north around the British Isles. Storms and high winds wrecked many ships off Ireland's coast, and only about half of the fleet returned to Spain. Of the other half, there was no word. In a history of the Spanish Armada, Neil Hanson summarizes, "English losses were nil." As a result of the defeat, Philip was declared bankrupt.[7]

IN THE YEAR that Spain's armada was crushed, a child was born on a country manor in Groton, England, far from the great halls of kings, queens, and popes. The boy's grandfather, a London cloth merchant, had purchased the manor in 1544. It had once been part of a monastery called Bury St. Edmunds. But when King Henry VIII broke with the Vatican, he had confiscated the Church's lands and properties, many of which were then sold to men such as merchant Adam Winthrop. In 1588, the former monastery became the birthplace of John Winthrop, the future governor of the Massachusetts Bay Colony.

Part II

Hannah's Escape

1607   Jamestown, Virginia, the first permanent English settlement in America, is founded.

1608   Samuel Champlain settles Quebec.

1611   Publication of a new English-language Bible, authorized by King James.

1612   Dutch traders establish trading post on Manhattan.

1619   Virginia's first elected assembly, called the House of Burgesses, meets; African slaves carried on a Dutch ship are sold as "servants" in Jamestown; a shipload of marriageable young women arrives in Virginia and planters pay 120 pounds of tobacco for each woman's passage; a hundred London slum children are sent to Virginia as servants.

1620   On November 11, Pilgrims aboard the *Mayflower* sign the Mayflower Compact; it outlines rules for a rudimentary democracy. After exploring Cape Cod, the Pilgrims establish Plymouth Plantation on December 21.

1622   Powhatan Indian attacks devastate Virginia.

1625   Charles I ascends the British throne.

1629   King Charles I dissolves Parliament.

1630   The great Puritan emigration begins; Massachusetts Bay Colony is founded with Boston as its capital.

1634   Maryland founded as a refuge for English Catholics by Lord Baltimore.

1636-1637   Pequot War fought in New England.

1638   Religious dissenter Anne Hutchinson is tried in Massachusetts.

1642   The English Civil War begins. In 1649, Charles I is beheaded; his son Charles II is defeated by the forces of Puritan leader Oliver Cromwell and escapes to France.

1653   Oliver Cromwell takes on dictatorial powers as "Lord Protector" and holds power until 1658.

1660   The Restoration brings King Charles II, a Roman Catholic, back to claim the British throne.

1664   English seize Dutch New Amsterdam and rename it New York.

June–August 1676   King Philip's War devastates New England.

1682   The Frenchman La Salle descends Mississippi River to its mouth and claims the Louisiana Territory for France.

1685   King James II becomes England's last Roman Catholic ruler.

1688   In the Glorious Revolution, King James II flees to France; the constitutional monarchy is restored under William and Mary, James' daughter.

1689–1697   The Second Indian War, or King William's War.

1692   Salem witchcraft trials.

1702–1711   Queen Anne's War (known as the War of the Spanish Succession in Europe). In 1704, French and Indians massacre English settlers at Deerfield, Massachusetts; English forces massacre Apalachee Indians at Spanish missions in Florida.

Mrs. Hutchinson, you are called here as one of those that have troubled the peace of the commonwealth and the churches here; . . . you have spoken divers things as we have been informed very prejudicial to the honour of the churches and ministers thereof, and you have maintained a meeting and an assembly in your house that hath been condemned by the general assembly as a thing not tolerable nor comely in the sight of God nor fitting for your sex.

—Governor John Winthrop
during the trial of Anne Hutchinson (1643)

The New-Englanders are a People of God settled in those which were once the Devil's Territories; and it may easily be supposed that the Devil was exceedingly disturbed, when he perceived such a People here.

—Cotton Mather,
The Wonders of the Invisible World (1693)

There was a type of man whom the Puritan never tired of denouncing. He was a good citizen, a man who obeyed the laws, carried out his social obligations, never injured others. The Puritans called him a "civil man," and admitted that he was "outwardly just, temperate, chaste, carefull to follow his worldly businesse, will not so much as hurt his neighbours dog, payes every man his owne, and lives of his owne; no drunkard, adulterer or quareller; loves to live peacably and quietly among his neighbours." This man, this paragon of social virtue, the Puritans said, was on his way to Hell, and their preachers continually reminded him of it.

–Edmund S. Morgan,
The Puritan Family (1944)

Puritanism–the haunting fear that someone, somewhere, may be happy.

–H. L. Mencken (1949)

I N THE COLD DARKNESS OF a late winter New England morning, Hannah Emerson Dustin was lying in. Six days earlier, the forty-year-old mother and farmer's wife had given birth to a girl, her eighth child. The infant, named Martha, was being tended by Mary Neff, a widow who served the frontier village of Haverhill as nurse and midwife.

As winter's grip lingered on this bleak Ides of March, spring's promise must have seemed very remote in Haverhill. Situated near the New Hampshire border, the small town still shuddered from a brush with witchcraft a few years earlier. Accusations of sorcery and spectral doings had sent a chill of fear through Haverhill, although the town had escaped the notorious trials and mass executions that had shattered nearby Salem village during its witchcraft crisis at about the same time.

Adding to Haverhill's unease, the town bordered Indian country, and with war in the air, that was no small threat. Overwhelmed by the English influx, the Algonquian-speaking "people of the dawnland"— the Abenaki, who were spread across northern New England—had been pressing English frontier settlements with growing ferocity for nearly ten years. Just two years earlier, Haverhill had barely fended off an attack by eighty Indians. In York, Maine, the people had been less fortunate. In what was called the Candlemas Massacre, more than fifty settlers had died and another hundred had been taken captive in the early winter of 1692. That the settlers believed that the Indians were actually in league with the devil only served to heighten the climate of fear. The connection between witches, magic, and Native Americans was not coincidental. Contemporary scholars have much more closely connected the outbreak of New England's witchcraft hysteria in the 1690s with the growing threat from local tribes who were widely viewed by Puritans as demonic agents.

For Haverhill's residents, these dangers—both the spiritual and the worldly—simply confirmed the constant admonishments of their Puritan preachers: they were hopeless sinners with little chance of redemption, in this life or the next. As the Reverend George Burroughs, a minister from Wells, Maine, wrote after the devastating surprise attack on York, "God is still manifesting his displeasure against this Land."[1]

On this cold March morning, Thomas Dustin, Hannah's forty-five-year-old husband, suddenly burst into the house in a panic. Haverhill was under attack. Half a dozen nearby houses were already burning. An Abenaki raiding party was heading for the Dustin home. Hannah implored her husband to collect their other children and get them to safety. She and Mary Neff would fend for themselves and the baby.

After what must have been a torturous moment in which he had to choose between trying to save his wife and newborn and saving the rest of his family, Thomas Dustin did as his wife asked. Rushing from the house, he gathered his seven other children, ranging in age from two to seventeen, and managed to shepherd all of them to safety. Desperately holding off the Abenaki warriors who followed his family as they fled, Thomas Dustin kept the Indians at bay without actually firing his musket, which might have spelled his doom. Had he gotten off a shot, the Indians would have certainly overwhelmed him before he could reload. The little group reached the town's designated garrison, the fortified house of veteran Indian fighter and Salem witch trial judge Nathaniel Saltonstall, about a mile away.

Barely moments after Thomas rushed off, some twenty Abenaki raiders, armed with war axes and muskets, came crashing into the farmhouse where Hannah cowered by the hearth. Hannah and the nurse, clutching newborn Martha, expected death. Instead, they were pulled from the house, which was then set ablaze. One of the raiders grabbed newborn Martha from Mary Neff's arms and brained the six-day-old baby against a nearby apple tree.

In this inconceivable moment of terror, shock, and grief, the two women were spared. Taken captive along with at least ten other prisoners from Haverhill, they began a wilderness trek. According to the most famous contemporary account of this ordeal, "several of the other captives, as they began to Tire in their sad Journey, were soon sent unto their Long Home; the Salvages [*sic*] would presently bury their Hatchets in their Brains, and leave their Carcasses on the Ground for Birds and Beasts to Feed upon."[2]

As the raiders pushed over the rugged, snow-covered backwoods with their prizes, Hannah Dustin and Mary Neff's fate remained uncertain. Like the other captives, they might be killed in an instant simply because they could not keep up with the war party as it wound its way north in the late New England winter. They might be forced to become servants of an Indian family, or even adopted by one to replace family members lost in fighting.

Or, in what was perhaps their best hope, they might be turned over to the Abenaki's European allies, the French, who might pay the Indians a bounty for the English prisoners. The women would then possibly be ransomed back to the English or used as bargaining chips in a negotiated hostage exchange between the two contentious European nations as they battled for control of North America. In the big picture, this Abenaki raid on Haverhill was but a single, brief moment in a larger conflict, known in New England as the Second Indian War and later called King William's War, after England's reigning monarch. This running battle was a mere instant in a much longer drama of fighting between England and France that raged across North America for three-quarters of a century.

After several days' march, the women were taken to an island near the convergence of the Contoocook and Merrimack rivers (now known as Dustin Island, near Concord, New Hampshire) and handed over to a native family. Here they joined another captive, Samuel Lennardson, a young English boy who had been taken from his father's farm near Worcester, Massachusetts, a year and a half earlier. Like young Samuel, the two women were given as servants to this family of twelve Indians—two men, three women, and seven children. More distressing, as Puritan cleric Cotton Mather underscored in his account of the captives' plight, these Indians said their prayers three times a day and made their children pray before eating or sleeping, as the French priests had taught them. In other words, they were not merely what Mather termed "Salvages;" they were Roman Catholics to boot—"idolaters like their whiter Brethren Persecutors," by which Mather meant the French. One of Boston's most famous and influential preachers, Mather pointedly observed in recounting Hannah Dustin's story that some Puritan families might profit from the Indians' example of such rigorous devotion.

If the image of Indians faithfully reciting Catholic prayers seems at odds with the traditional view of Native American families in wigwams, consider the report of a French priest, Father Pierre Thury. Two years after the Haverhill raid, he described the scene as an Abenaki war party prepared to assault an English fort at Pemaquid, Maine: "Almost all our warriors, who numbered about one hundred, took confession before they left, as if they were going to die on this expedition. . . . The women and children also followed their example and took confession, after which the women recited an endless rosary in the chapel, taking turns one after another from the first light of dawn until night, asking God through the intervention of the Sainted Virgin, to take pity on them and protect them during this war."[3]

Shortly after Hannah Dustin and Mary Neff arrived at the island camp, one of the Abenaki men told young Samuel that the entire party would ultimately head toward Canada. There, at an Indian rendezvous, the three English captives would be stripped and forced to "run the gauntlet." As Cotton Mather described it, with what sounds like a mix of breathless horror and a slight frisson of wishfulness, "When they came to this Town, they must be Script, and Scourg'd and Run the Gantlet, through the whole Army of Indians. They said this was the Fashion when the Captives first came to a town; and they derided some of the Faint-hearted English, which they said, fainted and swoon'd away under the Torments of this Discipline."[4]

While the practice of running the gauntlet has provided Hollywood with some vivid moments, its true intent may not have been cruel torture for the tribe's entertainment. "Running the gauntlet was an initiation rite common among certain Indian tribes," notes historian Kathryn Zabelle Derounian-Stodola. "Many terrified captives described as torture what was apparently intended to test the survival of the fittest and to serve as an introduction—even a welcome—upon arrival at an Indian village."[5] This interpretation fits in neatly with another of colonial America's most famous captivity stories: after the founding of Jamestown in 1607, Captain John Smith lay prostrate with his head upon a stone, as he later told it, about to be brained by an Indian war club, when the maiden Pocahontas lay across his body and saved his life. The legendary incident is now acknowledged to have been an initiation ceremony rather than a threatened execution. Or, at most, it was a symbolic execution in which the Indians asserted their dominion over the captive Smith.

But for Hannah Dustin and Mary Neff, such distinctions would have offered small solace. To them, it must have seemed that death or survival as servants to the Indian family were their only prospects. Upon learning the Indians' plan to take them north to Canada, Hannah Dustin set her mind to escape.

In the predawn hours of March 31, as her captors lay asleep, Hannah roused Mary and Samuel. The three resourceful New Englanders found tomahawks and, with little difficulty or hesitation, dispatched ten of the sleeping Indians—six of them children—sparing only an old woman and a small boy.

At Hannah Dustin's suggestion, young Samuel Lennardson had acquired the grim skills to carry out this plan from one of the Indians. A famous later account imagined the deadly tutorial session: "'Strike 'em there,' said he placing a finger on his temple and he also showed him how to take off the scalp. . . . The English boy struck the Indian who had given him the information, on the temple, as he had been directed."[6]

Setting out from this horrific bloodletting, Hannah Dustin was sufficiently self-possessed to return to the wigwam to take the Abenakis' scalps in order to prove what she and the other two escapees had done. The Massachusetts Bay Courts had enacted a bounty for the scalps of Indians three years earlier, in 1694. Although the bounty had since been reduced and then repealed, Hannah Dustin thought it might be worth the effort if they not only made good their escape but profited from the ordeal as well. This extraordinarily plucky decision may have resulted from some mingling of Yankee thrift and Puritan work ethic, along with some of that legendary colonial American pioneer bravado—perhaps mixed with a measure of vengeance at the memory of what had been done to Hannah's newborn child. With ten scalps wrapped in a linen kerchief—later to be displayed in Haverhill's historical society—the trio scuttled all of the Indians' canoes save one, and in that one they started out on their journey back to Haverhill, about sixty miles downriver.

> Early this morning the deed was performed, and now, perchance, these tired women and this boy, their clothes stained with blood, and their minds racked with alternate resolution and fear, are making a hasty meal of parched corn and moosemeat, while their canoe glides under these pine roots whose stumps are still standing on the bank. They are thinking of the dead whom they have left behind on that solitary isle far up the stream, and of the relentless living warriors who are in pursuit. Every withered leaf which the winter has left seems to know their story, and in its rustling to repeat it and betray them. An Indian lurks behind every rock and pine, and their nerves cannot bear the tapping of a woodpecker. Or they forget their own dangers and their deeds in conjecturing the fate of their kindred, and whether, if they escape the Indians, they shall find the former still alive.
>
> —HENRY DAVID THOREAU,
> *A Week on the Concord and Merrimack Rivers (1849)*

The two women and the young boy eventually reached the safety of Haverhill, and when word of their escape reached Boston, they would be feted as heroes. Later brought to the seat of the Massachusetts Bay Colony, the redeemed captives received a grand welcome. Although the bounty for scalps had actually expired, the Massachusetts General Court made a special case for the brave mother and her compatriots. Accounts vary, but most agree that Hannah Dustin received a reward of £25, while Mary Neff and young Samuel split another £25—significant purses for colonial American farmers. All three also enjoyed hearty congratulations, along with a great many dinner invitations. In a short time, Hannah Dustin was the most famous woman in America.

This heroic tale of "redemption" and victory over the Indians, and by extension their French allies, was hailed in Puritan Massachusetts, possibly all the more because of Hannah Dustin's somewhat disreputable family history. Her father, Michael Emerson, had been in legal trouble for abusing his Haverhill neighbors and family, which included nine children; six other children had died in infancy. In a time when corporal punishment of children was the norm, Emerson had been convicted and fined for "cruel and excessive beating" of one of his daughters. Another Emerson daughter, Mary, had been sentenced, along with her husband, to be whipped for the crime of fornication before marriage, a crime taken very seriously in Puritan Massachusetts. As David Hackett Fischer notes, "Even in betrothed couples, sexual intercourse before marriage was regarded as a pollution which had to be purged before they could take [their] place in society and—most important—before their children could be baptized."[8]

Far more notoriously, Hannah's unmarried sister Elizabeth— the victim of the earlier beating at her father's hand and already the mother of one "fatherless" little girl—had been tried and convicted of infanticide for the strangling of infant twins; their paternity remained a secret she took to the gallows. At Elizabeth Emerson's hanging on June 8, 1693, Cotton Mather had preached a sermon he considered one of his best, using for his text Job 36:14: "They die in youth and their life is among the unclean."[9]

Before Hannah Dustin's exploits provided him with such a mother lode of material, Cotton Mather had gained great notoriety for his writings on witchcraft and for his central role in the Salem witch trials of 1692–93. His 1689 book, *Memorable Providences Relating to Witchcrafts and Possessions,* had practically served as a textbook for the Salem prosecutions, and three of the five judges in the Salem trials were friends of his and members of his congregation. The son of Increase Mather, the equally illustrious and influential Puritan leader and president of Harvard College, Cotton Mather would now serve as the chief instrument in turning Hannah Dustin's tale of captivity and vengeance into a Puritan parable of divine justice. In his accounts, Hannah's perseverance triumphed over the twin perils of popery and native savagery.

In several pamphlets and later in his landmark 1702 book known as *The Ecclesiastical History of New England,* Mather repeated Dustin's tale for its enormous propaganda value. It had all the ingredients the Puritan preacher needed for his purposes: depraved Indians—baby killers, no less—working in concord with the papist French, set against a virtuous Massachusetts wife and mother capable not only of saving herself and her fellow captives but also of striking a blow against the forces of idolatry and Satan. This despite the fact that Hannah Dustin was not a member of any church at the time. She officially joined Haverhill's congregation only in 1724, at age sixty-seven.[10]

Mather's account made Hannah Dustin a colonial-era icon. Although overlooked or entirely forgotten by more recent American history books, Dustin could lay claim to a singular distinction: a statue honoring her was unveiled in 1874, the first permanent statue of a woman erected in the United States. It immortalized Dustin, hatchet in one hand, scalps in the other.

While some details of Hannah Dustin's extraordinary escape were undoubtedly embroidered upon as the story grew over time into regional legend, there was nothing at all extraordinary in the fact that Hannah Dustin and the others had been taken captive by Indians. That was a risk that came with the territory in seventeenth- and eighteenth-century America, and throughout New England in particular. One scholarly estimate counted more than 1,640 New Englanders taken hostage by Indians between 1675 and 1763.[11] Not all reacted as Hannah Dustin did. According to Carol Berkin's history of colonial women, "at least one-third of the women taken to New France chose to remain, and at least 40 percent converted to Catholicism and married French husbands."[12] That was not a story Cotton Mather wished to explore.

THE THREAT OF attack and capture posed by Indians was so prevalent by the latter 1600s that the people of Massachusetts and other New England colonies must have slept with one eye open, a loaded gun at the ready. The reality of the perils they faced stands at odds with the comfortable, legendary American epic of the Puritan arrival, which extols rugged individuals seeking religious freedom in their "New Jerusalem" and sharing happy meals with the natives. The real story is, of course, far more complicated. It is a long, twisting tale of the struggle for power and land: the struggle between native Americans and European settlers; the epic contest among France, the Netherlands, Spain, and England for control of the New World; and the struggle of religious dissenters in a place that tolerated none.

Many of these threads come together in the history of another Puritan woman who did not share Hannah Dustin's fate or fame. Like tens of thousands of other Puritans, Anne Hutchinson and her family came to New England to escape religious and political persecution in their English homeland. No doubt she arrived with an impassioned dream of creating what Puritan leader John Winthrop famously called "a city upon a hill" when he led the great Puritan migration to New England in 1630. But for the outspoken, headstrong, and eventually rebellious Anne Hutchinson, that vision took a different course. She found herself locked in a contest of wills that captured all of the conflicting forces at play in early New England.

Born in Lincolnshire, England, in 1591, Anne Marbury was the daughter of a Cambridge-educated minister and Puritan reformer. Although most girls did not attend school then, young Anne did learn to read, at her father's insistence. Literacy, and the ability to read the Bible in particular, were essential to Puritans, who believed in the inerrancy of Scripture, and the rise of the printing press had made it possible for many people to own a Bible, if no other books.[13]

The exception also likely to be found in the Marbury household and other English Protestant homes at the time was John Foxe's *Book of Martyrs* (1563), a history of Christian martyrs through the ages, highlighting the worst excesses of the Inquisition and focusing especially on the persecution and gruesome torture of Protestants during the reign of Catholic queen Mary Tudor. A work of Protestant propaganda, the book included lurid descriptions of the racking, boiling oil, burnings, and other tortures suffered under "Bloody Mary" as she attempted to restore Catholicism to England. Foxe's treatise was an essential building block in the formation of a nationalist and Protestant identity in England. Queen Mary's successor, her Protestant half sister Elizabeth, ordered that a copy of *The Book of Martyrs* be secured at every parish lectern in England.

At age twenty-one, following her father's death, Anne married William Hutchinson, a prosperous cloth merchant, and the couple settled in Alford, where Anne began working as a midwife and healer who grew herbs and was familiar with their use, especially in childbirth. The Hutchinsons joined the congregation of Reverend John Cotton, a highly regarded young Puritan minister, who had been "born again" and attracted an avid following. Hutchinson became a devoted follower who proclaimed Cotton's message, especially to those women for whom she served as midwife.

The Hutchinsons' world was shaken at its foundations in 1626, when King Charles I succeeded to the English throne and began a new round of persecution of Protestants in an attempt to restore the Church of England's ties to Roman Catholicism. Adding in no small measure to the Puritans' unhappiness was a "forced loan" to the throne that the king had decreed. In 1629, when the House of Commons balked at these changes, Charles I dissolved Parliament, which was to English Puritans "the last bulwark against heresy and sin," in Edmund S. Morgan's phrase. The strife accelerated in 1633 when Charles' chief political advisor, William Laud, was appointed archbishop of Canterbury. Royal patronage and parish appointments were now in the hated Laud's hands.

England's Puritans howled. But with Laud's accession to the most powerful post in the Church of England, the suppression of Protestants accelerated. In addition to instituting changes in the decoration of churches and forms of Anglican worship, all of which reeked of popery to Puritans, Laud believed in the divine authority of kings—undoubt-edly an appealing notion to his patron, King Charles I. As archbishop, Laud also held to the theological belief that men could win salvation by their own willpower and acts. This went beyond the order of wor-ship and church decorations. To the Puritans, it was pure heresy.

Largely derived from Calvin's teachings, the Puritan view held that salvation—what they called "justification"—came only through God's grace. Believing that God had chosen before birth those who were to be saved, the "elect," the Puritans believed that no ritual, no purchase of indulgences, nor even good works made any difference. Even those granted divine grace had to constantly prove their worthiness by their actions. This endless striving to cleanse one's soul, called "sanctifica-tion," literally meant behaving like a "saint," which referred to those set apart by God, not the saints canonized by the Catholic Church.

This was no polite theological controversy to be argued inside uni-versities by whispering men in robes, poring over ancient Latin texts. These were some of the central ideas at the heart of the Reformation and Counter-Reformation and all the blood spilled in their wake. To English Puritans, the thought that salvation could be earned by works simply deepened a theological divide that further split England, forc-ing thousands of Puritans to leave. In 1634, Anne Hutchinson, her husband, Will, and their ten children (she had lost four others in early childhood) sailed for America on the *Griffon,* joining a decade-long Puritan migration that reshaped New England and with it American history.

The great migration had begun in 1630, when John Winthrop, aboard the *Arbella,* led a flotilla of seventeen ships bringing the first one thousand Puritan colonists to America. "They fled," wrote Carol Berkin, "the economic penalties imposed on them by the government they criticized and the threat of imprisonment for their religious views, but they also fled what they judged to be an increasingly immoral society, whose values alienated and isolated them as surely as any edicts of bishop or king. Their departure from England was a rejection of their countrymen's lasciviousness, idleness, and extravagance and the corrupt public life they saw around them . . . streets filled with drunks, prostitutes and beggars."[14]

Governor Winthrop carried the charter for a new colony, the Massachusetts Bay Colony, which was a commercial venture as well as a religious one. Besides God, the Puritans would answer to shareholders. Unlike the Pilgrims who had preceded them in 1620, this wave of Puritan settlers did not call themselves separatists. Certainly they wished to purify the Church of England, but they did not plan to abandon it. In fact, the Congregational Church, New England's core institution for centuries, was born out of this new American intermingling of Pilgrim and Puritan. As Nathaniel Philbrick put it, "The Puritans staunchly denied it, but their immigration to America had turned them, like the Pilgrims before them, into Separatists. They might claim to be still working within the Church of England, but as a practical matter with no bishops in New England, they were free to worship as they saw fit."[15] The distinction between the Pilgrims, those who came to Plymouth between 1620 and 1630, and the Puritans, who came after 1629, initially settling Massachusetts Bay and Connecticut, eventually disappeared as the great wave of Puritan settlers transformed the colony.[16]

Anchoring near Salem, a second English colony founded on the Massachusetts coast north of Plymouth in 1625, they were greeted with the news that eighty of Salem's colonists had died in the previous winter. The "starving times" that had halved the *Mayflower* Pilgrims' number in 1620 were not over. Spending their first winter in holes dug in the side of a hill and simple wooden lean-tos, two hundred of Winthrop's new emigrants died from cold and starvation that first year. Winthrop struggled to keep the colony alive in a settlement they called Boston—after the Protestant bastion in Lincolnshire, where John Cotton preached. The successive waves of Puritan settlers bringing fresh supplies kept the Massachusetts Bay Colony alive. John Cotton followed in 1633 and became the father-in-law of Increase Mather and grandfather to Cotton Mather, who was named in his honor. By most estimates, more than twenty-one thousand Puritans arrived in Massachusetts over the next few years, the Hutchinsons among them. Within a few years, Boston was the largest of some twenty townships flourishing in Massachusetts.

As a trusted midwife, Anne Hutchinson had always spoken with her charges about John Cotton's teachings as she guided them through labor and delivery—a captive audience, no doubt. Now in America, she did the same. Midwifery and the birthing process were one of the few women's preserves in the colonial world. But in its exclusion of men, its intimacy, and the midwife's use of herbs, there was also a faint hint of secret and possibly dark doings. And of course, the possibility that a dead or deformed infant was the devil's work also cast the midwife in a suspicious light—except to the women she tended.

Drawn by Hutchinson's extraordinary charisma and intelligence, women soon flocked to her home to hear her discussions of Scripture and John Cotton's sermons—informal religious gatherings that began the year after she arrived in America. In time, the women brought their husbands as well. By 1636, Anne Hutchinson was attracting enough listeners to expand to two evenings a week, sometimes to audiences of as many as eighty people. With the blessing of the influential

John Cotton, her followers grew to include the young Henry Vane, who had recently supplanted John Winthrop as governor of the Massachusetts Bay Colony. Politics and theology were never far apart in Massachusetts Bay. And that was the source of the trouble.

At some point, Anne Hutchinson had moved beyond simple scriptural readings to commentary on the teachings of some of the leading Puritan ministers of the day. It was this step, along with the changing tenor of the finer points of her theology, that brought down the wrath of the Bay Colony's Puritan fathers. As Anne Hutchinson honed her message, "sanctification" was not evidence of "justification." In other words, how someone behaved had no influence on whether that person was saved. While this notion was in keeping with fundamental Puritan theology, it made men such as Governor Winthrop worry that Hutchinson's teachings were potentially subversive. If taken far enough, Hutchinson's ideas might lead her followers to believe that they could shirk responsibility, since following church and civil orders was ultimately fruitless. Hutchinson also believed in "personal revelation," the idea that God spoke directly to people—or so her accusers claimed. This was a frontal assault on the bedrock Puritan notion that God's will was revealed only through a careful, literal reading of the Bible—"the fundamental conviction," as Edmund S. Morgan noted, "on which the Puritans built their state, their churches, and their daily lives."[17]

Considering this female teacher-healer as a danger to both their religious and civic authority—and they would have seen no difference between the two—the Puritan elders of Massachusetts put the several-months-pregnant Anne Hutchinson on trial in November 1637. It followed in the aftermath of recent vicious fighting against the Pequot Indians. In the eyes of the men who now sat in judgment of her, Anne

Hutchinson had not helped her cause by opposing violence against the Indians.

During the two-day trial in which judges were also prosecutors (and jury), most historians agree that Hutchinson bested her male accusers. "In nearly every exchange of words, she defeated [Winthrop], and the other members of the General Court with him," Edmund S. Morgan commented. "The record of her trial, if it is proper to dignify the procedure with that name, is one of the few documents in which her words are recorded, and it reveals a proud, brilliant woman put down by men who judged her in advance."[18]

Defending herself, Hutchinson closed with a prophecy that confirmed the men's view that she was challenging the authority of the judges, which in their logic was tantamount to heresy. "Therefore take heed what yee go about to doe unto me," she warned. "For I know that for this God will ruin you and your posterity, and this whole State." Strong words from a woman standing up to the most powerful men in her world. It was this sort of audacious self-assuredness and open challenge to authority that must have prompted one of the judges to say, "I am fully persuaded that Mistress Hutchinson is deluded by the Devil."

When she told the judges that she had received a divine revelation, "by the voice of his own spirit to my soul," Hutchinson provided the proof of heresy the court needed. Overwhelmingly convicted on the basis of "false revelations," she was judged "not fit for our society" and banished from Boston.

One immediate result of this trial was the decision to establish the colony's first college to train new clergymen. The school was built in Newtown, scene of the Hutchinson trial, and the area's name was changed to Cambridge, in honor of England's great university; the school itself would later be named for its first great benefactor, John Harvard. A Puritan minister and son of a London butcher and tavern owner, Harvard came to America in 1637 but died a year later at age thirty, bequeathing his four-hundred-volume library and half his considerable estate to the school. In essence, Harvard existed because of Hutchinson, as Harvard's own Peter Gomes wrote. "Mrs. Hutchinson was the mother of New England's first and most serious theological schism . . . ; in debate she bested the best of the Massachusetts Bay Colony's male preachers, theologians, and magistrates; and . . . as a result of her heresy the colony determined to provide for the education of a new generation of ministers and theologians who would secure New England's civil and theological peace against future seditious Mrs. Hutchinsons."[19]

Given her advanced pregnancy, the imposition of the sentence was delayed until the end of winter, and Hutchinson remained under what was essentially house arrest. After being excommunicated by her congregation, she and her husband, Will, along with their children, some of their spouses, and thirty other families, left Massachusetts in March 1638 for the island of Aquidneck, in the territory of the Rhode Island colony, which had been purchased from the Narragansett Indians by Roger Williams, another renegade Puritan chased from Boston. The Hutchinsons and their followers founded a settlement called Portsmouth. In June 1638, Anne Hutchinson's pregnancy ended with the birth of a deformed fetus, not uncommon among older pregnant women. This "unnatural pregnancy" was seized upon by Boston's elders as further proof of her links with the devil—and that God was punishing her.

After her husband's death in 1642, Anne Hutchinson moved with six of her children, settling in the Dutch colony of New Amsterdam.

She was permitted to homestead there by the Dutch, who were more tolerant in questions of faith than Boston's Puritans. Dutch governor Willem Kieft, already at war with local Indians, was happy to have more settlers, especially those he could place as a buffer in no-man's-land.

There, fatally, Anne Hutchinson and her family got caught in the crossfire. In the heat of a late summer day in 1643, Anne Hutchinson's nine-year-old daughter was gathering berries in a meadow that overlooked what is now called Long Island Sound. The child probably dallied and, as most children might, ate as many blueberries as she put in her basket. The last of Anne Hutchinson's fourteen children born in England, Susan Hutchinson lived with her mother and extended family in what was then New Amsterdam—to be renamed New York when the Dutch capitulated to the British in 1664. The area in which the Hutchinsons were homesteading was later to be named after another early settler, Jacob Bronck.

As Susan went about her work, she must have heard screams and seen the smoke rising from the direction of her family's homestead. There is no account of the child's reaction. Legends told in this part of the Bronx long afterward held that when the Siwanoy warriors found her, Susan Hutchinson was hiding inside the cleft of a large glacial boulder, known as Split Rock. Her mother, other family members, and several servants all fell victim to the Indian war axes, their bodies then burned in the conflagration as their farmhouse was torched. Fifteen in all died that day when a Siwanoy war party swept through the Hutchinson homestead. An Algonquian-speaking people related to the Lenni Lenape (or Delaware) tribe, the Siwanoy lived in the area between the modern Bronx and Connecticut, covering parts of Westchester County along Long Island Sound. Their attack on the

Hutchinson farm was a reprisal for the massacre of a group of Lenni Lenape a few months earlier. It came during a two-year-long conflict known as Kieft's War, a localized conflict foolishly begun by the Dutch governor. Incompetent and cruel, the heavy-handed Willem Kieft had allowed the prospering trade relations with the local tribes to sour and then turn disastrous. In a series of battles fought between 1640 and 1643, hundreds of Indians and scores of Dutch settlers had been killed.

Ignoring warnings about the Siwanoy raiders, Anne Hutchinson had decided to stay put with her family: she had always enjoyed good relationships with Indians and was something of a pacifist. Since the time of the earlier Pequot War, fought in New England between 1636 and 1637, Hutchinson had argued against fighting with the Indians. As leader of a scripture study group in Boston, she had convinced some of her male disciples not to join a militia force at war with local Indians—making them some of American's earliest conscientious objectors.

But now she was fatally mistaken. According to Hutchinson biographer (and descendant) Eve LaPlante, "the Siwanoy took Susan captive, and their chief, Wampage, adopted her. Wampage also took on Susan's mother's name, calling himself 'Anne-Hoeck' from then on, for it was customary for a Siwanoy warrior to assume the name of his most illustrious victim. The neighboring land was called Ann-Hoeck's Neck. The river was given Anne's surname, and so the modern highway beside it is the Hutchinson River Parkway." Following the raid, nine-year-old Susan Hutchinson spent the next eight or nine years with the Siwanoy and, according to LaPlante, "is said to have left the tribe reluctantly." At eighteen, she arrived back in Boston, where her brother still lived, and married another settler a few months later.[20]

To the Puritan fathers back in Boston, the news of the Indian attack that resulted in Susan's capture and the death of much of her family gave great comfort. Indeed, one of their most heartfelt prayers seemed to have been answered. Longtime Massachusetts governor John Winthrop remarked, "Thus it has pleased the Lord to have compassion of his poor churches here, and to discover this great imposter, an instrument of Satan so fitted and trained to his service for interrupting the passage [of his] kingdom in this part of the world, and poisoning the churches here."

Another Puritan minister, Thomas Weld, saw God using the "devilish natives" for his handiwork: "I never heard that Indians in those parts did ever before this commit the like outrage upon any one family, and therefore God's hand is the more apparently seen herein. To pick out this woeful woman, to make her and those belonging to her an unheard-of heavy example of their cruelty above all others. Thus the Lord heard our groans to heaven, and freed us from this great and sore affliction."[21]

ONE "AFFLICTION" WAS relieved. But a much greater scourge remained. Every English man, woman, and child had heard tales of the Great Massacre of 1622, when Powhatans attacked a Virginia settlement, killing 350 colonists—a third of the population. In Virginia's early years, the losses were so profound that members of Parliament demanded an inquiry into what had become of thousands of British subjects.

But colonial America's "Indian problem" exploded most dramatically and violently in Puritan New England. After the arrival of the Pilgrims in Massachusetts in 1620, Native Americans had coexisted with the English in relative peace for some fifteen years. During this time, the Indians had helped the first Pilgrims survive—as every schoolchild well knows. Trade with Indians was a significant part of the early New England economy. And many English settlers carving out a life in the New England wilderness had learned the value of such everyday Indian necessities as the canoe, moccasins, snowshoes, and maple syrup.

But in time, relations between Indians and New Englanders soured. Many strands were woven into these ties, which were far more elaborate than the simplistic "trinkets-for-wampum and peace pipe" view once offered by schoolbooks and Hollywood. Of enormous import was the reality that there were many Indian nations, often divided by deep rivalries and ancient animosities. The first English to settle Massachusetts quickly grasped this truth and learned to play these intertribal rivalries to their advantage.

The Pilgrims' alliance with Massasoit, chief of the Wampanoag, for instance, was more than amiable friendship. The English understood that their firepower could help Massasoit overcome some of his traditional enemies. Welcoming the Pilgrims and joining the first Thanksgiving feast as a goodwill gesture, Massasoit knew all too well that the English advantages of cannon, musket, sword, pike, and powder could just as easily be turned on his people.

Nor were the Pilgrims reluctant to demonstrate that they were ready and willing to use that force. In a raw display of violence, Miles Standish, the *Mayflower*'s soldier-for-hire and military leader—although perhaps best known for his role in the fictitious Longfellow poem *The Courtship of Miles Standish*—had once grabbed the knife of an Indian and slit his throat, a brutal demonstration of the English will to tamp down Indian resistance.

As with almost all things Puritan, theology played a role in relations with the Indians. Of enormous importance to many Puritan ministers was the hope of converting Indians. The most vigorous Puritan missionary to the Indians, John Eliot, believed that Native Americans might be one of the biblical lost tribes of Israel. Arriving in Boston in 1631, Eliot devoted his life to converting the Indians. After completing a dictionary of the Algonquian language—the most widely spoken language among the northeastern tribes—Eliot set about translating both Old and New Testaments into a phonetic version of Massachusetts, an Algonquian dialect. Completed in 1663, this was the first Bible printed in North America. By then, there was a significant number of converts, known as "praying Indians," and in 1651 Eliot established the first "praying towns." Set up across Massachusetts, these villages accommodated these converts, many of whom were willing to assimilate. When Harvard College, founded in 1635, was officially incorporated in 1650, its charter specified a commitment to educate "the English and Indian youth of this country in knowledge and godliness." (Despite the good intentions, only a handful of Indians attended Harvard in its earliest years.)

As far as the Puritans were concerned, Richard Francis points out, "the biggest favor they could do the Indians, indeed anybody, was to convert them to Christianity, to their own Puritan doctrines. . . . Most Puritans believed the Second Coming of Christ was imminent. It would take place when the scattered tribes of Jews were reunited and converted to Christianity. A place would be made for them in the glittering New Jerusalem that would then come into being. . . . If the American Indian should prove to be the lost tribes of Israel, then it might well follow that the New World, in geographical and historical terms, might prove to be the New World in redemptive terms as well, the culmination of both earthly and spiritual history, the site of the New Jerusalem. . . . This made the task of converting the Indians one of the utmost urgency: the destiny of Christendom might depend on it."[22]

Though not as zealous as Spanish and French missionaries had been in the Americas, some early Puritans, including Eliot, believed converting the Indians was their duty. But they planned to do so without the brutal tactics employed by the Spanish, for whom the threats of slavery and death were early tools of conversion. As part of the "Black Legend," a long Protestant propaganda war against Catholicism, the English attempted to distinguish themselves from the Spanish by printing the landmark accounts of the torture and mistreatment of Caribbean natives by Bartolomé de Las Casas. A Dominican priest whose 1552 *Brief Account of the Destruction of the Indies* catalogued the brutal subjugation of Cuba, Las Casas had sparked some nominal reforms by the Spanish throne. Using the words of Las Casas, retitled *The Tears of the Indians* and referred to as the "Spanish Cruelties," the English tried to claim the moral high ground. As historian Jill Lepore wrote, "Part of the mission of New England's 'city on a hill,' then, was to advertise the civility of the English colonists and to hold it in stark contrast with the barbarous cruelty of Spain's conquistadors and the false and blasphemous impiety of France's Jesuit missionaries."[23]

But as New England villages spread and grew into towns, and as the Puritans pushed further inland and south from their initial coastal toeholds at Plymouth, Salem, and Boston, the number of English settlers exploded. The Indians saw their hunting grounds, farmlands, and sacred territory being overrun. Settlers who sought more acreage to pass on to their children—the chief reason, alongside religion, that many of them left England—were pressing the bounds of the frontier further and further west. With increasing frequency, this was accomplished through questionable real estate dealings with the natives, many of whom possessed no tradition of land being bought and sold. Instead they saw land as a shared resource, to be utilized but not owned. Often the sellers had no real right to offer the land. Eventually, some deeds were simply forged; others were obtained after the Indians had been liberally supplied with alcohol.

Assessing this period in English-Indian relations, Colin Calloway observed, "Europeans used a broad repertoire of devices to obtain land, one of which was to encourage Indians to run up large debts in trade. The tribe's accumulated bill then could be settled only by cession of territory. Indian leaders sometimes used land sales as a strategy to keep colonists at bay, hoping that this time their land hunger would be satisfied, but the pressure on Indian lands was unrelenting, a constant source of friction."[24]

Fueling that pressure was the prodigious fertility of the Puritans, who clearly observed the biblical admonition to "be fruitful and multiply" in their New World utopia. Seven or eight children in a Puritan family was typical, and much larger families—Anne Hutchinson's fourteen or the Emersons' fifteen, for instance—were hardly unusual. "The emigrants who came to Massachusetts in the great migration became the breeding stock for America's Yankee population," David Hackett Fischer writes. "They multiplied at a rapid rate, doubling every generation for two centuries. Their numbers increased to 100,000 by 1700, to at least one million by 1800 . . . —all descended from 21,000 English emigrants who came to Massachusetts in the period from 1629 to 1640."[25]

This swelling tide of colonists, doubling and trebling their numbers, threatened the existence of the dwindling tribes, already decimated by smallpox and other diseases that swept Indian villages with the ferocity of Egypt's plagues—another biblical connection not lost on the Puritans. Epidemic disease—most likely introduced by the traders and fisherman who had plied North America's coastal waters well before the Pilgrims arrived—emptied many northeastern coastal Indian settlements in 1616. That was why the *Mayflower* Pilgrims found a deserted village at the site of their Plymouth landing. In the 1630s, another severe epidemic had a similar effect, as Massachusetts Bay governor John Winthrop reported back to England. "For the natives in these parts, God's hand hath so pursued them as for 300 miles space the greatest part of them are swept away by the smallpox."[26]

Eventually this Puritan population explosion pressed the Indians to fight back for survival. The relative peace, first crafted by the Pilgrim fathers and cultivated by later arrivals, was first shattered during the Pequot War of 1636–37, a brief but brutal conflict that was complicated by the intertribal rivalries among several groups: the Pequot, a coastal Algonquian group based along the Connecticut River; their traditional rivals, the Mohegan, based around the Thames River near modern Norwich, Connecticut; and the Narragansett, of Rhode Island. Along with other area tribes, they were struggling to control their traditional lands and the lucrative fur trade with the competing English and Dutch.

The immediate cause of the war lay in the killings of several English traders and sea captains, blamed on Pequot tribesman. Operating in the belief that the Pequot were harboring those responsible for the deaths of these Englishmen, and convinced that a show of force was needed to deter further attacks, a ninety-man Puritan force attacked a Pequot village on Block Island in August 1636, burning it to the ground.

Leading this army was John Endecott, the fiery Puritan father later described by Nathaniel Hawthorne as "the severest Puritan of all who laid the rock foundation of New England." Endecott might have been the closest colonial American equivalent to an ayatollah or modern jihadist. He had arrived in Massachusetts in 1628 and was made governor of the fledgling Salem settlement established by Roger Conant a few years earlier. When Endecott landed with a fresh group of settlers, Conant turned over the reins of power to the military man.

A veteran of the Protestant wars against Catholics in the Netherlands, Endecott was usually seen carrying his thirty-inch steel blade. It was the same sword he had used to hack down a "pagan" maypole shortly after his arrival in Massachusetts, a story recounted by Governor William Bradford, retold by Nathaniel Hawthorne in *The Maypole of Merry Mount,* and very much at odds with the traditional view of the first English in Massachusetts.

At the center of the maypole drama was Thomas Morton, a London lawyer and partner in a new crown-sponsored trading venture. Morton was among the colonists with interests that were more commercial than spiritual. He sailed to America in 1624 and quickly decided that life among the Puritans—including the diminutive Miles Standish, whom Morton derided as "Captain Shrimp"—was not for him. Leaving Plymouth with a band that consisted mostly of freed indentured servants, Morton moved to a nearby settlement called Mount Wollaston, renamed it Merry Mount, and soon earned a reputation among the Pilgrims as a libertine. As Pilgrim chronicler William Bradford recorded, "After this, they fell to great licentiousness and led a dissolute life, pouring out themselves into all profaneness. And Morton became Lord of Misrule, and maintained as it were a School of Atheism."[27]

Morton also earned the ire of the Pilgrim fathers because he was trading guns and powder with the Indians. He was arrested, put in the stocks, and later shipped back to London; his Merry Mount settlement was renamed Mount Dagon, after a god of the dreaded biblical Philistines. In 1629, the recently arrived John Endecott raided the town, destroyed the remains of the "pagan idol" maypole, and burned the settlement to the ground. (The site of Merry Mount, or Mount Wollaston, is marked in present-day Quincy, Massachusetts.)

Five years later, Endecott argued that the women of the Bay Colony should be veiled in public, harking back to the Apostle Paul's early church admonition for women to cover their heads. His proposal failed and Massachusetts goodies, as they were known, were spared the colonial-era equivalent of the Islamic chador. But Endecott was undeterred. That same year, he used his sword to filet an English flag in order to remove the red cross of St. George. Endecott believed "that the red cross was given to the king of England by the pope, as an ensign of victory and as a superstitious thing, and a relic of Antichrist."[28]

In 1636, Endecott set out after the Pequot Indians with the fury of an avenging angel. After destroying their village on Block Island, Endecott's combined Massachusetts Bay Colony and Indian force moved on to the fortified English settlement at Fort Saybrook, Connecticut, and burned a nearby Pequot village before returning to Massachusetts. Endecott may have thought himself victorious. But as soon as his militiamen departed, the Pequot struck back, besieging Fort Saybrook and raiding other Connecticut towns, killing as many as a third of the colony's settlers. In response to these raids, another militia army was gathered, now joined by Narragansett and Niantic Indian allies, and attacked a Pequot village on the Mystic (Misistuck) River. Most of the village's warriors had left on a raid, leaving behind six hundred or seven hundred Pequots, most of them women and children.

Mayflower Pilgrim William Bradford recorded this Puritan search-and-destroy mission. His memorable telling appears in *Of Plymouth Plantation*:

> They approached the same with great silence and surrounded it both with the English and Indians, that they might not break out; and so assaulted them with great courage, shooting amongst them, and entered the fort with all speed. And those that first entered found sharp resistance from the enemy who both shot at and grappled with them; others ran into their houses and brought out fire and set them on fire, which soon took in their mat; and standing close together, with the wind all was quickly on a flame, and thereby more were burnt to death than was otherwise slain; It burnt their bowstrings and made them unserviceable; those that scaped the fire were slain with the sword, some hewed to pieces, others run through with their rapiers, so as they were quickly dispatched and very few escaped. It was conceived they thus destroyed about 400 at this time. It was a fearful sight to see them thus frying in the fire and the streams of blood quenching the same, and horrible was the stink and scent thereof; but the victory seemed a sweet sacrifice.[29]

The Mystic raid shattered the Pequot resistance, and most of the aftermath was a grim mopping-up effort. Although the Pequot chief, or sachem, Sassacus, continued to fight, many Pequots abandoned their villages and went to join other southern Algonquian tribes. In June 1637, a mixed force of English and their Mohegan allies, led by their chief, Uncas, caught one of the last large bands of Pequots in a swamp near Fairfield, Connecticut.[30] Although several hundred women were allowed to leave, most of the warriors were killed or captured. Many of the surviving Pequots were eventually absorbed by the victorious Mohegan and Narragansett as slaves. Some others were shipped to Bermuda and Barbados to be sold as slaves, or forced into servitude in Puritan New England households. Sassacus was later caught by the rival Mohawk and beheaded; the Mohawk sent his head to the English in tribute.

In the eyes of the Massachusetts colonists, this was a "just war."[31] Just or not, the Pequot War guaranteed a measure of peace between colonists and Indians, despite a brief flare-up of hostilities with the Narragansett. Allied with the colonists during the Pequot War, the Narragansett could see the handwriting on the wall. Their turn would soon come. "You know our fathers had plenty of deer and skins, our plains were full of deer, also our woods, and of turkies, and our coves full of fish and fowl," the tribe's sachem, Miantonomi, told the Montauk of Long Island. "But these English have gotten our land, they with scythes cut down the grass, and with axes fell the trees; their cows and horses eat the grass, and their hogs spoil our clam banks, and we shall be starved."[32]

Miantonomi attempted to unite several rival tribes against the colonists, but he was unsuccessful in convincing others to join an alliance. Instead, with the support of the colonists, the rival Mohegan went to war with the Narragansett, and Miantonomi was captured and killed, ending another native threat. For the next three decades, the colonists enjoyed a measure of peace, until another tribal sachem accomplished what Miantonomi had dreamed of doing in 1642—uniting some of New England's Algonquian-speaking tribes against the English settlers. In 1675, the simmering hostilities between native and colonist boiled over in the colonial era's most catastrophic conflict, King Philip's War.

Brothers, these people from the unknown world will cut down our groves, spoil our hunting and planting grounds, and drive us and our children from the graves of our fathers, and our council fires, and enslave our women and children.

—ATTRIBUTED TO METACOM,
also called King Philip[33]

In Hannah Dustin's day, painfully fresh memories still would have lingered of the terrible fighting of a generation earlier, when Metacom went to war with the English settlers in the summer of 1675. Metacom (also called Metacomet) was the second son of Massasoit, sachem of the Wampanoag and the chief who had allied himself with the *Mayflower* Pilgrims. Metacom had been given the English name Philip, and his older brother, Wamsutta, had been renamed Alexander after the famous kings of Macedon. There have been disputes for centuries over the exact provocation for King Philip's War. But there is no question that the underlying cause was the reality that the Indians could see the end of life as they knew it. Hunting grounds lost to pasture and unscrupulous land deals had soured relations between Metacom and the English. When Alexander died in 1662 while in English custody, Philip was convinced that the English had poisoned his older brother. Once elevated to sachem, Philip began to prepare for war, selling land to acquire more guns and powder, which some enterprising colonists were all too willing to peddle.

The breaking point came with the execution of three of Philip's tribesmen, convicted in the murder of John Sassamon, a Harvard-educated "praying Indian," and one of John Eliot's most enterprising converts. Working as a mediator between Wampanoag and the English, John Sassamon—related by marriage to Philip's sister—revealed to colonial authorities that the Wampanoag were planning to ally themselves with their traditional enemies, the Narragansett, to attack the English. Since the English first arrived, they had been able to skillfully finesse the rivalries between New England's tribes. Now, the prospect of Indian tribal alliances set alarm bells ringing for the Massachusetts authorities.

After John Sassamon was found dead in an icy pond, three of Philip's tribesmen were quickly tried and convicted of murder, based on the claim of a single Indian eyewitness—contrary to English law, which at the time required at least two eyewitnesses. During the execution on June 8, 1675, after the first two men were hanged, the rope of the third condemned man broke. Promised a reprieve, he confessed to the crime, giving the guilty verdict the second witness required by law. (The reprieve was short-lived; a month later, he was taken from his cell and shot.)

The executions were the final provocation Philip's warriors needed. Although Philip wanted to delay his offensive until he had time to stockpile more food and weapons, he could not keep his men back. On June 24, 1675, the Indians, many now armed with flintlocks against colonists with older, less reliable matchlock guns, began their attacks at Swansea in Rhode Island. Lasting from June 1675 to August 1676, King Philip's War was a devastating conflict that cost the lives of thousands on both sides, soldiers and civilians alike. As one English town after another was attacked and destroyed, the colonists retaliated against Indian settlements. Neither side spared women or children. In what was known as the Great Swamp Fight of December 19, 1675, the army of the united colonies attacked a palisaded Indian fort and burned all the wigwams inside, killing some six hundred Narragansetts, half of them women and children.

It was not simply a settler-versus-Indian war, as some New England tribes remained allied with the English. Philip's army had also been pressed up against another enemy to the west, the Mohawk of New York, part of the Iroquois alliance, traditional enemies of the Algonquian-speakers of New England.

In *Mayflower*, an account of King Philip's War, Nathaniel Philbrick appropriately summarizes the devastation. "The English had suffered casualties that are difficult for us to comprehend today. . . . During the 14 months of King Philip's War, Plymouth Colony lost close to 8 percent of its men. But the English losses seem inconsequential when compared with those of the Indians. Of a total Native population of approximately 20,000, at least 2,000 had been killed in battle or died of their injuries; 3,000 had died of sickness and starvation, 1,000 had been shipped out of the country as slaves, while an estimated 2,000 eventually fled to either the Iroquois to the west or the Abenakis to the north. Overall, the Native American population of southern New England had sustained a loss of somewhere between 60 and 80 percent."[34]

Survivors on both sides were left widowed, orphaned, homeless, impoverished, and, in the case of the natives, often in slavery. Many Indian children were sold as indentured servants to Puritan families, and others—apparently including Metacom's son—were shipped to the West Indies slave markets. The war nearly wiped out the last remnants of the Wampanoag—the confederation of tribes whose assistance had helped keep the first Pilgrims alive back in the winter and spring of 1621 and who then sat down to enjoy the first harvest feast of legend in October 1621. Other tribes allied with Philip's Wampanoag, such as the Nipmuc and Narragansett, also suffered devastating losses. Their crushing defeat signaled the end, as Neal Salisbury wrote, "of the legal and political autonomy of the region's Native Americans."[35] The war also led to the introduction of a royal governor in New England, greatly diminishing the New England colonies' near autonomy, with far-reaching consequences.

Philip was killed on August 12, 1676, shot by an Indian fighting with the English. Captain Benjamin Church, who commanded the forces that had captured Philip's wife and son and then killed Philip, ordered that his corpse be drawn and quartered and then decapitated. The chief's head was then carried back to Plymouth, where a great thanksgiving feast of another sort was celebrated. Philip's head was then staked on a pike for the public to see. It remained there for years, until a young Cotton Mather is supposed to have snuck up to the skull and removed its jaw.[36]

King Philip's War generated a flood of colonial accounts—a cottage publishing industry in war diaries and histories, including those of both Increase and Cotton Mather. Colonel Benjamin Church, an independent-minded settler who emerged as one of America's first "war heroes," wrote a memoir of his role in capturing Philip, helping to make him a prototype for such legendary Indian-fighters as James Fenimore Cooper's Natty Bumppo. But the postwar publishing boomlet also created the era's first icon of Puritan faith and resilience in the wildly popular account of the captivity of Mary Rowlandson, whose story certainly would have been familiar to Hannah Dustin. In February 1676, a Nipmuc war party attacked the small town of Lancaster, in central Massachusetts, and carried off Mary Rowlandson. The thirty-eight-year-old wife of Lancaster's minister, she and her six-year-old daughter were taken captive, along with another two dozen of Lancaster's settlers. Rowlandson was separated from her two other children, taken by a separate band of raiders.

Oh the dolefull sight that now was to behold at this House! . . . Of thirty seven persons who were in this one house, none escaped either present death, or a bitter captivity, save only one, who might say as he, Job 1.15. And I only am escap'd alone to tell the News. There were twelve killed some shot, some stab'd with their Spears, some knock'd down with their Hatchets. When we are in prosperity, Oh the little that we think of such dreadfull sights, and to see our dear Friends and Relations ly bleeding out their heart-blood upon the ground. There was one who was chopt into the head with a Hatchet, and stripped naked, and yet was crawling up and down. It is a solemn sight to see so many Christians lying in their blood, some here, some there, like a company of Sheep torn by Wolves. All of them stript naked by a company of hell-Hounds, roaring, singing, ranting and insulting, as if they would have torn our very hearts out; yet the Lord by his Almighty power preserved a number of us from death, for there were twenty-four of us taken alive and carried captive.

I had often before this said, that if the Indians should come, I should chuse rather to be killed by them than be taken alive, but when it came to the tryal my mind changed; their glittering weapons so daunted my spirit that I chose rather to go along with those (as I may say) ravenous Beasts, than that moment to end my dayes; and that I may the better declare what Happened to me during that grievous Captivity.[37]

Like hundreds of other New Englanders before her—and later Hannah Dustin—Mary Rowlandson survived her captivity. But her six-year-old daughter, Sarah, died in Mary's arms from her wounds, a fate shared by most of her other neighbors taken captive. For three months, Rowlandson was held among the Indians—warriors, women, and children all moving together. As they traversed western and central Massachusetts and fought the Anglo-American colonists, she witnessed the celebration of a great Indian victory and was also among the first Europeans to see a "war dance."

Shortly after her daughter's death, Rowlandson was taken to a rendezvous of more than two thousand Indians, where she learned that her other children were nearby. Ten-year-old Mary was being held by a warrior who had purchased her for the price of a gun and would not allow Rowlandson to see the child. Then she found eleven-year-old Joseph, who had been taken to another village but was permitted to visit his mother. And she ultimately encountered Philip, who shared a meal with her. In May, over the objections of Philip, who did not actually control her fate, Rowlandson was ransomed and reunited with her husband in Boston; their two children were also eventually released. With encouragement from Increase Mather, *The Sovereignty and Goodness of God,* Mary Rowlandson's account of her experiences, appeared in print six years later, in 1682. One of the earliest books written by a woman in America, it was among the country's first best sellers.[38]

Rowlandson's extraordinarily successful memoir, like Cotton Mather's versions of Hannah Dustin's exploits in the late 1690s, was a prime example of popular Puritan propaganda that underscored the virtues of a brave woman standing up to "satanic savagery." Along with Hannah Dustin, Rowlandson gave New England an essential foundation myth upon which Puritan pride would be built. This was in sharp contrast to the legacy of Anne Hutchinson. Not long after her trial, Puritan Boston decreed a prohibition against Roman Catholics, Quakers, and other sects such as Anabaptists. All were banned under pain of death. Anne Hutchinson's youngest sister, who had become a Quaker, was thrashed with a whip for her "blasphemy." Another of

Anne Hutchinson's followers who joined the Quakers, Mary Dyer, and who also defiantly returned to Boston, was arrested, stripped in public, and severely lashed. When Dyer returned to Boston a second time with two Quaker men, all three were convicted of blasphemy and the two men were hanged. Told to leave Boston, Mary Dyer refused. On June 1, 1660, she too was executed.

Anne Hutchinson, Mary Rowlandson, Hannah Dustin—each woman's story carried its own moral for the people of New England. The Puritan fathers believed that the banishment of Anne Hutchinson—along with the execution of Quakers and the banning of Catholics in Massachusetts—would end dissent and bring God's blessings on the colony. After King Philip's War, it was thought that the death and dismemberment of Metacom and the symbolic triumph of Mary Rowlandson would end the cataclysmic wars with the Indians. And again in 1697, the victory of Hannah Dustin over the Abenaki and the end of King William's War was expected to bring peace with the French.

All were short-lived visions.

❧ Aftermath ❧

Any hope for the British to win peace with the French and their Indian allies was shattered when the next phase of fighting, known in America as Queen Anne's War, began in 1702.[39] With different tribes allying themselves with both sides once more, the conflict spread as far south as St. Augustine, which the English attacked and burned in 1702. In 1704, an English force moved out of South Carolina and attacked Spain's Florida missions in what became known as the Apalachee

Massacre. This phase of the war nearly wiped out the remnants of the tribes who had once battled Spanish conquistadors and eventually accepted the Spanish missions and Catholicism, and for whom the Appalachian Mountains were later named. Hundreds were killed, and many more were taken captive and sold as slaves. About eight hundred Apalachees fled west into French Louisiana, where they were greeted by yet another catastrophic epidemic.[40]

In the winter of 1704, a combined French and Indian force attacked the settlement at Deerfield, an English outpost in remote western Massachusetts. After a heavy snowfall built up a ramp that allowed the raiders to easily mount the village's palisade, the ensuing massacre left fifty-seven of Deerfield's settlers dead. Again, this episode produced captives and captivity accounts. Among the most famous of these stories was the tale of Deerfield's minister, John Williams, famed as the "redeemed captive." But as with the tale of Anne and Susan Hutchinson, the fate of another Deerfield captive went untold for a very long time. Eunice Williams, the daughter of the "redeemed captive," chose to marry her Indian captor and remain in Canada.

Queen Anne's War lasted until 1713, ending in the Treaty of Utrecht, which extended England's American possessions at the expense of France. But the French and English contest for America was far from over.

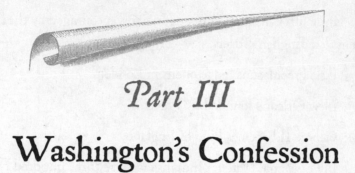

Part III

Washington's Confession

1714   George I becomes first Hanoverian king of England.

1715   In South Carolina, Yamasee Indians, encouraged by the Spanish, massacre English settlers.

1717   First Freemasons lodge opens in London.

1718   New Orleans founded by French.

1727   George II becomes king of England.

1729   In Louisiana, Natchez Indians massacre three hundred French soldiers and settlers.

1732   Georgia, last of the thirteen British colonies, is established as a defensive buffer against the Spanish in Florida; Roman Catholics are prohibited under its charter.

George Washington is born in Virginia.

1739   War of Jenkins' Ear fought between Britain and Spain, as part of the wider War of Austrian Succession, fought among European powers.

1741   Major Scots-Irish migration to America to escape persecution in Ulster, Ireland.

1743-1748   King George's War fought between British and French in North America, as part of the wider War of the Austrian Succession.

1753   French forces construct three forts in the Ohio River Valley.

1754   On April 16, the French expel the Virginians from the fort they are building at the forks of the Monongahela and Ohio rivers. On May 27, George Washington ambushes a French party; on July 3–4, the French force Washington to surrender.

1755   Defeat of British general Braddock by French and Indians in western Pennsylvania.

1756–1763   The Seven Years' War is formally declared in Europe.

1759   British capture Quebec; British general Wolfe and French leader Montcalm are both killed in battle.

1760   George III becomes king of Great Britain.

Montreal surrenders to British forces.

1762   Boston lawyer James Otis issues his first political tract, *A Vindication of the Conduct of the House of Representatives*, arguing that American colonists have the rights of Englishmen.

1763   Treaty of Paris is signed, ending the Seven Years' War (and the French and Indian War). Britain becomes the dominant power in the Americas; France retains New Orleans; Florida is ceded to Britain by Spain.

Associate yourself with Men of good Quality if you Esteem your own Reputation; for 'tis better to be alone than in bad Company.

—*Rules of Civility and Decent Behavior,*
Rule 56 (1640)

Formal attacks & platoon firing would never answer against the savages and Canadiens. It ought to be laid down as a maxim to attack them first, to fight them in their own way, and go against them light & naked, as they come against us.

—*Captain Adam Stephens,*
Virginia Ranger (1754)

I fortunately escaped without a wound, tho' the right Wing where I stood was exposed to & received all the Enemy's fire and was the part where the man was killed. . . . I can with trust assure you, I heard Bullets whistle and believe me there was something charming in the sound.

—*George Washington*
(May 31, 1754)

DEEP IN PENNSYLVANIA'S WESTERN WILDERNESS, with a small force of bad-tempered, ill-trained, rain-soaked Virginia militiamen and a group of Indians he barely trusted, twenty-two-year-old George Washington had a decision to make. Hundreds of miles from his superiors in Williamsburg, the young lieutenant colonel had been ordered not to engage any French forces should he encounter them—there was peace between the French and British. But now here he was, faced with a small detachment of French soldiers bivouacked in the Pennsylvania woods. Washington believed that many more French troops might soon follow. He could withdraw, report, and await orders. Or he could make a stand, stop this scouting party, and await reinforcements from Virginia.

Ambitious but untested in combat, headstrong, perhaps even foolhardy—the young Virginia planter's son chose to strike first, before the French could attack. He was urged on by his Indian ally, a Mingo tribal chief named Tanaghrisson, known to the English as the Half King.

In the early morning of May 28, 1754, with some of his men still lost and wandering in the thick Ohio River Valley wilds about sixty miles south of present-day Pittsburgh, Washington moved his forty backwoodsmen and their Indian allies through the dense woods. There would be no close-order march or precise firing lines accompanied by drums and pipes, in European military textbook fashion. Instead Washington's men moved Indian-style, stealthily surrounding the French from a rock cliff overlooking the small clearing where they were camped.

All through the night before, a steady, pouring rain had soaked the men. Now they readied their powder and dried their "Brown Besses," the notoriously inaccurate flintlock muskets they carried. In the clearing below them, the thirty or so Frenchmen began to wake, creeping from beneath blankets or out of rough lean-tos made from tree branches to start fires and cook breakfast. A Frenchman spotted one of the Virginians and cried out in alarm. In an instant, two shots rang out. The Virginia militiamen had, without a direct order from Washington, begun to fire on the French camp. In the pandemonium and thick fog of acrid gunsmoke hanging over the scene, the French soldiers gamely tried to return fire. Washington's Indian allies cut off any escape. The firefight lasted a mere ten or fifteen minutes. When it was over, one of Washington's men was dead and another three had been wounded. The French had suffered fourteen dead and wounded. Another twenty Frenchmen had been captured unharmed. Among the French wounded was a thirty-five-year-old ensign named Joseph de Jumonville.

What happened then has been the subject of conjecture and debate for more than 250 years. But these next few moments changed history—of that there is no doubt. Far from the halls of power in London and Paris, a world war had begun.

After the confusion of battle, as clouds of musket smoke—the thick bluish gray haze that inspired the phrase "fog of war"—slowly lifted, and as the wounded lay around him moaning, Washington struggled to understand the French officer. Translators on either side provided little help. Jumonville gestured frantically, waving some papers at the Virginian. Only after considerable misunderstanding did his purpose become clear. This small detachment and the injured Jumonville were not scouts, the vanguard of a French invasion force, as Washington suspected. Carrying a message to the English colonial authorities in Virginia, Jumonville was on a diplomatic mission. The letter the young officer waved at Washington was from the French governor in Canada and warned the English that the Ohio River Valley was French territory. It went on to threaten that no English expeditions should enter the area and that France would accept no English settlements in the area.

As Washington's interpreter struggled to make out the gist of the Frenchman's diplomatic letter—a thinly veiled threat aimed directly at the English crown—there was a flurry of motion. The chief who had guided and advised Washington, the Half King, moved beside Jumonville. Without warning, the Half King swung his hatchet, burying it in the wounded Frenchman's head, saying in French, "Thou art not dead yet, my father." Reaching into Jumonville's shattered skull, the Half King pulled out some brain matter and smeared it on his hands. As if on signal, the rest of the Half King's warriors fell on the wounded French captives. The Indians methodically scalped and stripped the Frenchmen as they were killed. One French soldier's decapitated head was then impaled on a stick.[1]

George Washington's later descriptions and reports of this seemingly minor battle and its horrific aftermath were brief and lacked these grim details. The twenty-two-year-old planter's son with precious little military experience first simply reported, "The French sent a detachment to reconnoiter our Camp and obtain intelligence of our strength & position; notice of which being given by the Scouts [Indians], GW [Washington] marched at the head of the party, attacked, killed 9 or 10, & captured 20 odd." In a more expansive follow-up letter written the next day to his superior, Governor Robert Dinwiddie, Washington mentioned Jumonville's death almost in passing. After spending considerable time complaining about the "trifling pay" received by colonial officers and the dissent this was causing within the ranks, Washington noted only that Jumonville was "amongst those that were killd." It was not an outright lie by the man later immortalized as the relentless truth-teller of cherry tree fame. Perhaps, at this moment, Washington thought, the less said the better.[2]

Two days later, Washington wrote a much more buoyant description of this "most signal victory" to his brother Jack, in which he added, almost as a postscript: "I fortunately escaped without a wound, tho' the right Wing where I stood was exposed to & received all the Enemy's fire and was the part where the man was killed & the rest wounded. I can with truth assure you, I heard bullets whistle and believe me there was something charming in the sound."[3] (When King George II later read of this account, he supposedly retorted, "He would not say so had he been used to hear many.")

Washington's terse description of a questionable decision on his part—clearly at odds with his orders not to engage in hostilities— made no mention of the Half King's grisly attack on Jumonville, a wounded prisoner. Reports detailing the death of Jumonville and how the Mingo warriors then scalped the wounded French captives only emerged afterward. Apparently the Half King was eager to avenge the death of his own father at French hands. Nor did Washington's account agree with the one delivered by the only French survivor of the battle, whose version of the events placed the blame for killing the wounded French soldiers squarely on Washington and his Virginians. The lone Frenchman who had escaped the ambush and watched the massacre of the French company from hiding, had made his way back to the French command. Eager for vengeance, a company of French troops was dispatched to track down Washington's Virginians. They were led by Captain Louis Coulon de Villiers, the brother of the dead Jumonville. When the French pursuers reached the scene of the battle in the clearing, they found the unburied bodies of their comrades and one severed head gazing at them from a pole.

The incident to which Washington had given his "spin" in such convenient brevity set off a chain of events that started a war about which the French Enlightenment philosopher Voltaire later wrote, "Such was the complication of political interests that a cannon shot fired in America could give the signal that set Europe ablaze." That war, the Seven Years' War—known in American history as the French and Indian War—cost the lives of some 853,000 soldiers and perhaps hundreds of thousands more civilians worldwide.[4]

In America, this deadly conflict's repercussions would ultimately carry the thirteen colonies on the road to revolution. This brief battle, involving a young colonial officer in an utterly remote backwater of England's great empire, altered the course of American history. It led to the demise of France as a competing force in North America. The policies that flowed from England's ultimate victory would also alter the course of American history, as fledgling Americans saw themselves in a new light and increasingly balked at decisions handed down in London. And it would provide many young colonial officers and soldiers with their first battlefield tests, perhaps even hinting that Britannia might rule, but was not invincible.

The battle at what became known as Jumonville's Clearing (or Jumonville's Glen) also begged another question: Was young George Washington fit for command? And, in a more controversial modern context, was the "Father of His Country" a war criminal culpable for the death of Jumonville, as the French eyewitness claimed, or at least permitting the actions of his Indian allies? It is not a question usually posed by history books, which tend to gloss over this phase of Washington's life and early career, moving almost directly to his leading the troops in the American Revolution.

But the experiences that the twentysomething future general and president had during the "Old War," as the Revolutionary generation called it, were Washington's "forge of experience," in biographer James Thomas Flexner's apt phrase. Washington's headstrong—or misguided—and mostly disastrous misadventures in the Pennsylvania wilderness, and later in wartime Virginia, were crucial moments in shaping the skills, personality, and command experience he brought to his leadership of the Continental army more than twenty years later. That he survived numerous brushes with death during this time might have been viewed by some as proof of his destiny.

In 1754, at the time of Washington's surprise attack on the French diplomatic party, England and France were officially at peace. But this was a cold-war atmosphere, the relative calm before an all-engulfing storm. Following the 1748 Treaty of Aix-la-Chapelle, ending the War of the Austrian Succession (called King George's War in America), there was a temporary lull in the on-again, off-again fighting that had preoccupied the two countries and their various European and American Indian allies for more than fifty years. Under the treaty's terms, the British had won some additional Canadian coastal territory from France. Left unresolved was the much larger question of control of a vast and valuable swath of North America's largely unexplored interior, the Ohio River Valley.

Things would soon come to a head over this prized piece of American real estate, claimed by both countries. Sparsely inhabited by Indians—mostly members of the powerful Iroquois Confederacy, along with bands of Shawnees and Delawares forced from their coastal homelands—the vast Ohio Valley had begun to lure settlers from the colonies of Pennsylvania, Maryland, and Virginia. Most of them were Scots-Irish and German squatters, homesteading on the unsecured land in a largely uncharted wilderness. Approximately two hundred thousand square miles of territory that encompasses parts of modern Indiana, Ohio, Kentucky, and West Virginia and smaller portions of several other states, the Ohio River Valley was richly forested and watered by a system of rivers that eventually emptied into the Mississippi River. (The Ohio River rises at modern Pittsburgh and empties into the Mississippi at Cairo, Illinois.) Ripe for settlement, the territory was also teeming with enormous reserves of highly prized beaver, by this time largely extinct in Europe. And the fur trade with the Indians who lived there—a source of great fortunes made in Europe and America—was a crucial piece of the spoils that finally brought the two countries to war.

When it came, the war gave George Washington his first taste of command, a harsh introduction to combat, and a measure of celebrity that carried him to leadership of the Continental army in 1775—along with some up-close and personal experiences of how disastrous and unglorious the business of war could actually be.

※

BARELY A YEAR before the brief ambush that altered the destinies of America and Europe, the twenty-one-year-old Washington had no actual experience or training as a soldier. He was a young man of relatively modest circumstances and precious little formal education. Although he possessed a small farm, it yielded little income and was still in the hands of his overly controlling, widowed mother, Mary Ball Washington. Young Washington's only brush with military life had come through the war stories told by his half brother Lawrence, fourteen years his senior.

The firstborn of Augustine "Gus" Washington's first marriage, Lawrence Washington had joined a regiment of Virginia volunteers assigned to a British navy ship during the War of Jenkins' Ear, a conflict between Spain and England begun in 1739, but eventually part of the larger War of the Austrian Succession.[5] Lawrence Washington commanded a marine detachment on the flagship of Admiral Edward Vernon, known as "Old Grog," who had earned everlasting infamy as the man who ordered his sailors' daily ration of rum diluted with water. This cost-saving measure was also meant to reduce the incidence of drunken brawls, but British tars cursed Vernon's name, and "three-water rum," meted out in two daily rations, became the British navy standard.

Although Admiral Vernon was a hero early in the war, he commanded during one of the greatest British naval disasters in history at the battle of Cartagena (off Colombia, South America). In a catastrophic campaign in the spring of 1741, the British lost some eighteen thousand men—more than half of them from tropical diseases—and fifty warships were destroyed. Aboard Vernon's flagship, Lawrence witnessed this debacle. When he returned home, Lawrence Washington was given command of training Virginia's militia—a largely honorary post. Dashing in his dress uniform, Lawrence enthralled his younger half brother with exciting tales of naval cannons booming, glorious combat, and the spit-and-polish romance of the officer's life. Most likely, he skirted the less appealing realities of what he had seen—the ravages of typhoid, yellow fever, scurvy, and dysentery, and the routinely brutal life of sailors on board British warships.

Soon after Lawrence's return, in 1743, when George was eleven, his father, Gus Washington, died. As the oldest son, Lawrence received his father's larger plantation, Little Hunting Creek, renaming it Mount Vernon in honor of the admiral with whom he had served. As the oldest son of his father's second marriage, young George was willed the smaller Ferry Farm, which would remain in his mother's hands until George came of age at twenty-one. Although he lived there with his mother, George was far happier with Lawrence at Mount Vernon, and he spent most of his time with his older brother, who essentially became his surrogate father.

Unlike Lawrence and his other half brother, Augustine junior, George was not sent to England for schooling. Instead, he received a rudimentary grammar school education in Virginia. His schoolboy notebooks contain his careful copying of a popular colonial-era combination of Miss Manners and *How to Win Friends and Influence People.* A collection of 110 maxims, *Rules of Civility and Decent Behavior in Company and Conversation* was composed by a Jesuit priest in 1595 to instruct French aristocrats. Its pithy advice and tips on etiquette were translated into English in 1640. Whether young George was honestly devoted to these principles or merely setting them down to hone his penmanship is uncertain. But he did have a lifelong appetite for such maxims, and there is little question that throughout Washington's adult life, he publicly exhibited the sort of ordered civility that had been prescribed by this strict set of principles for "decent behavior," among which were included these rules:

1st Every Action done in Company, ought to be with Some Sign of Respect, to those that are Present.

2d When in Company, put not your Hands to any Part of the Body, not usually Discovered. . . .

24th Do not laugh too loud or too much at any Publick Spectacle. . . .

66th Be not froward [*sic*] but friendly and Courteous. . . .

87th Let thy carriage be such as becomes a Man Grave Settled and attentive to that which is spoken. Contradict not at every turn what others Say. . . .

98th Drink not nor talk with your mouth full neither Gaze about you while you are drinking. . . .

110th Labor to keep alive in your Breast that Little Spark of Celestial fire Called Conscience.

Lawrence suggested that "boy George" become a midshipman in the Royal Navy, and plans to send him to England were set in motion. But in a decision that may well have rewritten the course of history, Washington's cantankerous and, by every account, extremely controlling mother put her foot down. She was said to believe—correctly, it seems in retrospect—that an American farmer's young son would be considered little more than a country bumpkin by the English and could never rise through the rigidly stratified, aristocratic world of the Royal Navy. An English uncle agreed, and a disappointed George unpacked his bags.

His next few years were largely spent in Lawrence's orbit, and when Lawrence married Ann Fairfax, daughter of Colonel William Fairfax, young George Washington gained entree into one of the richest and most powerful families in Virginia's plantation ruling class. Although far from poor, and with substantial holdings in land and slaves, the Washingtons were still not counted among Virginia's most elite families. The first Washington to settle in Virginia was John—George's great-grandfather—who left England for America in 1657, following the English Civil War and the execution of King Charles I in 1649. At this time, Oliver Cromwell's Protectorate held rein and Puritans exerted sway over the defeated royalists and Anglicans—known as "Cavaliers." John Washington's father, an Oxford-trained Anglican minister, was one of those who lost his job under Cromwell's Roundhead regime.

Virginia's population would explode under a "Cavalier migration" as those loyal to the throne and the Church of England fell from political grace. During the 1650s, as David Hackett Fischer put it, "Virginia's Royalist immigrants were refugees from oppression, just as New England's Puritans themselves had been."[6]

Having settled in Virginia, George Washington's great-grandfather earned the name Conotocarious, meaning "town taker," from some local Indians. It was neither a polite nor admiring honorific. Apparently John Washington had swindled some of the Indians out of land. The taste for acquiring land seems to have run thick in the Washington bloodlines, and John Washington and Washington's own father eagerly added to their real estate holdings. When Gus Washington died, he left behind an estate of some ten thousand acres and forty-nine slaves, along with a small iron foundry. Impressive, perhaps, but far from aristocratic.

The connection to the Fairfaxes gave Lawrence—and George by extension—a leg up in that world. The titular head of the family, Thomas, Lord Fairfax, was Virginia's largest single landholder—although mostly an absentee landlord. He remained in England and his cousin, Colonel William Fairfax, managed the Fairfax properties, a grant totaling some five million acres. When the childless bachelor Lord Fairfax did arrive from London for a visit to his Virginia holdings, his immediate and single-minded interest was in fox hunting. An experienced rider, the strapping, six-foot-tall George was invited to ride with his lordship. Suddenly, the unschooled and quiet teenager was transported into a whole new world of wealth and privilege.

Colonel William Fairfax, Lawrence Washington's father-in-law, also took a liking to young George Washington, and he was invited to join a surveying party, accompanying George Fairfax, the colonel's son, on an expedition into the wilderness of the Blue Ridge Mountains and the Shenandoah Valley beyond. Perhaps, as he set off, Washington may have recalled Rule 56 from *Rules of Civility and Decent Behavior:* "Associate yourself with Men of good Quality if you Esteem your own Reputation; for 'tis better to be alone than in bad Company." Aligning himself with powerful and wealthy friends would be a hallmark of Washington's career. If not to the manor born, Washington had learned the necessary eighteenth-century networker's skills.

Spending days on horseback, putting his native mathematical skills to use in learning the science of surveying, and encountering the rough backwoods families who were homesteading in the unmapped—and largely unregulated—wilderness, Washington was captivated and completely at home. He filled an early journal with a record of his experiences. Among other adventures, Washington reported on an encounter with Indians:

Wednesday 23d Rain'd till about two oClock & Clear'd when we were agreeably surpris'd at the sight of thirty odd Indians coming from War with only one Scalp. We had some Liquor with us of which we gave them Part it elevating there Spirits put them in the Humour of Dancing of whom we had a War Daunce. There Manner of Dauncing is as follows Viz. They clear a Large Circle & make a great Fire in the

Middle then seats themselves around it the Speaker makes a grand Speech telling them in what Manner they are to Daunce after he has finish'd the best Dauncer Jumps up as one awaked out a Sleep & Runs & Jumps about the Ring in a most comicle Manner.

—GEORGE WASHINGTON
"Journal of My Journey"

Washington put his newly acquired surveying skills to profitable use. By the time he turned eighteen, he was earning more money from surveying than he could as a farmer. And like his own father and his father before him, the young surveyor was converting cash into property, buying land whenever he could. His first purchase was a 1,459-acre plot. The teenager had become a land speculator.

The next great turn in Washington's life came when Lawrence fell ill. Having returned from the war with a hacking cough, Lawrence was diagnosed with consumption—what is now called tuberculosis. In October 1751, the half brothers sailed for Barbados in the hopes that the climate would improve Lawrence's health. Lasting four weeks— George Washington's only sojourn outside America—the trip was at first idyllic. Washington enthusiastically filled his personal journal with reports of sighting dolphins and other sea creatures. Then George himself took ill, in his case with the severe fever and telltale red pustules that accompany smallpox. George Washington was fortunate to survive this brief bout with one of the greatest killers in American history. His mild case effectively inoculated Washington against a viral disease that would prove to be the deadliest threat during of the American Revolutionary era, a seven-year epidemic that took vastly more lives than actual combat did.[7]

When Lawrence chose to sail on to see if the air in Bermuda might have more beneficial effect than that of Barbados, George returned to Virginia. But the ocean air and warm weather did not provide Lawrence with the hoped-for cure. He returned to Mount Vernon a few months later, only to die in July 1752. In his will, Lawrence left Mount Vernon to his wife, Ann, in trust for their infant daughter. George Washington would inherit the estate only if the child, Sarah, should die.

Ambitious, knowing that surveying would not bring the wealth or social standing he sought, and saddled with a small and somewhat unprofitable farm—as well as a mother who lorded over him—Washington decided to try for a military career. He applied to acting governor Robert Dinwiddie of Virginia for a commission in the colonial militia, essentially seeking to fill his late brother's post. Dinwiddie instead divided the command into four separate commissions and put them out to bid. In a day when such a commission went for a high price, George Washington could ill afford to purchase his position, but he still had powerful friends. Despite his obvious inexperience and meager finances, Washington turned to the Fairfaxes. William Fairfax pulled some strings, and in December 1752 George Washington commenced his military career. He was made a major and charged with training militias in the southern Virginia district. His preparation for this new post apparently involved reading books on military drills and tactics. At the time, most males—at least white ones—between sixteen and sixty were required to participate in local militia companies, and they could be compelled to train as often as once a week.

At this point in his life, George Washington made another choice that has inspired conjecture, controversy, and conspiracy theories for centuries. In August 1753, at age twenty-one, he became a Freemason, joining the lodge in Fredericksburg, Virginia. An ancient fraternal order, Freemasonry took on a new life in eighteenth-century Europe during the Enlightenment, when it grew increasingly hostile toward organized religion, Catholicism in particular. A mélange of religion and ancient fraternal rituals, Masonry recognized a supreme deity, but it also celebrated universal brotherhood, works of charity, and individual liberty. Its deistic ideals may have appealed to Washington, whose devotion to Anglican (later Episcopalian) beliefs seemed tepid at best. It has been oft noted that Washington routinely left church services before partaking of communion. Although this peculiarity has been cited as evidence of Washington's deism, and perhaps even his refutation of the notion of Jesus' divinity, other commentators have remarked that it was not unusual for colonial Anglicans to skip the Eucharist.

Like many men of his day—including Benjamin Franklin, John Hancock, James Madison, and several other Founders, as well as many British officers—Washington may have simply been drawn to Masonry's "old boys" club atmosphere. As David L. Holmes wrote in *Faiths of the Founding Fathers,* his excellent overview of religion's impact on the Revolutionary generation, the Masons were "a fraternal organization that provided a club for men at a time when clubbing represented a principal form of entertainment."[8] Born in England out of an old craft union that guarded the trade secrets of masons, the movement had morphed into an Enlightenment-era secret society that was concerned with moral and spiritual improvement, accompanied by a rejection of clerical dogma. By the eighteenth century, it had become more antagonistic toward Roman Catholicism, and the Vatican had long prohibited Catholics from joining the Masons.

As with almost everything else about Washington's life, his personal religious beliefs became shrouded in a mixture of mythology and speculation almost instantly upon his death. Fabricated tales of axes taken to cherry trees were conflated with nonexistent prayer vigils in Valley Forge to assert Washington's religious ardor. Yet he had taken the presidential oath of office with a Masonic Bible, wore a Masonic apron at the laying of the Capitol's cornerstone, and was buried with both Masonic and Episcopal funeral rites, the latter perhaps for his wife's benefit. Masonry was, after all, a gentleman's preserve. On the other hand, his Masonry seems to have fallen far short of fanatical devotion to a secret society pledged to a "new world order," as some critics of Masonry persist in suggesting. According to H. Paul Jeffers' account of Washington's Masonry, "Records indicate that he attended at most three meetings, and possibly fewer or none. He may have attended the dinners, but he seems not to have participated in meetings of the lodge of which he was the first master under its Virginia charter. . . . While master of the lodge, he did not assist in the work of the lodge."[9]

Young Washington's big break came as the cold war with France heated up considerably. The English had staked a claim to the Ohio Valley territory as part of its western frontier. The French had other ideas. From their base in Quebec, the French loosely controlled an American trading empire that arced from eastern Canada past the Great Lakes to the Mississippi River and down to the port city of New Orleans, established by the French in 1718. Their claims were based on the discoveries made by French explorers, including La Salle, who had traveled the length of the Mississippi River during a 1682 expedition. In June 1753, the governor of Canada, the Marquis de Duquesne, announced that France exclusively owned this territory and ordered all trespassers—meaning principally English settlers—out. He dispatched three hundred French regular soldiers, twelve hundred militiamen, and some two hundred Indians to build three forts: Fort

Presque Isle, on the southern shore of Lake Erie (present Erie, Pennsylvania); Fort Le Boeuf, at the head of French Creek (Waterford, Pennsylvania); and Fort Venango (now Franklin, Pennsylvania), at the point where French Creek joins the Allegheny River. These fortresses would solidify a water route from Lake Erie to the Ohio River and ultimately to the Mississippi, allowing French troops to move easily by river into the territory.

In Virginia, Governor Dinwiddie was alarmed at these French maneuvers. Complicating matters, settlers from the English colonies of Virginia, Pennsylvania, and Maryland had begun to push across the Appalachian Mountains into the Ohio River Valley. In exchange for furs, they began to sell guns, ammunition, and whiskey to the Indians. Influential Virginians, including Dinwiddie, the late Lawrence Washington, the Fairfaxes, and other Virginian aristocrats such as the Lees, wanted to secure a grant of a half million acres out of this territory for their "Ohio Company," formed in 1747. When George Washington learned that Governor Dinwiddie was looking for an emissary who could carry a message to the French military commander in the Ohio River Valley, warning the French to withdraw from the region, he volunteered.

The mission was no stroll in the park. The trip meant traveling through unmarked wilderness, upriver, and across the Allegheny Mountains, then returning south with the rivers—some five hundred miles each way through Indian country. And winter was not far off. In spite of his relative youth and inexperience, Washington was chosen by Dinwiddie because he possessed a unique skill set. He knew the wilderness, was an excellent horseman, and, although far from aristocratic, ranked sufficiently high on Virginia's social ladder through his connections to the Fairfaxes to qualify as a suitable royal messenger.

An experienced surveyor with a good eye for real estate, Washington could also fulfill another part of the job. Essentially, he would be spying on the French as he reconnoitered the territory. Washington could competently map the area and survey possible routes for roads or locations for a fort the English planned to build to counter the French advance. He was accompanied by Jacob van Braam, a Dutchman with a sparse knowledge of French, as an interpreter, and was joined by veteran fur trader and Ohio Company employee Christopher Gist, who would communicate with the Indians they expected to meet. Part of Washington's mission was to demonstrate to the French that the English had a strong alliance with the Iroquois Confederacy. The party was rounded out with four backwoodsmen and a string of pack horses.

Setting off in November 1753, Washington went ahead of the main party and reached the point where the Allegheny River joins the Monongahela River, which rises in the Allegheny Plateau (in modern West Virginia) and flows north to form the Ohio River at the site of present-day Pittsburgh. Washington explored the area for two days until finding what he considered the best site for a fort, a judgment later confirmed by separate French and British efforts to erect fortresses precisely at the location that Washington had singled out.

After the others caught up to him, the little expedition moved on to an Indian village called Logtown, where Washington first encountered the Iroquois chief Tanaghrisson, the Half King. Taken captive as a child by the French and their Indian allies, Tanaghrisson had been adopted by the Seneca. He had become a subchief among the Iroquois Confederacy in the Ohio Valley, the reason he was later dubbed the Half King by the English. Although Washington hoped to convince the Indians to bring a large force of warriors to his meeting with the French, only the Half King and three other elderly chiefs accompanied Washington to meet the French and deliver Dinwiddie's ultimatum.

At the first of the French forts he reached, Washington was treated cordially and invited to dine with the officers. As they supped, Washington drank more modestly than his French hosts, and he later recorded the results:

> The Wine, as they dosed themselves pretty plentifully with it, soon banished the Restraint which at first appear'd in their Conversations, and gave a Licence to their Tongues to reveal their Sentiments more freely.
>
> They Told me That it was their absolute Design to take possession of the Ohio, and by G—— they would do it; for that they were sensible the English could raise two Men for their one, yet they knew, their Motions were too slow and dilatory to prevent any Undertaking of Theirs. They pretend to have an absolute right to the River, from a discovery made by one La Salle 60 years ago.
>
> —GEORGE WASHINGTON,
> *"Journal to the River Ohio"*

Soon after his first encounter with these well-oiled Frenchmen, Washington was taken to Fort Le Boeuf, where the main French force had already established a fort Washington would later describe as "bristling with cannons." Hundreds of canoes were also beached nearby. The French were not trying to disguise their strength or intentions from Washington.

When the young colonial envoy delivered Dinwiddie's message, the French commander rejected the letter, which contained King George's ultimatum to the French. A veteran soldier of the wars in Europe, the French general minced no words. All lands drained by the Ohio River belonged to France. Any outsider would be arrested—if the Indians did not get them first. With little ceremony, Washington was sent packing.

Washington knew that it was urgent that he get the information about the disposition of the French to Dinwiddie. But the trip back to Virginia was far more difficult than the journey out had been. Now late December, it was bitterly cold, and heavy snow fell, slowing the horses, which had to be rested frequently. Unwilling to delay, Washington decided to continue on foot, so he and the trader, Christopher Gist, set off together. At least twice on this return journey, Washington was very nearly killed. First he and Gist were set upon by a group of "French Indians" and one of them shot at the two Virginians at close range—according to Washington, "not 15 Steps, but fortunately missed." Washington and Gist captured their Indian assailant but then let him go, deciding instead to walk all night and put more distance between themselves and the Indians.

When they reached the Allegheny River, expecting it to be frozen over, the pair discovered that it was only half iced and set about building a raft. Working for a whole day with what Washington called "one poor hatcher," the men constructed a rough raft to cross the river. But almost as soon as they set out across the ice-choked river, the raft was caught in an ice jam and Washington was tossed into ten feet of icy water. After pulling himself back aboard, Washington poled the raft with Gist's help to a nearby island, where they spent the night. As temperatures plunged during the night, Washington shivered in his wet clothes and Gist suffered frostbite on his fingers and toes. But in the extreme cold, the river had frozen solid overnight. The two men were able to set off on foot, and early in January 1754, Washington reported back to Dinwiddie in Williamsburg.

Bringing the French response, along with his assessment of French strength and detailed maps he had made of the territory, Washington urged Dinwiddie to build a fort where the Ohio River formed at the fork of the Monongahela and Allegheny rivers. His completed report, including his accounts of the Indians and his several brushes with disaster, was sent on to the Virginia legislature, the House of Burgesses. It was later published as a pamphlet, *The Journal of Major George Washington,* and this brief but exciting adventure narrative, filled with descriptions of the wilderness and Washington's close calls with Indians and frozen rivers in the wild interior of America, made the little-educated, backwoods colonial something of a celebrity on both sides of the Atlantic. His next act caused much larger waves.

Dinwiddie's interests were divided between what was good for Virginia, what was good for England, and what was good for himself as a shareholder in the Ohio Company. With Washington's report in hand, the governor got the burgesses to authorize a three-hundred-man army and construction of a fort at the location Washington had detailed. Acknowledging that he lacked the experience to command, Washington accepted the post of second in command, but was promoted to lieutenant colonel. As James Thomas Flexner, one of Washington's greatest biographers, admiringly put it, "Although only twenty-one, George Washington carried the manifest air of one born to command." Yet, as Flexner also put it, he would find himself in "situations that proved both politically and militarily far beyond his depth."[10]

In April 1754, Washington was ordered back to the Ohio Valley, leading the 159 troops and construction force that had been raised so far. As they moved west over the Allegheny Mountains, they built a rugged wilderness road for their cannons and wagons, the first road constructed in the Ohio Valley. It was difficult, backbreaking work for which the men were poorly paid. They let Washington know of their unhappiness. The men knew that they were ill-paid soldiers in the employ of a distant king and that the chief beneficiaries of their labors would be the colonial gentlemen who ran the Ohio Company. Their unhappiness hinted at the festering class distinctions between the mostly Scots-Irish western backwoods settlers and the landed gentry of Virginia's eastern planter class.

As Washington's combined road crew and army slowly moved west, they met up with the construction crew that had been sent ahead to begin building the fort. These men reported that eight hundred French soldiers and their Indian allies had captured the unfinished English fort and ordered them back to Virginia. The French had begun to construct their own fort—to be named Fort Duquesne—at the same spot. About this time, the Half King appeared on the scene and told Washington that about thirty French soldiers were camped nearby in a hidden ravine. Washington also learned that Half King despised the French—they had supposedly boiled and eaten his father. This was the moment in which Washington made the fateful decision to attack the French, believing that it was an advance party of an invasion force. As James Flexner commented, "Overlooking the fact that England and France were not officially at war, forgetting that the French had not attacked the party at the Forks and that Dinwiddie had ordered him to warn all Frenchmen away before he engaged in hostilities, Washington allowed himself to be persuaded to use the Indian tactic of a surprise attack."[11]

After the ambush, Washington must have quickly realized that he was responsible for the murder of an ambassador. With some eight hundred Frenchmen not far off, Washington decided to retreat to the nearby meadow where he had left the bulk of his troops, about sixty miles south of Fort Duquesne, and quickly throw up a rudimentary defense. Built as much out of desperation as necessity, it was appropriately christened Fort Necessity. But the word *fort* implies something far more substantial than the simple, rugged structure Washington's militiamen threw together. Washington's Fort Necessity was little more than a small rectangular wooden shed for storing ammunition and supplies, surrounded by a circle of rough-hewn upright logs about seven feet tall.

Reinforcements under the command of a British army captain had arrived in the meantime. While Washington and the captain argued over who was in charge, the French drew closer. Outside the log palisade, trenchworks were dug and most of the approximately three hundred men now at Fort Necessity would be placed in these trenches rather than inside the fifty-foot-diameter circular compound, which could hold only about sixty men. When the Half King saw what he called "that little thing in the meadow," he and his warriors beat a hasty retreat.

On July 3, about eleven hundred French and Indian troops, some of whom had recently been allied with the English, surrounded Fort Necessity. Commanded by the late Jumonville's brother Captain Coulon de Villiers, the French and Indians took positions in the thick woods around the fort, unleashing a withering fusillade on Washington's position. A night of driving rain soaked his ammunition and filled his trenches with water and blood, and the young colonel had little food for the troops. With ill-trained, poorly equipped men, many of them sick and all of them hungry, Washington's position was hopeless. It was made worse when discipline among his troops disintegrated. Certain that they would be massacred in retaliation for the deaths of the Frenchmen, Washington's militiamen broke into the rum stores. "It was no sooner dark," Captain Adam Stephens, one of Washington's company commanders, later recorded, "than one-half of our Men got drunk."

About midnight, Washington agreed to surrender Fort Necessity, the first and only time he surrendered in his military career. With his men low on ammunition as well, and fearing English reinforcements that might shortly arrive, Coulon de Villiers mercifully allowed Washington—the man he surely held responsible for his brother's death a few weeks earlier—to march out of the fort and return to Virginia with his men and guns. Washington only had to sign a formal parole, a written agreement that he and his men would not fight again for a year. It was July 4, a date that must have carried a most unpleasant association for George Washington for many years to come.

What Washington did not know or perhaps did not understand was that the letter of parole said that Washington had "assassinated" Joseph de Jumonville. In essence, Washington had signed a confession of murdering a French diplomat, which was cause enough for war. For the rest of his life, Washington would argue that he misinterpreted the agreement and completely disavow the charge.

Disconsolate in defeat, Washington returned to Williamsburg. Trying to salvage the situation, Dinwiddie and William Fairfax convinced the Virginia burgesses to recognize Washington and his officers for "gallant and brave behavior." The disaster at Fort Necessity was turned into Anglo-American propaganda—a heroic stand against the depredations of the French and their "savage" allies. If nothing else, Washington must have been learning from firsthand experience that even disasters could be useful if presented with the proper public face.

During Washington's absence, his niece Sarah, Lawrence Washington's daughter, had died and her mother had remarried. Washington was able to lease Mount Vernon from his former sister-in-law, Ann, for fifteen thousand pounds of tobacco a year. When Ann later died, the house and estate became his.

When the burgesses failed to vote new taxes for another expedition against the French, Washington's unit was disbanded and he resigned his commission. Disillusioned, he wrote to his brother, sounding more like a petulant adolescent with his nose out of joint than the heroic figure of American legend: "I was employed to go on a journey in the winter (when I believe few or none would have undertaken it) and what did I get by it? My expenses borne! I then was appointed with trifling pay to conduct a handful of men to the Ohio. What did I get by this? Why, after putting myself to a considerable expense in equipping and providing necessaries for the campaign—I went out, was soundly beaten, lost them all-came in, and had my commission taken from me, or in other words, my command reduced, under pretense of an order from home. . . . I have been on the losing order ever since I entered the service."

IT MIGHT HAVE all ended there—a bitter, complaining young colonial upstart who saw slights at every turn. But history had more in store for Washington.

In February 1755, British major general Edward Braddock arrived in Virginia to command a new campaign against the French, and it would be launched with an assault on Fort Duquesne. The choice of Braddock to lead the assault came, according to historian Fred Anderson, "not because he was an able tactician or even a particularly ex-

perienced battlefield leader, but because he was a noted administrator
and disciplinarian who was also politically reliable."[12] Sensing opportunity, Washington asked to join Braddock's campaign in March, and
Braddock agreed to allow him to serve as an aide-de-camp. Among
the other officers in Braddock's command were Lieutenant Colonel
Thomas Gage, who would later command British forces in North
America between 1763 and 1775 and face Washington in Boston, and
Captain Horatio Gates, later to be a general with mixed success—and
a thorn in General Washington's side—in the Continental army.

Braddock had assembled the largest invasion force yet seen in North
America to challenge the French, and he prepared to do it in the style
to which he was accustomed. Ignoring the advice of colonial soldiers
with experience fighting the French and Indians, Braddock rejected
the use of Indian allies. He planned to bring an immense European-
style army to bear on the French. More than two thousand soldiers
and wagoneers—along with camp followers, the women who inevita-
bly follow at the rear of most armies to cook, clean, and perform other
nonmilitary "services"—set out. With twenty-five hundred horses and
hundreds of wagons, Braddock's force stretched out for more than six
miles. As this large, slow-moving army snaked its way through hundreds of miles of virgin territory, the men had to hack a road through
wilderness and forage for their food. They were constantly harassed
by Indians, who had no difficulty finding the massed British troops in
their bright red uniforms.

On July 9, 1755, disaster struck with a vengeance. The British had
nearly reached Fort Duquesne. Bunched like commuters in bumper-
to-bumper traffic, the ponderous British formation provided an easy
target for the French and Indians, who launched their assault from the
forest cover. In Washington's own words, "We were attacked (very un-

expectedly I must own) by about 300 French and Indians; our numbers consisted of about 1300 well armed men, chiefly regulars, who were immediately struck with such a deadly panic, that nothing but confusion and disobedience of orders prevailed amongst them. . . . The English soldiers . . . broke and ran as sheep before the hounds. . . . I luckily escaped without a wound, though I had four bullets through my coat and two horses shot under me."

Out of a total force of thirteen hundred men, the British and Americans suffered more than nine hundred casualties. During the battle, Washington raced to the front and was able to organize an orderly retreat that was credited with saving many more lives. He also collected the wounded Braddock, who died three days later. Washington buried his body and had wagons roll over the grave so that the general's remains would not be desecrated.

It was a disaster he would never forget. Thirty years later, Washington remembered the battle's aftermath: "The shocking scenes . . . the dead—the dying—the groans—lamentations—and cries along the road of the wounded for help . . . were enough to pierce a heart."

Many of the British and American soldiers captured by the Indians were taken back to Fort Duquesne. There they were stripped and tortured by the Indians, screaming at the touch of red-hot irons, in the account of one eyewitness, before being put to death.

In spite of this devastating defeat, Washington's stature was actually enhanced. His actions in rallying the survivors was hailed as heroic. Still only twenty-three, Washington would be given command of the newly created Virginia Regiment, charged with the colony's defenses for the duration of the war.

Along with his increased fame in the colony, Washington acquired a new reputation. Following the strict British code of military discipline, Washington became known as a martinet for harshly doling out five hundred lashes for laziness or a thousand for drunkenness. He even boasted of building a gallows forty feet high on which to hang deserters. After executing two deserters, Washington wrote to Governor Dinwiddie, "Your Honor will, I hope, excuse my hanging instead of shooting them. It conveyed much more terror to others; and was it for example sake we did it." Similarly harsh measures were applied to Indians attacking Virginia's frontier. Washington had no objection if his Rangers left Indian scalps staked to trees. These were the rules of war in the eighteenth century, and Washington adopted them with ease.

Not only did the young colonel learn about command during this time, he would also be schooled in the politics of war. With the French threat fading as the bulk of fighting moved north toward the Great Lakes and Canada, Washington struggled constantly with the colonial legislature for funds to properly outfit his regiment. In Williamsburg, the House of Burgesses was controlled by landed men far more concerned with protecting their interests, property, and pocketbooks than with protecting clusters of backwoodsmen on Virginia's western fringes. The gentlemen in Virginia's colonial administration were more interested in equipping and training the militia that was charged with providing security against any slave insurrections, such as the one at Stono, South Carolina, in 1739. There, slaves encouraged by the Spanish in Florida had killed more than thirty whites before being hunted down and executed.

Although the heavy action in the war had moved north to the Great Lakes, New York, New England and eventually Canada, Washington was present when his Virginians—now outfitted in blue uniforms of Washington's design—joined a large British force for another assault on Fort Duquesne in the fall of 1758. By the time they arrived, the French outpost was deserted and burning, abandoned by the outnumbered French. The British took it over, rebuilt it, and renamed it in honor of the prime minister who now led the war effort, William Pitt; the settlement nearby would eventually be named Pittsburgh in his honor as well.

Afterward, Washington returned to the battlefield where Braddock's army had been so devastated. One of his officers described the scene: "Men's bones were lying about as thick as leaves do on the ground." Washington ordered his men to collect some 450 skulls and bury them. He then returned to Williamsburg and, late in 1758, resigned his commission.

Assessing these years, historian Fred Anderson summarized Washington's experience in the Virginia theater's fighting:

It would be merely silly, if it were not morally repugnant, to maintain that war builds character. And yet it ought not to be denied that, for better or for worse, military service and combat mold the views and the character of those who experience them. . . . He [Washington] was a man for whom the strains of command and the experience of seeing men killed and wounded as a result of his orders had burned away the delusion that courage and valor—or even victory—will necessarily make the decisive difference that commanders long to achieve. . . . He had gained self-confidence and self-control, and if he could not honestly number humility among his virtues, he had at last begun to understand his limitations. George Washington, at age twenty-seven, was not yet the man he would be at age forty or fifty, but he had come an immense distance in five years' time. And the hard road he had traveled from Jumonville's Glen, in ways he would not comprehend for years to come, had done much to prepare him for the harder road that lay ahead.[13]

ᴥ Aftermath ᴥ

The French and Indian War, the North American phase of the Seven Years' War, concluded with the fall of Quebec in 1759, a battle in which the French general Montcalm and British general Wolfe both died, and the capture of Montreal the following year. Elsewhere around the rest of world, the fighting continued until the Treaty of Paris was signed in 1763. Under its terms, France surrendered almost all of its North American territory to England. In Nova Scotia, the British forced out all of the French living in what was called Acadia. Most of these displaced Acadians traveled south to the vicinity of New Orleans and would later be known as Cajuns.

By the time the war was over, Great Britain also had a new monarch in George III, who had taken the throne in 1760. And in Boston, a feisty American lawyer named James Otis would issue his first political tract and argue that American colonists possessed all the rights of an English citizen.

Meanwhile back in Virginia, the retired Colonel Washington, not yet turned thirty, had slipped into the new and much more comfortable role of country squire. After leaving Virginia's service he had made his match, marrying Martha Dandridge Custis on January 6, 1759. Barely five feet tall and plump, the twenty-five-year-old Martha, widow of one of Virginia's wealthiest men, Daniel Parke Custis, gave

George Washington the property, slaves, and wealth he had dreamed of, along with her two children, whom he treated as his own. Now securely numbered among the "well-read, well-fed and well-wed," as a historian once described the Founding Fathers, Washington became a member of the House of Burgesses, experimented with crops, and turned his attention to other concerns of Virginia's planter class—such as the problem of runaway slaves.

Fairfax County (Virginia) August 11, 1761

The last of these Negroes were brought from an *African* Ship in *August* 1759, and talk very broken and unintelligible English; the second one, Jack, is Countryman to those, and speaks pretty good English, having been several Years in the Country. The other, Peros, speaks much better than either, indeed has little of his Country Dialect left, and is esteemed a sensible, judicious Negro. . . .

. . . Whoever apprehends the said Negroes, so that the Subscriber may readily get them, shall have, if taken up in this County, Forty Shillings Reward, beside what the Law allows; and if at any greater Distance, or out of the Colony, a proportionable Recompence paid them, by

George Washington

N.B. If they should be taken separately, the Reward will be proportioned.[14]

At the time George Washington placed that advertisement seeking the return of some runaway slaves in 1761, the gentleman farmer probably did not foresee a future note he would pen, with its reference to a different sort of "slavery." At the end of a business letter dated May 31, 1775, Washington wrote from Philadelphia to his old friend George William Fairfax:

Before this letter can reach you, you must, undoubtedly have received an Account of the Engagement in the Massachusetts Bay between the Ministerial Troops (for we do not, nor cannot yet prevail upon ourselves to call them the King's Troops) and the Provincials of that Government. But as you may not have heard how that affair began, I inclose you the several Affidavits that were taken after the action. . . .

Unhappy it is though to reflect that a Brother's Sword has been sheathed in a Brother's Breast, and that the once happy and peaceful plains of America are ether to be drenched with Blood, or Inhabited by Slaves. Sad alternative! But can a virtuous man hesitate in his choice?[15]

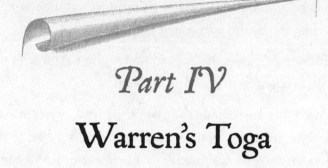

Part IV
Warren's Toga

1763   The Treaty of Paris ends the Seven Years' War.

Pontiac's Rebellion. Indians overrun British forts on the western frontier, including the British garrison at Detroit.

1764   Parliament passes the Sugar Act to collect American revenue on molasses brought from non-British colonies.

James Otis condemns Britain's "taxation without representation" at a Boston town meeting; In June, the Massachusetts House of Representatives organizes a Committee of Correspondence to communicate with the other twelve colonies over their common grievances; in August, Boston merchants agree to boycott British luxury imports and are soon joined by the other colonies.

1765   The Stamp Act is passed by Parliament, the first direct tax on the American colonies. Passage of the tax is met with opposition in all thirteen colonies.

The Quartering Act goes into effect. Under it, colonists must provide housing for British troops stationed in America. It provokes further discontent.

Secret groups called Sons of Liberty form to resist the Stamp Act.

1766   The Stamp Act is repealed that same day that the Declaratory Act becomes law, asserting that the British government has the complete power to pass laws governing the American colonies.

1767   The Townshend Revenue Acts place a tax on tea, paper, and other imports.

John Dickinson publishes *Letters from a Farmer in Pennsylvania to the Inhabitants of the British Colonies.*

1768   British warships arrive in Boston to reinforce the customs officials, and two regiments of infantry are billeted in Boston.

1770   On March 5, British troops kill five Boston civilians in what becomes known as the Boston Massacre. Defended by John Adams, the British soldiers charged in the massacre are tried; the commander and six men are acquitted by the civil jury.

1773   The Tea Act is passed. In December, Boston militants hold the Boston Tea Party, destroying British tea in protest.

1774   The Coercive Laws (Intolerable Acts) are passed by Parliament.

On September 5, the First Continental Congress convenes in Philadelphia.

1775   On April 18–19, American militias make stands at Lexington and Concord. On May 10, the British Fort Ticonderoga on Lake Champlain is captured with its rich arsenal of munitions. The Second Continental Congress meets in Philadelphia. On June 14–15, after voting to raise six companies and authorizing salaries for soldiers, Congress unanimously appoints George Washington to lead the Continental army.

Battle of Bunker Hill fought on June 17.

After a twelve-day journey from Philadelphia, George Washington reaches Cambridge, Massachusetts, on July 3 and takes command of the Continental army.

That a Revenue be raised in Your majesty's Dominions in America for defraying the expenses of defending, protecting, and securing same.

—Preamble to the Sugar Act (1764)

What a glorious morning for America!

—Samuel Adams,
remark after the battles of Lexington and Concord (April 1775)

Our men inlist very slow and our Enemy have got a Reinforsement of five Regiments and if the New army is not Reased in season I hope I & and all my townsmen shall have virtue anofe to stay all winter as Volentears.

—Joseph Hodgkins,
cobbler and minuteman (November 1775)

ONE OF THE ASSASSINS CARRIED an egg. It was not the weapon of choice. It was merely the signal to begin a brawl, a melee intended to provide cover for the killings. A word spoken against the king was all it would take. The egg would be thrown, a riotous uproar would follow, and in the ensuing panic and confusion, the American rebels targeted for death would either be carted away or finished off. The British officers on hand would see to that. If a few treasonous, upstart Yankee skulls were cracked in the offing, all the better.

The conspiracy was set to unfold during a memorial held on the fifth anniversary of the Boston Massacre, that signal event of March 5, 1770, when a company of British soldiers, pressed by an angry crowd, had opened fire, killing five of Boston's "town-born." The memory of those deaths—kept alive by Paul Revere's engraving, an icon hanging in many patriot homes—had been elevated to something approaching a high holy day on Boston's civic calendar. The service planned for this evening was part solemn remembrance of the dead and part political theater for a crowd whose mood was more combative than somber. The event would serve as a propaganda platform for a town that savored a good public donnybrook every so often and relished any chance to thumb its nose at the occupying British regulars, the hated "lobsterbacks."

As the huge audience filled Boston's Old South meetinghouse to overflowing, some of the more volatile members of the crowd may have had more in mind. One observer, a British lieutenant, reported that "almost every man had a short stick or bludgeon in his hand . . . many of them were privately armed."[1] After all, these were the same people who had hanged royal tax officials in effigy, chased a stamp tax collector from office, riotously ransacked the home of Lieutenant Governor Thomas Hutchinson, burned a British ship, and tarred and feathered more than a few royalists.

For the portly, palsied fifty-three-year-old patriot firebrand Samuel Adams, chief organizer of the evening's proceedings, this memorial provided a fresh opportunity to goad the British. Adams knew that another deadly attack on Americans might be the spark to galvanize the cause of independence in Massachusetts and throughout the colonies. He also knew Old South and the crowd well. Baptized into this Congregational bastion, Samuel Adams had been there on December 16, 1773, the fateful date of the Tea Party, using his canny genius for focusing and even manipulating the street anger of Boston's underclass. "This meeting can do nothing more to save the country," he had told the thousands in attendance, his words sending the Sons of Liberty into action. Their faces blackened and poorly disguised as native Americans, some eighty men with axes had climbed aboard three British ships and dumped 342 chests of tea into the harbor.

Responding in raw fury, the powers in London and a new military governor, General Thomas Gage, had clamped a mailed fist around Boston and then squeezed harder, issuing a series of punishing laws that crippled the port's economy. The harbor had been closed, forcing thousands of men out of work. Food supplies were cut short, sending prices skyrocketing and leaving pantries bare. As basic necessities disappeared, malnutrition worsened a smallpox epidemic that grew more deadly with the onset of New England winter. And thousands more

British troops streamed into the city's already close quarters, comman-deering beds in private homes and further unsettling a tense, fright-ened population.

So it was an uneasy Boston on this March evening in 1775, a little more than a year after the Tea Party and its brief celebratory after-glow. Accustomed to the sight of British troops drilling and marching around Boston—and often competing with them for jobs, which also stuck in the craw of Boston's working class—the crowds gathering to commemorate the massacre must have been stunned by the sight of some three hundred British regulars arriving at Old South. These were the same occupying redcoats who had perpetrated the Boston Massacre in the first place, who had opened fire when unemployed townies, some fresh from the tavern, threw stones and snowballs at some British sentries. Now at the service marking those deaths, many of these townspeople—some hungry, angry, and out of work—had to mingle with equally aggrieved British soldiers whose disdain for their American "cousins" was deep and often on display. Both sides were clearly spoiling for a fight.

Forty or so seemingly bored British officers ominously pushed to the front of the meeting hall, exuding the air of superiority and ar-rogance that only stoked American antagonism. Attempting to ease tensions, Samuel Adams asked people to surrender their seats to the redcoats. Adams didn't know he was the chief target of their plot. The British soldiers had arrived at this Boston Massacre memorial expecting to put a stop to the mob of treasonous Americans before the situation disintegrated any further. They had no sympathy or regard for the Americans and came expecting to end the simmering rebellion and get back home to England with the traitorous rebels in chains—or dead. Samuel Adams' biographer Mark Puls described the mood: "With war plans gearing up, the Whigs lived in daily fear that Adams, Hancock and Dr. Warren and other provincial leaders would soon be arrested or perhaps shot. Gage held warrants for the arrest of Adams and Hancock. Adams suspected that as soon as more regiments appeared in Boston, they would be arrested, chained and sent to England."[2]

The British soldier carrying the egg that night was supposed to throw it at the moment any treasonous or otherwise incendiary remarks were made in the meetinghouse. With one swift blow, the British hoped to take out the three most dangerous provocateurs, the purse, head, and heart of the Massachusetts rebels: wealthy merchant-shipowner John Hancock, politician Samuel Adams, and charismatic physician Joseph Warren.

Despite the growing threat of violence or arrest, Warren had volunteered to serve as the evening's chief speaker. The thirty-three-year-old surgeon was, in the words of one British officer, "the greatest incendiary in America."[3] Blocked by the crowds milling around Old South, Warren circled the building until he found a ladder and an open window. The sight of Warren clambering up the ladder must have been comical; dressed as Cicero, the Roman orator, he had arrived wearing a white toga over his suit.

Dr. Warren's toga wasn't part of some amusing colonial-era masquerade. Among the intelligentsia of America's patriots and Sons of Liberty, there was a keen philosophical devotion to the glory of Rome's republic, considered the zenith of republican history. For many of the Founding Fathers, the Roman republic represented their idealized vision of government, as Gordon S. Wood explains in *The Radicalism of the American Revolution*: "According to classical republican tradition, man was by nature a political being, a citizen who achieved his greatest moral fulfillment by participating in a self-governing republic. Public or political liberty . . . meant participation in government. And this political liberty in turn provided the means by which the personal liberty and private rights of the individual . . . were protected."[4]

Statesman, philosopher, and senator, Cicero was considered Rome's greatest orator. He was also viewed by American patriots as the greatest martyr of republicanism. After his assassination by antagonists, Cicero had been decapitated, his head and hands displayed in the Roman Forum. This dramatic demise might have served as a warning to Warren. But it was Cicero's republican ideals, not his fate, that Warren had in mind as he stood and spoke in Old South.

After a rousing and flowery oration, Warren was thunderously applauded by the partisan crowd. Then Samuel Adams stood to introduce a second speaker to the increasingly rambunctious audience. But when Adams said the words "Boston Massacre," several British officers sitting in front immediately rose and hissed. Another shouted disapprovingly, "Fie, fie." But to the overflow crowd, the British officer's words sounded instead like a shout of "Fire." The packed house panicked. People jumped through windows and pushed for the doors. At that very moment, a British military unit marched by, and the sound of drums and pipes only added to the confusion and fear. It seemed as if the long-expected British assault on Boston was in full gear.

But the moment fell laughably short of Armageddon. According to a later report about the incident, the officer given responsibility for starting the violence by throwing the egg had fallen down while entering the meetinghouse. He had dislocated his knee and the egg had broken. As the crowd quickly dispersed in the general mayhem of the false alarm, the evening, fraught with such violent possibilities, ended not with a bang but a whimper. In a Boston on tenterhooks, expecting a battle or perhaps even a war, this single broken egg—to contradict the familiar expression—would make no omelets. It was more like a stage prop in the final scene of an opéra bouffe or an absurd ending to some Gilbert and Sullivan costume drama with dashing uniformed soldiers and a toga-clad orator, except that the stakes were much higher. And the farcical conclusion of the events on that Boston night in March 1775 did not conceal the deep and dangerous divisions that were pushing the American colonies and Great Britain ever closer to war.

Such a state of affairs would have been inconceivable to the people of Massachusetts a mere dozen years earlier. When the Seven Years' War formally ended in 1763, American colonials had just spent years fighting side by side with British regulars in the North American phase of the conflict, the French and Indian War, between 1754 and 1760. More accurately, they fought beneath their British counterparts, who were usually in command. Americans, including Massachusetts men, had fought in many of the war's chief engagements, including the crucial battles of Quebec in 1759 and Montreal in 1760. New Englanders were overjoyed by the complete defeat of the French and the dismantling of their American empire, eliminating what had been the greatest single threat to colonial New England for a century. The victory also blunted the power of France's traditional allies, the northeastern Indians.

When the Treaty of Paris ended the worldwide fighting in 1763 and secured Great Britain's imperial triumph around the globe, it was seen as a victory for America as well. After years of intermittent warfare, the peace of 1763 ushered in a new era of optimism. As Fred Anderson described the moment: "To many of the inhabitants of New England, the successful conclusion of the war heralded nothing less than the beginning of the millennium. Even the most worldly of the colonists undoubtedly agreed that the elimination of New England's perennial antagonist and the accession of immeasurable tracts of virgin land could hardly fail to produce a thousand years of peace and prosperity in North America."[5]

But the prosperity was short-lived. And the peace lasted barely a decade. How, then, did those men and women who crowded into Old South go from dutiful royal subjects to armed insurrectionists in the space of a dozen years? What great ground shift sent people with connections of kinship and common traditions to the barricades? Was it ever just about tea, stamps, and sugar?

There is no question that Enlightenment philosophy played a key role in firing the independent spirit of the Revolutionary generation. The upheaval in religious, scientific, and political thinking that elevated reason above dogma and the traditional authority of church and state profoundly influenced the political leanings of such men as Samuel Adams, Benjamin Franklin, Thomas Paine, and Thomas Jefferson. Whether found in the physics of Newton or the skepticism of Scottish philosopher David Hume and French philosopher Voltaire, these radical new ways of thinking and observing had broken what historian Peter Gray described in *The Enlightenment* as "the sacred circle."

But for most Americans, these were largely the inconsequential musings of those fortunate enough not to have to work for a living. There were many other bread-and-butter issues that struck at the purse strings of Americans at every rung on the social ladder. At its heart, the conflict boiled down to real estate, taxes, and property—and the power to control them.

The downward spiral in America's unlimited fealty to London began almost immediately after the Treaty of Paris ended the Seven

Years' War in 1763. The ink on the treaty was not yet dry when British forts in the western frontier around the Great Lakes and near modern Detroit came under Indian attack in what was called Pontiac's Rebellion, named for the Ottawa chief who was one of its most prominent native leaders. The most prolonged and deadly conflict between Native Americans and British Americans since King Philip's War, this series of battles was costly in lives lost and royal expenditure. It was not the battles themselves that stirred the trouble, however, but the royal reaction. To prevent further disputes with the midwestern tribes, King George III decided to restrict development of the vast interior territories that were now part of England's American empire. News of his Proclamation of 1763 did not sit well with American land speculators, including George Washington, who had formed the Mississippi Company to purchase these newly available lands, which Americans felt they had fought to win.

As historian Colin G. Calloway wrote, "George Washington, Thomas Jefferson, Arthur Lee, Patrick Henry, and others saw tyranny in Britain's interference with their freedom to make a killing in the West. . . . Colonists who had fought and bled in the war were not about to be deprived of the fruits of victory by a distant government. Land speculators would not watch their investments in Indian country slip away. The clash of French and British ambitions gave way to a clash of British and American ambitions."[6]

Struggling under a massive government debt after the Seven Years' War, and confronted by the ongoing cost of committing armies to the defense of the American colonies, Parliament and the king made another fateful decision that left the American "cousins" far from pleased. Reasoning that the colonists should foot the bill for their own defense, Parliament passed the Sugar Act on April 5, 1764, to collect American revenue on molasses brought from non-British colonies. A month later Boston attorney James Otis had condemned this "taxation without representation" at a town meeting, and in July he published "The Rights of the British Colonies Asserted and Proved."

By August, Boston merchants had agreed to boycott British luxury imports and were soon joined by other tradesmen. New York and the other colonies followed suit, in the first coordinated political action by Americans. In March 1765, Parliament passed the Stamp Act, the first direct tax on the American colonies. Again designed to fund the cost of maintaining British armies in America, this tax applied to all printed materials and was met with stiff opposition in all thirteen colonies. Later that year, the Quartering Act, which required Americans to provide housing for British troops stationed in the colonies, went into effect, provoking further discontent.

For America's large and growing lower classes, "No taxation without representation" was an empty phrase. These working poor had little if anything to tax. Without property, they often couldn't vote. They didn't drink tea, the beverage of the wealthy. Nor did they have to worry—as George Washington or Thomas Jefferson did—that the king's proclamation was keeping them from buying up western land. But they did have to face the prospects of impressment—essentially being kidnapped into service—by the Royal Navy and losing jobs to off-duty British soldiers who were permitted to look for work around Boston Harbor. In this antagonism toward British authority, the Boston "street" could link arms with upscale patriots, as they did at the Boston Tea Party.

That act of civil disobedience, repeated in several other colonies with considerably less fanfare, had brought the wrath of King George III and his acquiescent Parliament slamming down on Boston, seedbed of America's rebellious spirit. The colonial governor Thomas Hutchinson, a direct descendant of dissident Anne Hutchinson, who had been parrying for control of Boston's politics with the likes of attorney James Otis and Samuel Adams for more than a decade, was recalled to London. He was replaced by General Thomas Gage, survivor of Braddock's disastrous march and now commander in chief of British forces in North America. Additional troops were dispatched to garrison the port city, bringing their number to more than three thousand in a city of some twenty thousand.

At Gage's insistence, Parliament issued the Massachusetts Government Act, which substituted royally appointed judges, sheriffs, and justices of the peace for locally elected ones. Officials elected in town meetings were also replaced by appointed royal councilors. And the town meetings, the beating heart of individual rights and local democracy since the Massachusetts charter was revised in 1691, were now subject to the consent and approval of the royally appointed governor.

This act had sparked outright rebellion in many rural Massachusetts towns, including Springfield and Worcester, where five thousand armed farmers had shut down the new royal Court of Common Pleas, and with it the authority of the British crown. Taking control of the courts themselves, groups of angry, disenfranchised farmers had, in essence, established the first popularly elected, independent government in America.[7] Moderates, accommodationists, and royalists in the other colonies might still be wavering or hoping for reconciliation with Great Britain. But rural Massachusetts had taken the lead in openly declaring its independence from the British throne.

And the contagion was spreading, largely through Samuel Adams' Committees of Correspondence. A grassroots community of letter writers—an eighteenth-century quill-pen blogosphere—these committees had created an effective, efficient patriot network throughout the colonies. By the end of 1774, the royal governor of Virginia reported to London that every county was "arming a company of men for the avowed purpose of protecting their communities. There is not a justice of peace in Virginia that acts except as a Committee man."[8]

When Boston's bustling port was closed in retaliation for the Tea Party, essentially cutting off the town's lifeline, some thirty-five hundred men were put out of work. Parliament decreed that the harbor would remain closed until Massachusetts paid for the dumped tea as part of the Coercive Laws, passed to bring the defiant Americans back into line. Coincident with passage of these Intolerable Acts, as they were known in America, was the onset of another deadly epidemic. "Smallpox continued its gradual but inexorable spread as the political insurgency mounted," Elizabeth Fenn records in *Pox Americana,* her history of the smallpox outbreak that raged across America parallel with the Revolution. According to Fenn, rumor had it that General Gage was deliberately spreading the disease in Boston, as he supposedly had done to native Americans during the French and Indian War.[9]

With the privations caused by the harbor shutdown, growing fears of an epidemic, and the ominous threat of harsh military action by the British—the warships in the harbor could provide plenty of eighteenth-century-style "shock and awe"—Boston's mood was bleak. As John Adams, Samuel's second cousin and the more temperate of the two, wrote to his wife, Abigail, "The Town of Boston, for ought I can see, must suffer Martyrdom: It must expire: And our principal consolation is, that it dies in a noble Cause. The Cause of Truth, of Virtue, of Liberty and of Humanity."[10]

Each heavy-handed British reaction only seemed to strengthen patriot resolve. Parliament's vindictiveness also heightened sympathy for Massachusetts among the other colonies, which began shipping food and supplies to beleaguered Boston in a show of solidarity. When news of this reached England, King George and Parliament simply ratcheted up the tensions by extending the Quartering Act to all of the colonies in June 1774 and shutting other colonial ports. It was the news of these royal reactions reaching Virginia's legislature that prompted delegate Patrick Henry to rise and proclaim, "Give me liberty, or give me death."

The draconian British response to the Tea Party had also been one reason the First Continental Congress had convened in Philadelphia in September 1774, a meeting largely inspired by Samuel Adams. Taking his lead, the Continental Congress approved an embargo resolution, halting all trade with Great Britain, Ireland, and the West Indies. All but the most radical Americans still hoped that an economic war could avert a shooting war.

But the point was moot. Plans for a shooting war were already being laid. Well before the Egg Plot had fizzled on that March 1775 night, a Committee of Safety, formed by Adams and other patriot leaders, was training an extralegal militia under the direction of wealthy merchant John Hancock. Calling themselves "minutemen," the best of these militia fighters were prepared to be ready for action in sixty seconds. Across Massachusetts and in other New England colonies, other groups of militiamen began stockpiling weapons and gunpowder.

In a daring provocation to British power, hundreds of New Hampshire men had descended on Fort William and Mary, in Portsmouth Harbor, and seized muskets, cannons, shot, and a hundred barrels of gunpowder on December 14, 1774, nearly a year to the day after the Tea Party. Warned by patriot rider and spymaster Paul Revere that a large British force was moving to secure the munitions, the four hundred New Hampshire militiamen assaulted the fort, garrisoned by a handful of invalid British soldiers, too ill or injured for regular duty, in what might truly be called the first battle of the American Revolution, albeit a bloodless one. There were no casualties more severe than a bloodied nose and some bruised British egos.

As word of this audacious attack on British might and sovereignty spread, thousands more minutemen descended on New Hampshire's chief port, to the astonishment of the British. Patriot militias in several other New England towns and ports soon did the same, attacking and confiscating powder and guns from British armories. To General Gage, New England was essentially in open rebellion. Urgently requesting reinforcements, he wrote late in 1774 to surprised officials in London, "If you think ten thousand men sufficient, send twenty; if one million is thought enough, give two; you save both blood and treasure in the end." This was a far cry from the easy assurances that had earlier been voiced in Parliament, when it was scoffingly suggested that a few British regulars would quickly send any ill-trained and inexperienced Americans flying from the field at the first cannon shot.

Lost powder and the volunteers flocking to join the American insurgency were not General Gage's only vexing problems. Gage, who had been back in England when word of the Boston Tea Party reached London, thought he knew America. And even if he didn't especially like a great many Americans, he had married one, a beautiful New Jersey heiress, Margaret Kemble. Having invested wisely in property in the North American colonies and the West Indies, Thomas Gage had become a wealthy man, and he believed that peace and prosperity went hand in hand. Hoping to avoid war, Gage had recommended most of the Coercive Laws, believing that a stiff show of resolve would break the insurgency. With this stick in one hand, Gage also held out the carrots of bribes and titles to anyone who would betray or desert the patriot cause.

In the wake of the Tea Party crisis, Gage was dispatched to Boston as military governor in 1774. As the city struggled under the British embargo Gage himself had recommended, British forces and their Tory sympathizers were also forced to do without. With fresh supplies slowed to a trickle and fewer American farmers willing to sell to the British occupiers, Gage's troops suffered as their rations were cut. The British soldiers were also constantly taunted; daily barrages of salty insults sailed down from the ranks of the unemployed fishermen, dockworkers, and sailors hanging around the harbor.

Food supplies may have been low, but rum flowed freely. Drinking was about the only entertainment available to the troops, and one English officer reported alarmingly about the situation to London: "The rum is so cheap that it debauches both navy and army, and kills many of them," wrote Major John Pitcairn, soon to acquire notoriety on Lexington Green. "Depend on it, my Lord, it will destroy more of us than the Yankies will."[11]

As the winter of 1774–75 approached, infectious diseases swept the city, and neither smallpox, diphtheria, nor any of a host of other deadly illnesses showed any regard for uniforms. Morale among the British troops—malnourished and lacking proper winter clothing, with New England's weather showing no mercy—was even darker than that of the townspeople. As David Hackett Fischer described it, "The men were increasingly bored, angry, and hungry—a recipe for disaster in any army."[12]

Some of the British soldiers had sold their guns, and many others had begun to desert. General Gage was facing a crisis of daily losses severe enough for him to double the guards around town to keep his soldiers from leaving. In many cases, they were encouraged by patriots, as word of help—a sort of Underground Railroad for deserters—spread through the British ranks. Plots of farmland in New Hampshire were also offered as an inducement for deserters. Ultimately, Gage was forced to resort to public lashings and finally executions. A private who had attempted to desert three different times was shot in the public square, to the shock of Bostonians. Another was shot on Christmas Eve.

Through Boston's bleak winter months in 1775, Gage watched and waited. He was doing his best to avoid the bloodshed of all-out war, but increasingly he expected trouble. A few weeks after the failed Egg Plot in March, General Gage received a letter from Lord William Dartmouth, King George's secretary responsible for American affairs. Alarmed at the reports of growing stockpiles of patriot powder and guns and the swelling ranks of militias in Massachusetts and other colonies, Lord Dartmouth ordered a preemptive strike. General Gage was ordered to arrest the ringleaders of the rebellion and disarm the colonists.

On April 15, the day after Gage received Lord Dartmouth's letter, he was also given a report from his most useful, industrious, and well-placed spy that the Massachusetts Provincial Congress had voted to send delegates to the other New England provinces to discuss the creation of a New England militia army. The spy confided, "A sudden blow struck now would overset all their plans."[13]

The information came from one of the most trusted members of the patriot inner circle, Dr. Benjamin Church. Grandson of his namesake Colonel Benjamin Church, the famed hero of King Philip's War, Church was privy to the most sensitive information about patriot plans and strategy. As a physician, he moved easily between patriot meetings, Tory patients, and the lodgings of his mistress. His motive for betraying the cause was simple and as old as history: he was being amply bribed by Gage. The British commander was more than willing to spread royal silver around in hopes of averting war. He had offered Samuel Adams similar inducements in the summer of 1774, including an annual salary and a patent of nobility in the American peerage that England was planning to establish. But Adams had flatly rejected the temptation.[14]

From other loyalist spies, Gage learned that the patriots had hidden approximately one hundred barrels of gunpowder in nearby Concord. It was a laughably small amount for an army that the New Englanders hoped would soon number fifteen thousand men. But Gage thought that by capturing both powder and patriot provocateurs, he could put an end to the rebellion before it really began.

General Gage's planned sally into Concord would not be his first attempt to disarm the rebels. Six months earlier, on September 1, 1774, the British commander had ordered the seizure of an arsenal of weapons stored in Charlestown, just north of Boston. After the British successfully removed 250 barrels of powder to Boston, thousands of armed Massachusetts and other New England militiamen had descended on the city, quickly responding to the rapid alarm system and expecting a fight that never came. In the aftermath of this event, known as the Powder Alarm, wild rumors spread all the way to Philadelphia, where the First Continental Congress was in session, that war had begun, and Americans were dying as British guns leveled Boston.

In February 1775, after learning that carriages for cannons were being built in the Salem forge, General Gage sent twelve hundred men to the port town, just north of Boston. To Gage, such expeditions and seizures of stores not only reduced the rebel militia's ability to fight but also familiarized his troops with the terrain over which they might eventually be forced to campaign. Gage knew that minuteman companies kept the British under close observation. Using large troop movements, Gage hoped to intimidate the minutemen—or at least make them tired of responding to false alarms. Instead, these forays by the British amounted to valuable war games, exercises that increased rebel confidence that they could muster large numbers of fighting men on short notice.

Landing at Marblehead, Massachusetts, on a Sunday in February 1775, while most townspeople were in church, the British troops marched toward Salem. By the time they approached the town, however, the alarm had been spread. The British found themselves confronted by a large and growing crowd of men and women who had raised the drawbridge over the North River to prevent the British from reaching their target. Soon hundreds of militiamen streamed into Salem from all directions, and the long-expected confrontation seemed set to begin.

When Colonel Leslie, the British commander, ordered the townspeople to allow his men to travel on "the King's Highway," a feisty old transplanted Englishman, James Barr, replied, "It is not the King's Highway; it is a road built by the owners of the lots on the other side, and no king, country or town has anything to do with it."[15] Barr's simple declaration was as ringing a statement of the American mood and what average Americans were ready to fight for—the primacy of individual and property rights—as any document now stored in the National Archives.

Faced down by the old man, and responding to a local minister's appeal not to fire on the civilian crowd even as armed militiamen continued to surge onto the scene, Colonel Leslie agreed to a compromise. Acknowledging that it was too late in the day to carry out the search, Leslie asked to be allowed to march across the bridge about a hundred yards into Salem and then march out again so he could fulfill the letter of his orders, if not his actual mission. As the British troops trooped back to their transport ship, they were taunted at every step by an army of mocking militiamen and townspeople. Having forced a British retreat without firing a shot, the Salem militia not only preserved its munitions and cannon carriages but achieved another propaganda coup. The story of Salem's people turning back a large detachment of British soldiers further emboldened the patriots with the belief that they could face down British regulars, who would not fire on them.

By mid-April 1775, with direct orders from London to end the insurgency, Gage was of a different mind. The search and seizure raid aimed at Lexington, where his spies had reported that Adams and Hancock were staying in the parsonage of Reverend Jonas Clarke, and neighboring Concord, where the munitions were supposedly hidden, was not a dry run for show. Gage chose his best troops—light infantry, grenadier companies, and Royal Marines. He also selected Lieutenant Colonel Francis Smith, an experienced officer, to command. Second in command was Major John Pitcairn, a battle-toughened Scot with nineteen years of service and little sympathy for the "Yankies."

"Within twenty-four hours the expedition was the poorest-kept military secret in history," Thomas Fleming writes of this legendary night in Boston. "Dozens, possibly hundreds, of Bostonians, noticed that the light infantrymen and grenadiers had been relived from routine duty. They also noted that the British had collected numerous longboats from the fleet and tied them up to a man-of-war near the shore, suggesting that Gage was going to send his men across the Back

Bay to Cambridge instead of marching across Boston Neck. While Gage knew that these plans would not remain secret, he believed that he could keep the expedition's aims and destination from being leaked, along with its departure time: a night march."[16]

Not only were Gage's secrets leaking, but his entire ship of state was about to run aground. Historians have long known that the spy game was far from one-sided. Gage had his sources, but it has been widely speculated that Dr. Joseph Warren also was receiving regular reports from a secret ally inside General Gage's headquarters. Most likely the spy was Margaret Kemble Gage, the general's beautiful American wife. Given to lecturing her husband on liberty, Mrs. Gage was suspected of patriot sympathies by several officers on Gage's staff. Others hold that there was no need for Mrs. Gage to betray her husband, as thousands of eyes around Boston were focused on every move the British made.

At 9:30 P.M. on April 18, 1775, the British assembled at the foot of Boston Common for the boat trip across Back Bay. After receiving word of the troop movements, Dr. Warren directed Paul Revere and tanner William Dawes to ride to Lexington and warn John Hancock and Samuel Adams that Gage had ordered their arrest and was preparing to march on Concord. He gave them both written messages: "A large body of the King's troops (supposed to be a brigade of about 12, or 1500) were embarked in boats from Boston, and gone to land at Lechmere's point."[17]

Dr. Joseph Warren and silversmith Paul Revere represented the extremes of the American independence movement; one from the ranks of the Puritan elite for whom the term "Boston Brahmin" would be coined; the other from the working class of "mechanics." The tall, handsome Warren had set his sights on a medical career at age fourteen, when he saw his father fall from a ladder while picking apples on his Roxbury farm. With no physician nearby, his father died. After opening his surgery, Warren married Elizabeth Hooten, a wealthy teenage heiress, in 1764, and the couple had four children. Warren was prosperous, much admired, and progressive in his thinking—one of the chief proponents of the controversial practice of inoculations to prevent the spread of smallpox. In modern American terms, Warren might be said to "have it all." It would hardly seem to be the profile of one of Boston's most prolific dissidents and patriot organizers.

Yet by the end of the 1760s, Warren had emerged as a committed idealist at the center of patriot politics, and his home served as a gathering place for the inner circle of Boston's most visible leadership, including Samuel Adams; his younger cousin, attorney John Adams; the legendary but increasingly erratic attorney James Otis, who would soon go completely mad; and fellow physician Dr. Benjamin Church, the doctor who had tended Crispus Attucks, the half-African, half-Indian man who had been mortally wounded in the Boston Massacre. Warren frequented the Green Dragon, a tavern that was one of the chief incubators of the revolutionary spirit in Boston. It would later become the home of the Masonic lodge in which Warren was made Grand Master. Dr. Warren also began to write articles for the *Boston Gazette,* the patriots' chief propaganda voice, whose offices were another locus of Boston's rebellious mood. In fact, Warren could often be found in one of Boston's several patriot hotspots.

Despite his young wife's death in 1772, the physician helped Sam Adams draft a document that year detailing the rights of Americans under the British constitution. In it, Warren composed a section reciting a litany of complaints against Great Britain, a document that presaged many of the sentiments found four years later in Jefferson's

Declaration of Independence.[18] While the First Continental Congress was in session in Philadelphia, Warren had also issued the Suffolk Resolves, a document adopted by a convention of Massachusetts towns. Drafted by Warren and Samuel Adams, the Resolves derided Britain's coercive measures as "the attempts of a wicked administration to enslave America." They also called for the creation of a militia, withholding taxes to cripple British authority, and a renewed embargo on trade with Great Britain. Carried to the Continental Congress in Philadelphia by Paul Revere, who covered the three-hundred-mile journey in a prodigious and nearly unthinkable six-day ride, Warren's Suffolk Resolves were read on September 17, 1774, to Congress, which then unanimously endorsed them. Immediately afterward, Congress also adopted the embargo on trade with Great Britain. Revere returned to Massachusetts with news of this reaction, further cheering and emboldening the Massachusetts rebels.

Warren and fellow Freemason Paul Revere were widely thought to have led the Sons of Liberty on December 16, 1773, the night of the Tea Party. At least that was what the author of a popular Boston ditty thought. Sung on the streets of Boston, the ballad went, in part:

> *Our Warren's there, and bold Revere*
> *With hands to do and words to cheer.*
> *For Liberty and laws.*[19]

Although successful, Paul Revere came from the other end of Boston's economic spectrum, the "mechanic" class of tradesmen, laborers, and dockworkers. He was the son of Apollos Rivoire, a French Huguenot immigrant who arrived in Boston at age thirteen, bound as an indentured apprentice to a New England silversmith. Expertly learning the trade, Rivoire purchased his freedom following his master's death and set up shop as a silver and goldsmith. When New Englanders struggled with his French surname, he changed it to Revere. In 1729, he married Deborah Hitchborn, whose large Yankee family was descended from an indentured servant who had arrived during the Puritan migration. On December 21, 1734, their first son, Paul Revere, was born.

Apprenticed to his father, Revere grew up in Boston's boisterous North End, receiving a basic education but acquiring a lifelong love of reading. His father died when he was nineteen, and Revere inherited the business. Working mostly in silver, he crafted buckles, a brandy cock for Samuel Adams, pins and other jewelry, and the tea sets and household items that now fill museum shelves. He also made frames for the miniatures painted by John Singleton Copley and learned the art of engraving and the setting of false teeth—he would later make a set for Joseph Warren. In 1757, he married Sarah Orne. After bearing eight children, she died in 1773. He remarried five months later.

Prosperous although never wealthy, Revere belonged to the colonial American version of the middle class. A regular church member and active in Boston's civic affairs, Revere was a joiner. He had served in the militia during the French and Indian War and became an active Mason. In a fitting summary of what Freemasonry may have meant to men such as Revere, David Hackett Fischer wrote, "All his life he [Revere] kept its creed of enlightened Christianity, fraternity, harmony, reason, and community service."[20] Revere also joined the North Caucus Club, the political organization founded by Samuel Adams' father. And in 1765, as resistance to the Stamp Act coalesced in Boston, he became a member of the newly formed Sons of Liberty. Turning his engraving skill to politics, he was an aspiring political cartoonist. But his greatest accomplishment may have been the engraving he crafted after the 1770 Boston Massacre. Showing the British soldiers firing point-blank at their prostrate victims, it was one of the most effective pieces of patriotic propaganda ever created.

With this substantial patriot resumé, Revere was eventually invited to join the Long Room Club, another secretive group that met above the print shop where the patriotic propaganda journal the *Boston Gazette* was published. He was now in the heart of Boston's patriot inner sanctum, along with some of Boston's most notable lawyers, doctors, and men of wealth. Most were products of Harvard. Lacking their education and status, Paul Revere was pulled into this tight-knit group as a link to Boston's "street." He became a trusted lieutenant to Samuel Adams, organizer of a group of fast-riding messengers who carried Adams' "circular letters." Revere also formed a ring of spies to shadow British troop movements. Drawn largely from Boston's world of laborers and other mechanics who moved almost invisibly past the aristocratic British, their intelligence was relayed back to Warren and Adams.

Given the order by Warren to warn Adams and Hancock that British troops were moving to arrest them, Revere still feared his own capture by Gage's troops. Through his spy network—and Benjamin Church in particular—Gage knew about Revere's corps of messengers and had dispatched patrols to intercept any patriot couriers on the roads between Boston and Concord. But Revere had made his own contingency plans. Once he knew how the British troops were moving, a signal would be sent using lanterns hung by trusted men in the tower of Christ Church, known as Old North Church. In Charlestown, riders from Revere's stable of messengers awaited the signal: a single light (the poetically famous "one if by land") if they were marching south across Boston Neck, the thin isthmus connecting the peninsula on which Boston was built to neighboring Roxbury; two lanterns meant the British were moving out of Boston in longboats ("two if by sea"). When the Charlestown Whigs saw the two signal lights in the steeple, they dispatched yet another rider for Lexington. His identity and fate remain a mystery.

Arriving in Charlestown by boat, Revere was given a fast, powerful mare named Brown Beauty. Around 11:00 P.M., he set off for Lexington but was nearly intercepted by a pair of British soldiers. The speedy Brown Beauty easily outdistanced them, and the silversmith was first to reach Lexington, where Adams and Hancock were staying before departing for Philadelphia and the Second Continental Congress. The pair were at the Clarke parsonage, built by Hancock's grandfather, who had been the minister in Lexington. When Revere arrived after midnight, the two patriot leaders were sleeping in the downstairs parlor. To a guard at the parsonage, Revere reported sharply, "The regulars are coming out."

William Dawes, active in the Boston patriot militia and a tanner by trade, arrived about half an hour later. He and Revere had both covered the approximately eleven miles from Boston before the British even finished crossing the Charles. The Royal Navy had failed to provide enough boats to transport all seven hundred troops, and no senior commander was on hand to organize the crossing. Not until four hours after they had first assembled, at 1:30 A.M. on April 19, did the British even finish the crossing. Then they faced a long march through darkness to Lexington and Concord.

By then, Revere and Dawes had delivered Warren's warning to Lexington and the town bell tolled, bringing members of the village's militia to form up on the two-acre common. There Captain John Parker, a much-respected townsman and veteran of the French and Indian War now suffering from tuberculosis, gathered his men. It was agreed that they would not "meddle with the regulars."

Dawes and Revere, in the meantime, left for Concord, where the munitions were hidden, to continue spreading the alarm. Along the way, they encountered Dr. Samuel Prescott, a twenty-three-year-old Concord doctor who had been courting his fiancée in Lexington. An avowed member of the Sons of Liberty, Prescott joined the other two and they began to knock on farmhouse doors, alerting the people in the countryside between Lexington and Concord. Their message was not, as poetic legend put it, "The British are coming," but "The regulars are coming out."

Out of the darkness, the trio was suddenly confronted by a British patrol near Lincoln, between Lexington and Concord. All three men were seized at gunpoint and held alongside a number of other locals captured by the British patrol. Some of them were patriots spreading the word, others merely innocents caught in the wrong place at the wrong time. As they were forced from the road into a nearby pasture, Prescott cried, "Put on," and broke away, galloping through the forest, familiar territory to the young man. Some of the British gave chase, but they soon quit as the young physician disappeared into the thick, swampy wood and made his way to Concord to sound the alert.

Back in Lexington, Hancock and Adams argued about what to do. Hancock wanted to join with the militia and face down the regulars.

"That is not our business; we belong to the cabinet," argued Adams. After considerable debate, the two men left for the safety of quarters in nearby Woburn before setting off for Philadelphia in Hancock's large, fashionable carriage.

Meanwhile, the British officers who had let Revere and the others go had encountered the advancing British troops as they neared Lexington. When they told Smith, the British commander, of the reports of as many as five hundred American militiamen gathering at Lexington, Smith sent word back to Boston requesting reinforcements. It would prove to be one of the wisest decisions he made. He then ordered Pitcairn to take six light infantry companies and march at top speed to take the bridges at Concord.

As this British advance guard approached Lexington, Pitcairn was told by locals that upward of one thousand men were now waiting to confront the British troops at Lexington—a gross exaggeration, but it put Pitcairn on high alert. When a lone American alongside the road discharged his musket—perhaps only a "flash in the pan," with no actual ammunition loaded—Pitcairn ordered his men to load their guns. In the distance, they could hear church bells tolling in Lexington and other nearby towns.

Over the course of the next hours, America was transformed. A still-mysterious shot fired on Lexington Green led Major Pitcairn to order a British volley into the ranks of the American militia. The first Americans to die in the Revolution fell there, most shot in the back. The action quickly shifted to Concord, where more Massachusetts men had rallied. Then smoke was seen rising above Lexington. The British had set fire to some stores, but the Massachusetts men thought that their homes were being torched. As a smattering of shots were exchanged in Concord, the British began to withdraw for the long march back to Boston. But thousands of Massachusetts militiamen were now streaming to the route that the British regulars would have to travel. For the next few hours, over miles of road surrounded by Massachusetts woods, the American minutemen fired on the British ranks, constantly harassing the British and inflicting sharp casualties.

The day's bloodiest fighting was not at Lexington or Concord but still to come in Menotomy (now Arlington), where American forces were being led by Brigadier General William Heath in a more disciplined attack. Using a moving "ring of fire," Heath directed a constant, withering rain of musketry down on the British troops. By the time British reinforcements finally reached the bloodied, exhausted redcoats and used cannons to drive off the patriot militia, the damage was done. As William Hallahan summarized, "One of the finest military units in the world—some 1,800 men—had been humbled, decimated in a shooting gallery slaughter by thousands of New England farmers. Some 73 soldiers were dead. Another 174 were wounded and 26 were missing (captured, in most cases). The casualty rate among British regulars was nearly 10 percent, while the casualty rate among the 3,500 militia was much lower—less than 2 percent. For the families and friends of the militia casualties, there was also much to mourn over—49 dead, 30 wounded, 4 missing."[21]

"It was a glorious morning for America," in Samuel Adams' (perhaps apocryphal) words. "The shot heard round the world"—as Ralph Waldo Emerson, whose grandfather was then the minister in Concord, would famously call it—had provided Samuel Adams with the deadly encounter he knew was needed. There would be no turning back. It was a glorious morning that turned into a struggle that lasted six and a half long and often desperate years, until major hostilities ended on October 17, 1781, at Yorktown.

The shooting war had now begun. But the propaganda war that would be even more critical to Americans' hopes for independence was also getting under way. Dr. Joseph Warren, who had rushed from Boston to join in the fighting in Menotomy, knew that how the story was told—both in America and England—was paramount. Quickly gathering depositions from witnesses, including the wounded British officers in patriot hands, Dr. Warren soon wrote a letter to town committees that began, "The barbarous murders committed on our innocent brethren, on Wednesday, the 19th instant, have made it absolutely necessary that we immediately raise an army to defend our wives and children from the butchering hands of the inhuman soldiery, who, incensed at the obstacles they met in their bloody progress, and enraged at being repulsed from the field of slaughter, will, without the least doubt, take the first opportunity in their power to ravage this devoted country with fire and sword."

The nearly one hundred depositions Warren had collected and a letter he addressed to the "Inhabitants of Great Britain" were dispatched on a speedy American schooner. Reaching London before General Gage's own official report of the battle could, Warren's open letter caused a sensation, painting the Americans as victims of an unprovoked British slaughter. All England was shocked at the concept of their finest troops—even though they were not, for the most part, battle-tested regulars—being sent flying by the raw Massachusetts militia. Having dismissed the American battlefield threat as of no consequence, the British government was put completely on the defensive. Friends of the American cause in England, while few, had powerful new arguments.

Back in America, the influence of Warren's propaganda coup was felt even more powerfully. As David Hackett Fischer noted: "This second battle of Lexington and Concord was waged not with bayonets but broadsides, not with muskets but depositions, newspapers and sermons. In strictly military terms, the fighting on April 19 was a minor reverse for British arms, and a small success for the New England militia. But the ensuing contest for popular opinion was an epic disaster for the British government and a triumph for American Whigs. In every region of British America, attitudes were truly transformed by news of this event."[22]

In the immediate aftermath of the fighting of April 19, a hodge-podge, ragtag army of New England militiamen began descending on the outskirts of Boston. They came not only from Massachusetts but from neighboring colonies as well. In Connecticut, portly, aging Israel Putnam, a legend for his heroism during the French and Indian War, left his farm to join the Connecticut men who streamed off to Massachusetts. From Pennsylvania came a contingent of buckskin-clad backwoodsman, led by Daniel Morgan and toting the long rifles that would add to their legendary stature as American marksmen who would take such a heavy toll on British officers. These were among the farmer-minutemen of Revolutionary War mythology, but some did not stay long: they had farms to tend, or their terms of enlistment would expire in a few months.

But many of the others trooping into Cambridge were the poor, the unemployed, the young, and the restless, looking for adventure and a payday. These recruits would become the core of Washington's Continental army. Lacking organization or experienced leadership, it was essentially a rapidly growing small town, numbering between fifteen thousand and twenty thousand men, short on supplies and lacking any sense of basic sanitation. But they would succeed in bottling up the bloodied British troops still licking their wounds in Boston under a shocked, crestfallen General Gage.

Meanwhile in Philadelphia, Congress dithered. That the other colonies would join in the rebellion was still not, in a modern phrase, a "slam dunk." Conservatives and moderates eager to avoid war held sway in Congress. The Massachusetts delegates, already viewed as radical troublemakers, had to lie low and keep their counsel, although the ambitious, egotistical John Hancock hoped to be named commander of the American forces. His dream was dashed by the Adamses, who had agreed on another candidate. As Samuel Adams biographer Mark Puls recounts it, "John Adams rose to argue for the need for Congress to adopt the army around Boston. John could see a satisfied expression cross Hancock's face; he believed he was about to be nominated commander-in-chief of the Continental army. When John Adams then nominated George Washington, Hancock was astonished. 'I never remarked a more sudden and striking change of countenance. Mortification and resentment were expressed as forcibly as his face could exhibit them.' Samuel Adams seconded the motion."[23]

Grandson of Lexington's minister, John Hancock was one of the wealthiest men in Massachusetts and all of America. In spite of his prestigious Puritan bloodlines, he had not been born to wealth. His father, an impoverished Congregational minister, died when he was seven and the boy grew up in his grandfather's Lexington parsonage. The source of Hancock's fortune was his bachelor uncle Thomas, who had made a killing as a smuggler and supplier to the British army during the Seven Years' War. When Thomas Hancock died, John Hancock inherited both business and fortune in 1764, and by continuing its illegal pursuits, prospered in spectacular fashion. Around Boston, it was said that Hancock's true interest in wanting to be free of Britain was to get out from under the £100,000 in fines he owed for smuggling. Shortly after winning his inheritance, Hancock had been invited into the patriot inner circle by Samuel Adams, who had bankrupted just about every business endeavor he had put his hands on. More than a few Boston wags nudged and winked. With his deep pockets, Hancock became bankroller to Adams' cause. But the slight over Washington's selection, as Hancock perceived it, left a deep fracture between the Boston patriots. It was a bitter rift that was never completely repaired.

On June 15, the Continental Congress unanimously approved George Washington's appointment, and a day later he left for Boston. By this time, General Gage had been joined in Boston by three more British generals—"Gentleman Johnny" Burgoyne, Sir Henry Clinton, and Sir William Howe. Arriving with more reinforcements in late May, the trio also brought along fishing rods, as if planning for a country outing instead of a long campaign. They were shocked to discover that Gage's troops were pinned down by what they considered "rabble."

On June 16, 1775, the patriot militia erected a battery on Breed's Hill, near Bunker Hill. The next day, the British attacked the hill in what has come down in history as the battle of Bunker Hill. The British won the day, eventually chasing the rebel forces from the hill, but they suffered horrendous casualties, losing a third of their men. Among them was Major Pitcairn, killed when hit by a shot fired by Peter Salem, a freed slave and one of a number of blacks at Bunker Hill. Rhode Island militia leader Nathanael Greene is said to have quipped, "I wish we could sell them another hill at the same price." A Quaker who had learned his soldiering from the military books he shared with fellow Quaker and bookseller Henry Knox, Greene was shunned by the pacifist Society of Friends for his military pursuits. He would go on to become one of George Washington's most trusted and successful lieutenants.

But on the patriot ledger too, the price of Bunker Hill was steep. Among the losses was Dr. Joseph Warren. Although he had been named a general, Warren insisted on fighting in the front lines. Rallying some men to the hottest point of the British attack, Warren was struck in the head at point-blank range by a musket ball and died instantly. A British officer in charge of the burial detail who later reported finding his body said he had "stuffed the scoundrell with another Rebel into one hole and there he and his seditious principles may remain."[24]

On the day of the battle, Warren's four children were in the care of Abigail Adams in Quincy, where the doctor had sent them for safety, with Boston under siege. When she received word of Warren's death at Breed's Hill, she wrote to John in Philadelphia: "Not all the havoc and devastation they [the British] have made has wounded me like the death of Warren. We want him in the Senate; we want him in his profession; we want him in the field. We mourn for the citizen, the senator, the physician, and the warrior. When he fell, liberty wept."

Several months later, Paul Revere and a few other patriots went to the battle site in Charlestown to locate Warren's remains and provide a proper burial for the patriot leader. They were able to find his body, which Revere identified by the false teeth he himself had set in Warren's mouth, now credited as the first known instance of forensic dentistry in American history.

So much had changed since that March night in Old South. Like Cicero, Warren had died for his republican ideals. Now his toga was replaced by the mantle of a revolutionary martyr.

◄§ Aftermath §►

Not long after the events at Concord, General Gage packed his wife aboard a ship and sent her back to England. Following the Bunker

Hill disaster, Gage remained in America for more than a year, until October 1776, when he returned to London. Deemed responsible for the British calamities at Lexington, Concord, and Bunker Hill, Gage was the scapegoat. His own men essentially mutinied; he was replaced by General Howe as acting commander in chief. After his return to England, Gage became estranged from his wife, Margaret, and died in 1787. Margaret Gage survived him for more than thirty years, never revealing any role in the events in Boston. But leading historians, such as David Hackett Fischer, conclude, "All of this circumstantial evidence suggests that it is highly probable, through far from certain, that Doctor Warren's informer was indeed Margaret Kemble Gage— a lady of divided loyalties to both her husband and her native land."[25]

In Philadelphia, the war's outbreak cut both ways. For John Adams, who had walked through the devastation at Lexington and Concord before setting off for the Second Congress, there was no going back. To him, the key was how to bring the other reluctant colonies along. Many other more moderate voices still hoped for reconciliation with London. One of them was Philadelphia's John Dickinson, a wealthy but hesitant patriot and Quaker who drafted a petition that not only opposed taxation of Americans but demanded a guarantee of colonial rights and strictly prohibited any changes in provincial charters.

The king was not amused. After the hostilities in Massachusetts, King George III was not remotely interested in reading Dickinson's "Olive Branch Petition," as it was called. Instead, in August 1775, after the Continental Congress had adjourned for the summer, the king issued a proclamation, reading in part:

Whereas many of our subjects in divers parts of our Colonies and plantations in North America misled by dangerous and ill-designing men

and forgetting the allegiance which they owe to the power that has protected and supported them; after various disorderly acts committed in
disturbance of the public peace to the obstruction of lawful commerce
and to the oppressions of our loyal subjects carrying on same: have at
length proceeded to open and avowed rebellion by arraying themselves
in a hostile manner to withstand the execution of the law and traitor-
ously preparing, ordering and levying war against us; And whereas
there is reason to apprehend that such rebellion has been much promoted by the traitorous correspondence . . . We have thought fit by and
with the advice of our Privy Council, to issue our Royal Proclamation . . .
to suppress such rebellion and to bring the traitors to justice.

—*King George III, Proclamation of Rebellion (August 23, 1775)*

By the time King George issued his proclamation, George Washington had reached his newly minted army in Cambridge. He was ap-
palled at the condition of the camps and the behavior of the troops.
Washington found one militia officer shaving some of his men. A
barber before the fighting began, the man had been elected captain
of the company. Democracy might be a fine way to run a legislature,
in Washington's view, but no way to run an army. Over the next few
months, Washington would attempt to organize and discipline his
forces.

He was also confronted with another shocking reality in this new
"democratic" American army he had been presented with: it included
black men with guns. Some of them had fought at Lexington, Concord, and Bunker Hill. "Freedom" was a catchy tune, and although
slavery was still widespread in the northern colonies, the abolitionist
spirit was growing. That was not going to sit well with Washington's
southern planter friends, who were probably much more concerned

about slave rebellions than about the American Revolution. Washington initially balked at allowing blacks to serve. But as time went by and he needed every fighting man he could muster, he was forced to moderate his policies.

As Simon Schama wrote in *Rough Crossings,* "George Washington, despite the voiced hostility of fellow officers and civilian delegates to his camp at Cambridge, was reluctant to let black volunteers go, so he put the question to Congress. There, the horror expressed by Southern representatives such as Edward Rutledge at the idea of arming slaves predictably overcame the lukewarm gratitude for black service. Even armed free negroes were a worry. Could they be trusted not to spread the seeds of insurrection among the unfree? In February 1776 Congress instructed Washington that, whilst free negroes might be retained, no more should be enlisted."[26]

Recent scholarship, such as Schama's, has cast new light on a major turning point in American attitudes about the Revolution. In November 1775, Lord Dunmore, the last colonial governor of Virginia, issued a promise of outright liberty to all slaves who escaped and joined the British army. Clearly designed as a tactical maneuver rather than an abolitionist landmark, Dunmore's pledge became official British policy. To many slaves, Schama points out, "the vaunted war for liberty was . . . a war for the perpetuation of servitude."[27] Inspired by Governor Dunmore's promise, tens of thousands of slaves sought freedom with the British and were organized into British fighting units. Once Washington became desperate enough for more bodies, the Continental army became the most racially integrated American fighting force until the time of the Vietnam War.

A FEW WEEKS before George Washington reached the Cambridge front, the dashing captain of a force of Connecticut's militia had marched into the patriot camp. Arriving eight days after the battles of Lexington and Concord, their elected captain made an immediate impression on the Massachusetts troops and patriot leaders. A thirty-four-year-old apothecary, successful merchant, sea captain, and devoted member of the Sons of Liberty, he led the Foot Guards, impressively outfitted in their scarlet coats, with smart efficiency. He soon met with Joseph Warren and other leaders of the Massachusetts Committee of Safety, the de facto American government in Massachusetts. Given a secret military mission and a promotion, he left Cambridge on May 3. He would remain in close correspondence with Warren over the weeks leading up to the battle of Bunker Hill.

After that battle and Warren's untimely death, when both Massachusetts and the Congress failed to provide a pension for the martyred doctor's children, the young officer announced that he would see to it that Dr. Joseph Warren's orphaned children were properly provided for. This principled young officer's name was Benedict Arnold.

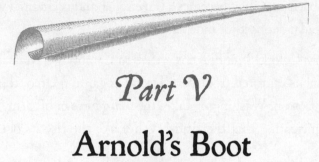

Part V

Arnold's Boot

1776   Thomas Paine anonymously publishes *Common Sense;* this forty-six-page pamphlet becomes a huge seller and is credited with creating popular support for independence.

In January, Colonel Henry Knox arrives in Cambridge, Massachusetts with cannons captured from Fort Ticonderoga. In March, the British evacuate Boston. Washington takes the main force of his army to New York, anticipating that the British will make the city its operational base.

In May, French king Louis XVI secretly begins to arm the Americans; Spain also supports the American rebels.

In June, a large British armada sails into New York harbor. By August, more than thirty thousand British troops and Hessian mercenaries have landed in New York.

Congress votes for independence on July 4.

On August 27–29, the British crush Washington's forces in the battle of Long Island.

The battle of Trenton takes place on December 25–26. In a surprise attack, Washington defeats a British-Hessian garrison at Trenton, New Jersey. The victory boosts morale for the struggling Continental army. A second important victory is won at Princeton, New Jersey, on January 3, 1777.

1777   On January 15, residents of the New Hampshire Grants declare an independent republic called New Connecticut. In July, the republic is renamed Vermont and adopts a constitution banning slavery and promising universal male suffrage.

In the battle of Saratoga on September 19, the first of two key battles fought in upstate New York, American forces under General Daniel Morgan and militia colonel Henry Dearborn defeat Burgoyne's forces.

At Saratoga on October 7, American forces defeat British General Burgoyne. On October 17, Burgoyne surrenders his fifty-seven-hundred-man army, which is marched to Boston upon swearing not to serve again in America. News of the victory encourages European support for the American revolutionary cause. In December, France officially recognizes American independence.

Washington leads his army into winter quarters at Valley Forge, Pennsylvania, on December 17.

1778   France declares war against Britain on July 10. Later that month, a French fleet arrives off the New England coast.

1780   On September 23, British major John André is captured near Tarrytown, New York, carrying plans for Arnold's surrender of West Point. Arnold flees and André is convicted as a spy and executed on October 2.

1781   The combined American and French army begins a siege of the British forces at Yorktown, Virginia, on September 28. On October 19, General Cornwallis surrenders to Washington at Yorktown.

1782   On February 27, the House of Commons votes against waging further war in America. In March, the prime minister, Lord North, resigns and is succeeded by Lord Rockingham, who seeks immediate negotiations with the Americans. Peace talks begin in Paris in April.

1783   The Treaty of Paris is signed on September 3, formally ending the Revolutionary War. On December 4, as the last British troops board ships in New York, George Washington takes leave of his officers at Fraunces Tavern.

Colonel Washington appears at Congress in uniform and by his great experience and abilities in military matters is of much service to us.

–John Adams,
in Philadelphia, to his wife, Abigail (1775)

Arnold has betrayed us! Whom can we trust now?

–George Washington
(September 1780)

THE VERMONTERS WERE DRUNK. THE men had been assigned to commandeer a schooner belonging to a local Tory, Major Philip Skene. A wealthy British officer, Skene owned a substantial chunk of the real estate bordering southern Lake Champlain, the slender thread of water separating what is now Vermont and upstate New York.[1] These midnight raiders were also supposed to scrounge up any other boats they could find on the lake. Instead, their foray had uncovered a private cellar that belonged to the self-styled "Governor" Skene. Finding the cellar stocked with "choice liquors," the men quickly abandoned the search for boats.[2]

It was about three o'clock in the morning on May 10, 1775, just three weeks after the battles of Lexington and Concord. America's first offensive against a British target in the nascent and still undeclared Revolution was off to an inauspicious beginning—if it would begin at all. In a cove on Lake Champlain's eastern shore, more than two hundred members of an American raiding party were hunkered down in a gloomy rain. They didn't know what had become of the thirty or so men who had been dispatched to "liberate" Philip Skene's boats. This raiding party needed those boats to carry them across Lake Champlain.

As the darkness that would cover their attack began to drift toward dawn, the joint commanders of the raid conferred. Should they postpone the attack? The two officers did not like or trust each other. They disagreed, and one of the men stoically and perhaps melodramatically declared that he would go it alone if necessary. Then, out of the dark-ness, a single thirty-foot scow appeared on the lake's ink-black waters. Instead of securing enough boats to carry all 230 men across Champ-lain, the drunken boatmen had managed to produce only one, capable of holding about forty men. The two commanders agreed that they would press on with the attack with as many men as they could ferry across the lake in the next hour. As the weather worsened, the over-loaded scow twice crossed Champlain's ice-cold, wind-whipped chop. From the cove in what is today Shoreham, Vermont, the boat deliv-ered fewer than ninety men to the New York side of the lake.

Stitched together out of militiamen from Massachusetts, Connecti-cut, and the future Vermont, this patchwork raiding party made its way to the target—the imposing citadel of Fort Ticonderoga. Loom-ing above Lake Champlain, Fort Ticonderoga, along with its smaller sister, Fort Amherst, some twelve miles to the north at Crown Point, was a valuable prize standing on blood-soaked ground. Although un-dermanned and suffering from years of neglect, the two British garri-sons were stocked with gunpowder, cannons, and other artillery pieces that the ill-equipped and dysfunctional patriot army camped outside Boston so desperately needed.

Holding Fort Ticonderoga, once called the "Gibraltar of North America," and the smaller fort at Crown Point would also mean se-curing control of a crucial waterway that linked Quebec and Mon-treal with New York City. Scraped out by the Ice Age glaciers, Lake Champlain and its adjoining valley of rich farmland and dairy pas-tures are wedged between New York's Adirondacks and Vermont's Green Mountains. From eastern Canada, boats carrying troops could travel down the St. Lawrence and Richelieu rivers to Lake Champlain, then sail south on the roughly 110-mile-long lake. A short portage from Lake Champlain's southernmost tip brought an army to nearby Lake George in New York, and once across that lake, it was a mere eight-mile march to the Hudson River, just above Albany.

This largely water route was far more manageable for an army with horses and artillery than negotiating the several hundred miles of northern New York's rugged Adirondack wilderness. It was also the fastest route between Massachusetts and Canada. Guns placed at Fort Ticonderoga and Crown Point could easily stop any boats that reached the southern stretch of Lake Champlain, where it narrows to its thinnest point. Although still unsettled frontier wilderness for the most part, the area's strategic value had been the reason for several devastating battles fought by the British and French around Lake Champlain and Lake George during the French and Indian War.

In August 1757, French forces under General Montcalm had defeated the British at Fort William Henry on Lake George. After surrendering the fort, a number of British civilians and "paroled" soldiers—soldiers who had agreed not to fight again for eighteen months under the European gentleman's code of military honor— had been killed by the Abenaki and other Indian allies of the French; countless others were taken captive. The exact number of dead in this "massacre" remains uncertain, but has been reliably estimated at between 70 and 184 British and Americans, as well as many more Indians allied with the British and black servants killed or taken prisoner.[3] But American and British wartime propaganda quickly inflated those numbers to more than a thousand, creating a wave of panic in New England and New York. More significantly, the "massacre" changed the rules of engagement between British and French during the rest of the war and further demonized native Americans. Finally, the incident also inspired the fictionalized version of events at the center of James Fenimore Cooper's 1825 novel *The Last of the Mohicans.*

A year later, in July 1758, a British counterattack on what was then called Fort Carillon, on Lake Champlain, had resulted in a disastrous bloodbath. Some twenty thousand British soldiers, the largest force yet assembled in North America, was ordered into an all-out frontal assault on Carillon's four thousand French and Indian defenders. The seven-hour battle saw wave upon wave of red-coated British soldiers decimated by French artillery as they attempted to cross the earthworks in front of Fort Carillon, littered with a forest of felled and sharpened trees. More than two thousand British soldiers died in what was called "one of the most incredible incidents of bravery and stupidity in the annals of the British army."[4] The French later abandoned Fort Carillon and the British moved in, renaming it Ticonderoga and then spending millions to fortify its defenses. After more than a decade of relative peace in what had become a colonial backwater, Fort Ticonderoga had fallen into disrepair. Now, taking this granite-walled citadel and securing Lake Champlain were crucial to any patriot hopes of containing Great Britain's might.

With two-thirds of their total force left behind on the other side of the lake, the two American commanders were relying on surprise instead of superior numbers. They led the assault party, clambering up the steep slope from the lake shore. It was well past four in the morning when the raiders finally reached the main gate of the lightly guarded fort. Some forty British soldiers manned the garrison, most of them "invalids," soldiers who were injured or otherwise unfit for regular army duty, along with some of their families. Despite a warning sent to Fort Ticonderoga a month earlier from Boston by General Gage, only a single sentry was posted, and he was asleep. Racing for the wicket gate, a small entryway through the fort's larger wooden door, both American commanders later claimed they had been first through the broken entry. Taking credit for victory (or being denied it) and assigning blame for disaster were going to be central themes in the turbulent futures of these two American soldiers—both of whom would be called traitors.

As the Americans swept into the fort, the startled sentry attempted to get off a shot, but in the early morning rain, his damp musket misfired. The British soldier threw down his weapon and raced for the barracks to raise the alarm. He was chased and caught by some of the Green Mountain Boys, led by one of the American commanders, Colonel Ethan Allen. A second sentry appeared and fired at Allen himself but missed. He rushed at Allen with his bayonet fixed, but the six-foot-tall, powerful backwoodsman swung his sword, striking the man a glancing blow on his head, which was protected by a comb that kept his powdered white hair in place.

Allen demanded that the man bring them to the fort's commandant, Captain Delaplace. But the junior of the two British officers at Ticonderoga, Lieutenant Jocelyn Feltham, was the first to emerge and confront the Americans. With time enough only to grab his jacket, the half-naked Feltham had tried unsuccessfully to awaken Captain Delaplace. Breeches in hand, the young officer audaciously, if improbably, challenged the eighty or so musket-bearing Americans standing before him: "By what authority have you entered His Majesty's fort?"

It was an excellent question. Still intent on finding the British commandant, Ethan Allen shouted, "Come out of there, you damned old British rat," according to the accounts of his men. But in the oft-quoted—and most likely apocryphal—post-Revolutionary version of events, Allen, who favored the cadences of an Old Testament prophet, is said to have replied, "In the name of the great Jehovah and the Continental Congress."

A noble sentiment, to be sure. But history can't confirm whether Ethan Allen actually made that bold statement at this astonishing moment when a disorganized, ragtag band of ill-disciplined backwoodsmen captured one of the most important British fortifications in North America. Nor can Jehovah's purported instructions to Allen be verified. The latter claim, however, was certainly untrue. The second Continental Congress was not yet in session and wouldn't formally place the colonies in a state of defense for another five days. George Washington would not be named commander for more than a month. And independence was more than a year away. The orders to carry out this assault on a British fort, before hostilities had been formally declared by anyone on either side, had actually come from two separate sources. Neither of them possessed any authority to issue such orders, which was part of a problem of command that would soon worsen.

Colonel Ethan Allen and his men were operating under a directive that had come by way of Connecticut's militia, even though Fort Ticonderoga was in New York's territory, and most of Allen's men were from the rugged Green Mountain wilderness that eventually became Vermont. Born in Litchfield, Connecticut, and bound for Yale when his father died suddenly, Ethan Allen and his Green Mountain Boys were freelancers with an agenda very much their own. For five years, this self-appointed militia force had been trying to wrest the disputed territory known as the New Hampshire Grants from the control of New Hampshire and New York, which both laid claim to the area. If taking Fort Ticonderoga fit that agenda, it suited Allen. If not, as his life would later prove, he would follow his own path. In the words of Michael A. Bellesiles, a generally admiring modern biographer, Ethan

Allen was "a scoundrel, a charismatic charlatan of enormous strength and courage, and a braggart of almost mythical proportions. In short, Allen was the ideal of the frontier redneck, Davy Crockett in a tricorne."[5]

Allen's co-commander carried orders issued in Cambridge and written by Dr. Benjamin Church, whose treachery to the patriot cause had not yet been revealed. The Massachusetts Committee of Safety, which also lacked any standing on which to send forces against a British fort in the neighboring colony of New York, was behind those orders. They had secretly elevated Connecticut militia captain Benedict Arnold to the rank of colonel, and he had ridden out of Cambridge with a satchel of cash, a handful of men, and the assignment to gather more troops to capture Fort Ticonderoga and its artillery. With a few dozen men recruited from western Massachusetts, Arnold had linked up with Allen's force. It proved to be an uneasy alliance.

With the fort in their control, Benedict Arnold listened as Ethan Allen issued a blustering threat that any resistance would mean the deaths of all of the British men, women, and children in the fort. Still resplendent in the scarlet uniform of Connecticut's Second Foot Guard, Colonel Arnold interceded, acting very much the gentleman-soldier. According to a British account of the incident, Arnold formally and more politely requested that Fort Ticonderoga's commandant, Captain Delaplace, surrender Ticonderoga. Left with no other choice, Delaplace gave up the fort, along with his sword and pistols. The British prisoners would later be sent on to Connecticut.

While those prisoners were collected in the fort's parade ground, more of Ethan Allen's Vermonters poured into the compound, ultimately reaching about four hundred in number. One of their first discoveries was the cellar beneath the officer's quarters, where they found ninety gallons of rum. Instead of stripping the fort of its cannons, the Vermonters soon got drunk and began to loot the barracks.

In his initial report on the capture of Fort Ticonderoga, Benedict Arnold wrote back to the Massachusetts Committee of Safety, "On and before our taking possession here I agreed with Colonel Allen to issue further orders jointly, until I could raise a sufficient number of men to relieve his people, on which plan we proceeded . . . since, which, Colonel Allen, finding he had the ascendancy over his people, positively insisted I should have no command, as I had forbid the soldiers plundering and destroying private property. The power is now taken out of my hands and I am no longer consulted."[6] Allen had relieved Arnold of his joint command at gunpoint.

The attack on Fort Ticonderoga under Ethan Allen and Benedict Arnold had been a misadventure of dueling orders, competing agendas and two considerable, conflicting egos. In short, it was entirely typical of the American effort in the earliest days of the Revolution, when nobody was actually in charge, there was not yet any thought of a grand strategy, and free spirits such as Ethan Allen sometimes reigned. Benedict Arnold's report to Dr. Joseph Warren about the capture of Fort Ticonderoga barely revealed the convoluted twists the New Haven merchant-turned-soldier had taken in carrying out the plan.

Dispatched by Warren and the Massachusetts Committee, Arnold carried orders that seemed to hold some legitimacy. What he didn't know was that while he had made the case for this attack to Warren, men back in Connecticut with whom Arnold had discussed Fort Ticonderoga and its easy pickings of cannons and powder, had moved to do the same thing. They sent sixteen Connecticut militiamen to meet up with Ethan Allen, in command of a group of irregulars who were, at that moment, wanted by the authorities in New York. In their efforts to liberate the future Vermont, Ethan Allen and his Green Mountain Boys had rankled the New York authorities, and there was a price of £100 on Ethan Allen's head. In the eyes of the "Yorkers," Allen's men were little more than backwoods banditti.

When Benedict Arnold first arrived in the town of Bennington and met some of the Green Mountain Boys in the Catamount Tavern, which they had proclaimed the "capital of Vermont," these backwoodsmen nearly shot the Connecticut dandy. First of all, Arnold wore a uniform that looked suspiciously like that of a British officer. He also possessed the haughty air of a gentleman that these backwoodsmen despised. When Arnold later met up with Ethan Allen, the leader of the Green Mountain Boys grudgingly deferred to Arnold and his orders from Massachusetts. But Allen's men refused to obey Arnold and threatened mutiny, so the two officers had agreed upon a joint command. Allen even gave Arnold an antiquated blunderbuss, since he was carrying only a saber and pistols. Mutual suspicion and the desire to take charge of the expedition colored every move they both made. But in spite of all the misadventures, the capture of Fort Ticonderoga would soon have enormous reverberations. When Dr. Joseph Warren received Allen's report a week later, he wrote, "Thus a War has begun."[7]

While Arnold chafed at what he considered the undisciplined banditry of the Vermonters under Ethan Allen, the cannons he had come to collect were left sitting. Some of them were actually under water, as the lake had risen from the snowmelt and spring rains. Arnold was also unaware that Ethan Allen—in collusion with some of the Connecticut militiamen who had axes to grind against the New Haven merchant Arnold—was already undermining Arnold's role in the capture of the fort. Dispatches critical of Arnold and placing Ethan Allen and other Connecticut men in the central role at Ticonderoga had made their way back to Connecticut. This sort of backstabbing, which diminished his accomplishments and authority, would torment Benedict Arnold throughout the war's early years.

Often it has been said—particularly when it comes to warfare—that while success has a hundred fathers, failure is an orphan. In the case of Fort Ticonderoga, there were many fathers. In truth, the idea of taking Fort Ticonderoga seems so obvious as to make the question of credit fairly meaningless. The fort's tactical value, its recent history, and the stores of munitions it held were all well known. But most immediate versions and the later legendary account of the Ticonderoga victory virtually ignored—or certainly diminished—the role of the man who played a key part in the attack's success, largely because he would become the most vilified man in American history. Like some Soviet general whose image was removed from photographs after a Stalinist purge, Benedict Arnold and his leadership at Fort Ticonderoga, along with his other accomplishments, were deliberately erased from history.[8]

Despite Arnold's broken reputation, much of that history is clear. In a document dated April 30, 1775, which he prepared for Dr. Warren and the Safety Committee in Cambridge, Arnold had specifically laid out the number of cannons and other guns at Fort Ticonderoga. He accurately noted that "Fort Ticonderoga is in a ruinous condition and has not more than fifty men at most." In addition, he pointed out, a British sloop was on the lake. Familiar with the lake from his travels to Canada as a merchant, Benedict Arnold was also an experienced sea captain capable of commanding and sailing a sloop. In other words, Arnold was uniquely qualified for the assignment of taking Ticonderoga and securing Lake Champlain. Perhaps others had the same idea at the same time, but Benedict Arnold had the information and abilities to carry out this mission. The question of credit for success—or blame for defeat—would weigh heavily in his saga of patriotism falling prey to pride, power grabs, ambition, and ego. It ended as a tale of a heroic, if deeply flawed, character gone terribly wrong in the American Revolution.

❧

FOR MORE THAN TWO CENTURIES, the name of Benedict Arnold has been synonymous with treachery. Arnold's modern biographies typically begin with the fact that he was the would-be betrayer of West Point, the crucial fortifications controlling the Hudson River just north of New York City. In most tellings, Arnold is dismissed as a turncoat who ruthlessly brought down havoc and destruction on several American towns. But Benedict Arnold had begun the war as an idealistic patriot. His military successes, including numerous instances of conspicuous bravery, were so remarkable that he had earned the respect, friendship, and committed patronage of George Washington. James Thomas Flexner, one of George Washington's greatest biographers and a man not usually given to hyperbole, wrote of him: "[A] genius in leading men and at fighting, Benedict Arnold was, in fact, the greatest combat general in the war on either side."[9]

In pre-Revolutionary Connecticut, Benedict Arnold had lived a childhood and young manhood that reads like a Dickensian invention. A fourth-generation American, Benedict Arnold was born into an influential New England family in Norwich, Connecticut. The first Arnold in America, William, arrived with the great Puritan migration. Chafing at the constraints of Puritan Massachusetts, William

Arnold and his son, the first Benedict Arnold, had moved to more tolerant Rhode Island. Benedict Arnold succeeded Roger Williams as the colony's governor and served several terms, all the while amassing a considerable fortune in land. At his death, his Rhode Island holdings were split among several sons, and Benedict II inherited one piece, also later split among his sons. By the time Benedict IV received a portion of the Arnold inheritance, the great fortune had been considerably whittled down by being spread among so many heirs. In spite of his illustrious ancestry, Benedict Arnold IV was forced to seek work in neighboring Connecticut. Landing in the bustling port of Norwich on Connecticut's Thames River, he found a job as a cooper, building barrels for merchant and trader Absalom King.

Enterprising and industrious in that fashion commonly described as the "Puritan work ethic," Benedict Arnold rose from making barrels to command one of King's trading ships, plying the waters of Long Island Sound, carrying timber, salt pork, and beef from Connecticut to the Caribbean in the 1730s, returning with molasses and rum. Eventually he became Absalom King's partner and, when the merchant died, Benedict Arnold IV married his widow, Hannah, member of an old and prosperous Norwich family. He now controlled King's ships, wharfs, and houses and the widow's fortune. Arnold built the town's grandest home and began a family. A son, named Benedict V, was born, but died in infancy.

On January 14, 1741, when the second Benedict Arnold V was born, his father was one of the most prosperous and admired men in Norwich, frequently elected to local offices. Wealthy, esteemed in the local Congregational church, and connected to the town's original settlers through his wife, Captain Arnold had achieved Puritan Connecticut's trifecta of social standing: money, godliness, or at least its appearance, and a connection to old blood. During the War of Jenkins' Ear—the same war in which George Washington's older brother had served—New England's shipping business boomed, and Arnold supplemented his trading income by outfitting his vessels with cannons and attacking French and Spanish ships as a privateer.

When young Benedict was four years old, the on-again, off-again war with France came to New England. During what was called King George's War in the colonies, the French and their Indian allies stepped up attacks on settlements throughout the Northeast. After Connecticut militiamen joined in the capture of the French fortress at Louisbourg in Nova Scotia in 1745, New Englanders remained constantly on alert for French or Indian attacks.

Still, the war had been typically good for the shipping and trading business, and Captain Arnold thrived. The Arnolds were sufficiently well-off to send young Benedict to boarding school in nearby Canterbury. During summers, he was taken on trading trips, sailing to the Caribbean with his father. But when another Anglo-French peace was made in 1748, the inevitable postwar bust followed. Captain Arnold's once-busy ships were idled in a colonial depression, and the captain took to drowning his miseries in rum. Several bad business ventures plunged the family into debt, and Captain Arnold became a very public drunk. The family's woes turned more tragic when two of Benedict Arnold's three younger sisters died in a 1753 yellow fever epidemic while he was away at boarding school.

Suffering from yellow fever as well as alcohol-induced dementia, Captain Arnold descended further into dissolution, financially and personally. The business collapsed completely when Benedict was thirteen, and he was forced to leave school. Through a family connection, he was apprenticed in the successful apothecary and general merchandise store in Norwich owned by his mother's cousins, Dr. Daniel Lathrop and his brother Joshua. Just before his fourteenth birthday, with his father in debtor's prison, Benedict Arnold was legally bound over as the Lathrops' indentured servant until he reached the age of twenty-one.

Instead of enduring the harsh and often cruel world of most eighteenth-century indentured servants, Benedict Arnold entered a halcyon period in the Lathrop household. A shrewd businessman, Daniel Lathrop received a contract to supply British troops when yet another Anglo-French war broke out in 1754, following Washington's defeat at Fort Necessity. The doctor was an expert horse breeder and taught Benedict the finer points of horseflesh. Lathrop's wife, Jerusha, who had also lost all three of her children to yellow fever, was generous, intelligent, and well-read. She had practically accepted Benedict into her house as if he was her own son.

In 1757, during the French and Indian War, the teenage Arnold enlisted in the Connecticut militia. At the time, indentured servants could join the militia only if granted permission, and Dr. Lathrop—himself a militia veteran during the previous war with the French—agreed to let him go. The decision came after the devastating defeat inflicted on the British at Fort William Henry, when the exaggerated reports of the massacre of British soldiers by the native allies of the French sent shock waves of panic through New England. The alarm after this defeat was short-lived, the militia was disbanded, and a disappointed sixteen-year-old Benedict Arnold returned to Connecticut without seeing action. But he had gotten a taste for army life and began to chafe at the tedium of being an apothecary's apprentice.

In the early spring of 1758, Arnold slipped away from Norwich and walked south to New York, enlisting in a Westchester County militia company—this time without Dr. Lathrop's permission. When his mother discovered what he had done, she arranged to have Benedict returned. Against his will, Arnold was brought back to the apothecary, embarrassed yet determined to make his way to the war. Again, he ran away to reenlist and was brought back, this time after Dr. Lathrop posted a reward for his return. On his third try, in 1759, Arnold finally joined the volunteers heading off to besiege Quebec and Montreal in the climactic battles of the French and Indian War.

Preparing another assault on Fort Carillon on Lake Champlain as a prelude for an invasion of Canada, Arnold's company marched to Albany, New York. While in camp, Arnold learned that his mother was gravely ill, and he went absent without leave—not an uncommon occurrence among colonial militiamen, who often left the lines to return to their farms or tend to family business. He returned to Norwich and was safely hidden from authorities, even when an advertisement offering a reward for the now eighteen-year-old deserter was published in a New York newspaper. When his mother died in the summer of 1759, Arnold became the man of the house, responsible for his ailing, alcoholic, and destitute father and fifteen-year-old sister, Hannah. Once more, he was welcomed back by the obviously charitable and forgiving Lathrops, who helped Benedict with his mother's funeral costs and then looked after Hannah when he returned to the army to finish his recruitment terms. The war was winding down, and Benedict Arnold had not seen action, but he had come to love the discipline of army life. When the North American phase of the fighting ended in 1760, the Lathrops took him back into the apothecary shop.

By the time he was twenty, Benedict Arnold was a hard-driving assistant with ambitions to open his own shop. With his father again jailed for public drunkenness, Arnold must have been humbled at how low the family's status had tumbled. Clearly, he set his mind to revive his own fortunes and make his way in the world. To complete Benedict's training in anticipation of opening another apothecary and general store, the Lathrops sent the young man to sea to learn the Caribbean trade. Eager to expand their businesses, they provided Benedict with cash to set up a shop after his father's death. A year later, Daniel Lathrop gave Benedict the deed to the Arnold family house, which he had taken over. Arnold sailed to London to acquire goods for his new apothecary shop, general store, and bookshop, established in New Haven, Connecticut, in 1762. The home of Yale College, New Haven was a growing port that also served as Connecticut's eastern capital. Arnold sold books, including medical texts, and surgical supplies to the Yale students. The shop offered the usual complement of eighteenth-century herbs and medicines, along with aphrodisiacs, including an exotic concoction called Francis' Female Elixir. For a prospering colony that was beginning to forsake its Puritan past for more continental fashions, he also stocked the latest in stylish items from London—cold creams and cosmetics, earrings, buckles, and buttons.

Advertising himself as "Dr. Arnold from London," the ambitious young merchant aggressively sought to expand. After paying off the last debts on his father's Norwich house, he sold it at a profit and moved his sister to New Haven to manage his shop. With the proceeds from the sale of the house, Arnold bought a sloop that he named the *Fortune,* and set up a lucrative trade with the West Indies. As biographer Willard Sterne Randall points out, "Although his business thrived, he yearned to go to sea. Not only was there more profit for the middleman-merchant than for the retail seller of imported goods, but Arnold loved the life on a ship. He wanted to . . . trade in the Caribbean and Canada, now that there was peace in America."[10] Arnold added more ships and began to sail as captain, his flourishing enterprise growing to include a specialty in horses, which he sold in Canada and the West Indies.

Arnold also gained a reputation for a hot temper and an unwillingness to back down. Once he caught a young Frenchman at home with his unchaperoned sister. Arnold chased the man from his house and fired a pistol at him. While on a trading voyage, he was insulted by a British ship captain. Already chafing at the dismissive attitudes of Englishmen toward Americans, Arnold challenged the man to a duel. After a polite exchange of shots missed, Arnold threatened to kill the man. A few years later, the captain's friends spread rumors that Arnold was involved with prostitutes and had syphilis. Those rumors reached all the way back to New Haven. Whether deliberate or accidental, deserved or not, Benedict Arnold had demonstrated a marked penchant for rubbing people the wrong way and creating enemies with long memories.

With the peace of 1763 another economic downturn hit New England hard, and in 1765 the Stamp Act further hurt American commerce. Like many New Englanders, Arnold simply ignored the requirements of the stamp tax. In essence, he had joined the ranks of such illustrious and successful American smugglers as John Hancock and the Brown brothers of Newport, Rhode Island. Arnold had also been drawn into Freemasonry, like so many men of the Revolutionary generation, joining New Haven's lodge in 1765. Aside from providing fraternity with like-minded men, membership in the Freemasons offered access to the upper reaches of New Haven's growing society, including the high sheriff of New Haven County. He introduced Arnold to his daughter, Margaret "Peggy" Mansfield, and the two married in February 1767. Soon they had three sons—Benedict, Richard, and Henry.

By 1767, the economic damage done by the taxes was threatening Arnold and other American merchants with ruin. Proud and ambitious, perhaps with a chip on his shoulder from seeing his father brought low, Arnold joined the growing ranks of Americans defying the Stamp Act. Emerging as a vocal political leader in New Haven, he began to write articles for the local press favoring American rights. Enlisting in the Sons of Liberty, he quickly demonstrated his natural leadership as the secret society grew more provocative and violent.

Arnold's fiery personality and his proclivity for making enemies, along with his dedication to the Sons of Liberty, all came together during a dispute over money with a man who had once sailed with him, Peter Boles. When Boles informed royal authorities that Arnold was a smuggler, Arnold and some of his crewmen beat the man for collaborating with the tax authorities. When Boles didn't leave town as he was told, he was given forty lashes by the Sons of Liberty, then ridden out of town on a rail. After hearing news of the Boston Massacre in March 1770, Arnold wrote to a friend, "Good God! Are Americans all asleep and tamely giving up their glorious liberties, or are they all turned philosophers, that they don't take immediate vengeance on such miscreants."

When Connecticut dispatched a delegation to the Continental Congress in Philadelphia in 1774, Connecticut sent three official delegates—chief justice of the colony's superior court, Eliphalet Dyer; merchant-magistrate Roger Sherman; and New Haven merchant Silas Deane. At Deane's invitation, Arnold unofficially joined the group.

Taller than average, handsome, with sharp, distinctive features, a talented horseman and reputedly a crack shot, Arnold clearly made an impression on other men. As one modern biographer puts it, "Quick-witted and articulate, full of energy almost to restlessness, bursting with confidence bordering on arrogance, Benedict Arnold was a force to be reckoned with."[11] In the first days after their arrival in Philadelphia, the Connecticut delegation and some of the other New Englanders including Samuel and John Adams, toured Philadelphia like country-cousins, taking in the sights of America's largest, most prosperous, and most well-organized city. Among their stops was a hospital and asylum administered by Dr. William Shippen, a physician and member of one of Philadelphia's leading families. William's nephew Edward Shippen, a judge, frequently entertained the congressional delegates during the next few months. It was here that Arnold first encountered Edward Shippen's youngest daughter, fourteen-year-old Peggy, by most accounts already a charming, precocious, and stunning beauty. Most assuredly he did not meet another recent arrival in Philadelphia, Second Lieutenant John André, a British army officer who had landed in Philadelphia in transit to his regiment in Quebec. The three would cross paths in the future.

Although there is no specific record of Arnold encountering George Washington in Philadelphia, the young merchant with military ambitions surely would have attempted to cross paths with one of America's most famous men. Now a wealthy planter and prominent member of Virginia's delegation, Washington had more in common than he might have realized with the Yankee merchant, ten years his junior. Both lost their fathers at a fairly young age, both were Freemasons, and each would have admired the other man's considerable horsemanship. Although Arnold's military service during the French and Indian War was scant, the pair might have shared a certain martial ardor as well. And perhaps they both would have recognized that each possessed that charismatic quality of leadership. Their paths, too, would cross again.

When fighting did break out in 1775, Arnold was thirty-four, successful beyond his wildest ambitions, disciplined, and hard-driving. He had already taken a leading role in the command of Connecticut's militia and, after Lexington and Concord, had been elected captain by the men, who included some Yale students with more enthusiasm than experience. Some of the more cautious leaders in Connecticut wanted to wait and see which way the winds would blow as patriot militia began to stream toward Boston, and they refused to give Arnold powder and guns from the colonial magazine. In another display of his fiery disposition, Arnold threatened to break into the armory and take them. He was given the keys to the magazine. Then he and his spiffily attired militia band set off for Boston.

IN THE WHIRLWIND OF EVENTS THAT followed the capture of Fort Ticonderoga in May 1775, Arnold had moved to reassert his command, especially as more of Ethan Allen's men drifted away, apparently losing interest in the somewhat decrepit fort. He secured several of Major Skene's boats, renaming two of them *Intrepid* and *Liberty*. Arming the boats with cannons and some swivel guns from the fort, Arnold sailed off to find the English sloop *George,* which he captured and renamed the *Enterprise.* With a handful of pilfered boats and captured artillery, Benedict Arnold had built what was essentially America's first navy, and for the moment he held control of the crucial Lake Champlain waterway. From this position, Arnold envisioned a grander scheme. Believing that Canada was lightly defended and ripe for invasion, he wrote a detailed campaign plan and sent it off to Philadelphia, unaware that Ethan Allen had made a similar recommendation to Congress. Still trying to find its footing, uncertain if it wanted to fight or negotiate, and months away from declaring independence, Congress initially rejected the plan to invade Canada and then, as suddenly, reversed itself and accepted the idea.

Personally bankrolling his operations on Lake Champlain as finances from Massachusetts or Congress were practically nonexistent, Arnold was blindsided when another Connecticut officer arrived to assume command at Fort Ticonderoga. He was one of the Connecticut militia officers who had earlier refused Arnold the keys to the armory, and there was bad blood between them. Unaware that he had been the subject of damaging reports and a whispering campaign meant to undermine his role in the capture of Ticonderoga, Arnold was furious at this treatment, which he saw as a slight to his achievements. His record of expenditures was also being questioned in Massachusetts. As Arnold viewed every one of these reversals as an assault on his honor, his famous pique took over and he quit his command.

"I have resigned my commission, not being able to hold it longer with honor," he wrote, just before learning that his plan to invade Canada had been accepted. Adding to the injustice in his eyes, New York's Philip Schuyler, one of the Continental army's new major generals, had been given command of the operation—*his* operation, to Arnold's thinking. On his way back to Connecticut, a dispirited Arnold met with Philip Schuyler, born into one of New York's most powerful families and wed into another. A veteran of the French and Indian War, Schuyler was a delegate to the Continental Congress and was chosen to command the Northern Department of the army when Washington was appointed commander in chief. Impressed with Arnold, Schuyler offered him a key staff position. But Arnold also received a much-delayed letter informing him that his thirty-year-old wife, Peggy, had died suddenly in his absence. He returned to New Haven and his three young motherless boys. Still intent upon a role in the invasion of Canada, he left the boys in the care of his sister, Hannah, and set off for Cambridge, where General Washington was now keeping the British at bay while attempting to mold a new American army.

Meeting Washington on August 15, 1775, Benedict Arnold laid out a plan for a secondary invasion of Canada while Schuyler, who had taken Arnold's Ticonderoga nemesis Ethan Allen into his command, pursued the assault on Canada up from Lake Champlain. Arnold's new plan called for a second attack aimed at Quebec, by traversing the Maine wilderness by canoe before winter set in. Confounded by the woes of the untrained, ill-fed army that had been presented to him, and the politicians he answered to, Washington apparently found Arnold a kindred spirit. As biographer Willard Sterne Randall commented, "Both understood . . . rule in war by an officer class which insisted on rank, order and discipline and emphasized leadership by personal example. Most of all, they were daring soldiers by inclination, and they sensed and admired this trait in others."[12] Washington gave Arnold a new commission as a colonel and more than a thousand men for his Canadian venture. But Arnold had to first endure a humiliating committee of investigation that was challenging his actions and expenditures, based on the innuendo spread about him by some old Connecticut enemies. Despite his successes, and his own opinion of his abilities which were admittedly considerable, Arnold found his path constantly blocked by forces who wanted to undercut him. He was also learning, as George Washington was, that all was fair in politics and war.

I also give it in charge to you to avoid all disrespect or contempt of the religion of the country and its ceremonies. Prudence, policy and a true Christian spirit will lead us to look with compassion upon their errors without insulting them. While we are contending for our own liberty, we should be very cautious of violating the rights of conscience in others, ever considering that God alone is the judge of the hearts of men and to him only, in this case, they are answerable.

—*George Washington, written orders to Benedict Arnold*

Washington's instructions to Arnold before sending him north hint at a little-noted aspect of America's independence movement, one not usually mentioned in the same breath as "life, liberty and the pursuit of happiness." That was colonial America's deeply held, sharp, and often virulent anti-Catholic (and anti-French) prejudices. Centuries of England's religious turmoil and Protestant propaganda had left many Americans, particularly the Puritan stock of New England, violently anti-Catholic. In Boston, Catholic priests had long been banned, and November 5 (known as Guy Fawkes Day in England, commemorating a failed Catholic plot against Parliament) had come to be celebrated as "Pope's Day." As the pope was paraded in effigy through the streets, mobs were encouraged to lustily express their contempt for Roman Catholicism, and Boston's authorities allowed South Side mobs to brawl in the streets against North Side gangs as a way to "blow off steam."[13] To America's vast Protestant majority, the long history of Spanish "perfidies," the purges of Protestants under Bloody Mary detailed in Foxe's *Book of Martyrs,* the anti-Catholic rants of clerics such as Cotton Mather, and the fresh example of French Catholic–allied Indians massacring English settlers and soldiers were all bitterly held memories.

This centuries-old religious animus took a sharp political turn in 1774, when England passed the Quebec Act, along with the Intolerable Acts. The former law's intent was to keep Canada's largely French Catholic population pacified so that England would not have to garrison the massive territory. While Catholics were not allowed to hold public office in Canada, the Quebec Act recognized the Roman Catholic religion and restored Canada's frontier borders. The law was not only considered a betrayal of Protestantism but also a direct assault on the land claims made by American speculators who had fought against the French and now felt stabbed in the heart by Parliament, creating another layer of American colonial resentment. After the Quebec Act was announced, Congregational minister (and later Yale president) Ezra Stiles screamed that it had established the "Roman Church and IDOLATRY." A seemingly otherwise enlightened Dr. Joseph Warren deemed the Canadian charter "dangerous in an extreme degree to the Protestant religion and to the civil rights and liberties of all America." New York's John Jay, a delegate to the Continental Congress, spoke for many Americans when he expressed his fears of a wave of Catholic immigration that would, "reduce the ancient free Protestant colonies to [a] state of slavery." Reacting to the act, Jay railed in "astonishment that a British Parliament should ever consent to establish . . . a religion that has deluged your island in blood and spread impiety, bigotry, persecution, murder and rebellion throughout every part of the world." (When later drafting New York's state constitution, Jay, the future first chief justice of the Supreme Court, proposed erecting what he called "a wall of brass around the country" to keep out Catholics.)

Credit George Washington with more temperate views, a tolerance of other religious traditions that was far from common in eighteenth-century Christian America. Besides, Washington knew that if a Canadian invasion were to succeed and French Canadians to join the Americans in rebellion, he needed the goodwill of the predominantly Catholic population.

While Arnold prepared for this wilderness march to Quebec, his rival Ethan Allen was already assaulting Montreal. With only a handful of men, Allen had foolishly attacked the city late in September 1775. The attack was a fiasco, and the hero of Ticonderoga was captured by the British. His Revolutionary military career was over. In roundabout fashion, Allen was transported by prison ship to Ireland, Madeira, North Carolina, Halifax, and finally New York, which had by then fallen to British forces. Ethan Allen remained captive for more than two years, until he was exchanged for a British officer. Allen returned to the Republic of Vermont, where he was appointed general of the still-disputed area's army by men with little love for either England or America, and lobbied for recognition of the state. When Congress refused, Allen began negotiating with the British governor of Canada for recognition of Vermont as a British province. For this, he was later charged with treason, but the charge was never substantiated. Allen always claimed that it had simply been a ploy to force Congress to recognize Vermont.

Following Allen's defeat and capture, Benedict Arnold's expedition into Canada deteriorated into a disaster of even greater proportions. With a force of eleven hundred men, Arnold had moved by river through Maine's wilderness and over the Appalachian Mountains. Among his command was a young volunteer from a prominent New Jersey family. Aaron Burr was accompanied by a nineteen-year-old Abenaki woman the other men had nicknamed "Golden Thighs."[14] Her presence might have provided the few moments of solace enjoyed on what otherwise became a hellish march.

When he reached the outskirts of Quebec in November 1775, Arnold had fewer than seven hundred men still with him. Those who finished the trek had endured six weeks of starvation and disease, reduced to eating dogs to survive. About 150 of his men had died, mostly sickened by dysentery, a debilitating disease that causes diarrhea. Hungry, sick, and injured, many others had deserted during the grueling expedition through 350 miles of Maine's rugged back-country. Arnold then linked his forces with those of General Richard Montgomery, a former British officer who had joined the rebels and had replaced General Schuyler, who had since fallen ill. A few weeks after Ethan Allen's failed attack on Montreal, Montgomery success-fully captured the French citadel on November 13, 1775.

In a howling winter storm on December 31, 1775, Montgomery and Arnold led an American attack on the well-fortified city of Quebec but suffered another grievous defeat. As Richard Ketchum succinctly wrote about the battle, "Just about everything that could go wrong, did . . . Montgomery was killed, Arnold badly wounded, and another exceptional officer, Daniel Morgan captured. Even at that, the rebels nearly brought it off."[15] Ultimately the British prevailed, with hun-dreds of Americans left dead or captured in the futile attack. In a winter that was as unforgiving for the 350 American survivors of the battle for Quebec as Valley Forge later proved to be for Washington's troops, the severely wounded Arnold maintained a halfhearted siege of Quebec, camped around the city.

Onto this abysmal scene, another old enemy arrived—smallpox. In *Pox Americana*, Elizabeth Fenn describes the state of the Americans outside Quebec: "The men were exhausted. Many were weak from starvation. They lived in close, unsanitary conditions, and with winter setting in, lodgings only became more crowded and contact more fa-miliar. Very soon after arriving, a Massachusetts-born fife player made an ominous journal entry. 'The small pox is all around us,' wrote Caleb Haskell on December 6, 1775, 'and there is great danger of its spread-ing in the army.'"[16] In a humane act in the midst of war, the British commander at Quebec took in many of the American sick in an attempt to properly care for them. Benedict Arnold initially enforced the Continental army's prohibition against inoculation, still a highly controversial expedient, but eventually looked the other way as the disease threatened his army.

In the spring of 1776, Arnold was relieved and returned to Montreal, where he continued to recuperate, having nearly lost his leg. By then, Henry Knox, a portly twenty-five-year-old bookseller from Boston, had finished the mission that Arnold had begun months earlier at Fort Ticonderoga. In doing so, Knox carried off one of the most extraordinary feats of the Revolution's early days. Between December 5, 1775, and January 26, 1776, "Ox" Knox and his men had managed to transport sixty tons of cannons and mortars from Fort Ticonderoga to Cambridge. In the dead of winter, moving with ox-drawn sleds, they had negotiated the frozen Hudson River and then crossed the Berkshire Mountains, delivering the artillery to an overjoyed George Washington. Knox earned Washington's permanent gratitude, friendship, and respect, and the bookish Quaker, with no real military experience, was placed in charge of Washington's artillery. He remained one of Washington's closest aides throughout the war, later becoming the nation's first secretary of war when Washington was elected president.

In a dazzling engineering feat, the cannons Knox delivered were placed overnight on Dorchester Heights, overlooking Boston. The sight of this artillery greeting them one morning astonished the British, and General Howe, who had replaced the disgraced General Gage, reportedly exclaimed, "My God, these fellows have done more work in one night than I could make my army do in three months."

The shocking new reality forced the British to abandon Boston, evacuating in hundreds of shiploads on St. Patrick's Day, March 17, 1776. They took along thousands of Boston's Tory loyalists, who were forced to leave behind almost everything they owned. Almost unbelievably, Boston was in patriot hands. The British sailed first for Halifax and ultimately to New York, where George Washington also moved the bulk of his army in preparation for the next great engagement of the war.

Back in Canada, the "quiet war" was about to give way to a curious attempt at diplomacy. On April 29, 1776, Benedict Arnold turned out his men for a welcoming ceremony. At Montreal's landing, he greeted a group of commissioners secretly sent by Congress hoping to persuade the people of Canada to unite with the American cause and create a fourteenth colony. The odd collection of dignitaries included a congressman, one of America's richest men, America's most famous man, the seventy-year-old Benjamin Franklin, and an American Jesuit priest. Having endured a rigorous winter journey from Philadelphia, Franklin, Maryland congressman Samuel Chase, and Charles Carroll, a wealthy Maryland patriot, carried gold to resupply Arnold's army and a printing press that would turn out propaganda to convince French Canadians to join the American cause.

The only Roman Catholic to sign the Declaration of Independence (also the last surviving signer; he died in 1832), Charles Carroll was said to be one of America's three richest men at the time. His grandfather had known Lord Baltimore, Maryland's founder, and the Carroll family was among Maryland's first rank, with extensive land holdings. Born in Maryland, young Charles Carroll was sent to France for a proper Catholic education, then unattainable in America, and returned to Maryland in 1764, fluent in French and heir to a massive estate called Carrollton. Drawn to the patriot cause, he became a leader of the opposition to the Stamp Act, persuading one owner of a ship loaded with tea to burn it rather than risk mob violence, as in Boston.

Although Carroll was not yet a member of Congress, his social status, his religion, and his fluency in French made him a clear choice to attempt to convince French Canadians to throw in with America. He brought along his cousin John Carroll, a Jesuit priest whose presence was meant to further reassure the Canadian Catholics, and especially their clergy, that their religion would be respected in America. (Father John Carroll became America's first Catholic bishop and is credited with founding Georgetown University, America's first Catholic university, in 1789.)

Whatever hopes the commissioners had of success were quickly dashed. The small, tattered American military presence in Canada was falling apart. A great many French Canadians who were asked to accept what was thought to be worthless Continental currency had been alienated by the Americans. The British, meanwhile, had moved to reinforce their garrisons in Canada, and within a few months the American army was driven out of Canada entirely.

With Canada lost, the recently promoted Brigadier General Benedict Arnold was ordered to block any British advance into New York from Canada. Having built a small flotilla on Lake Chaplain once before, he set about creating another navy on the lake. During the summer of 1776, Arnold built a collection of warships and gunboats with which to control Champlain's waters. Manned mostly by farmers and backwoods militia men with precious little sailing experience, Benedict Arnold's improvised navy accomplished the near-impossible: fending off a British fleet in a series of battles. Although ultimately chased from the lake after the battle of Valcour Island in October

1776, Arnold and his patchwork crews had sufficiently delayed the British advance. Faced by the onset of winter, and with Lake Champlain freezing over by November, the British abandoned the invasion of New York, which would have severed New England from the rest of the colonies, possibly putting an end to the Revolution. Like Bunker Hill, Arnold's campaign on the lake had ended in an American defeat, but it still had saved the rebellion from greater disaster.

Returning to New Haven, Arnold mustered a small Connecticut militia that harassed the British at Danbury, Connecticut, where Arnold was injured again when his horse was shot from under him. A bigger wound was to his pride. Congress bypassed him, promoting several other generals over Arnold to major general. In yet another fit of petulance, he offered his resignation in July 1777. When Washington asked Congress to recommission Arnold, they complied, and he was sent north to join the armies preparing to confront British General John Burgoyne who, after a year's delay created by Arnold, had embarked on the invasion of New York from Canada.

In a series of battles fought around Saratoga, New York, Arnold played a conspicuous and heroic role. At the battle of Bemis Heights on October 7, 1777, Arnold personally led his men who turned back part of Burgoyne's army for the last time. Rallying the American troops from horseback, Arnold was shot, wounded in the same leg that had been injured at Quebec. Having suffered tremendous losses, Burgoyne surrendered his army in the most stunning victory of an otherwise largely unsuccessful American military campaign. The shocking news that Burgoyne had surrendered and most of his five thousand men had been paroled was the key to bringing the French into the war as America's ally. With French troops, ships, and powder, the Revolution was given new life.

And Benedict Arnold had played a crucial role. He had demonstrated the courage and leadership skills that George Washington had recognized two years earlier in Cambridge. But once again, Arnold was denied glory. Another bitter feud, this time with General Horatio Gates, the American commander at Saratoga, meant Arnold received no official credit for his daring at Bemis Heights. Worse, he had been vilified by Gates for having disobeyed orders. Withdrawn to Philadelphia, where he convalesced, Arnold nearly lost his leg again. He continued his recovery with Washington at Valley Forge in the bleak winter of 1777–78.

Aftermath

Sir: The heart which is conscious of its own rectitude cannot attempt to palliate a step which the world may censure as wrong. I have ever acted from a principle of love to my country, since the commencement of the present unhappy contest between Great Britain and the Colonies. The same principle of love to my country actuate my present conduct, however it may appear inconsistent to the world, who very seldom judge right of any man's actions.

—*Benedict Arnold to George Washington, September 25, 1780*[17]

Standing on the Saratoga Battlefield in upstate New York is a statue of a single boot. Its worn dedication reads, in part, to "the most brilliant soldier of the Continental army." The statue anonymously honors the bravery and leadership of Benedict Arnold, the heroic officer who became the greatest villain in American history.

After Saratoga, Arnold's fall from grace was as stunningly dramatic as the rest of his incredible life had been. In June 1778, Washington appointed Arnold military commissioner of Philadelphia, which had earlier been captured by the British but was back in American hands. Embittered at being passed over for promotion, disgruntled at having Congress question his wartime expenses—he had borne many of the Quebec campaign's costs himself and expected reimbursement—Arnold threw himself into the whirl of Philadelphia's social life and swiftly fell into debt. His extravagances drew attention, and Congress investigated his financial dealings as Philadelphia's military commissioner. Faced with this investigation, Arnold complained to Washington, still a staunch defender, "Having become a cripple in the service of my country, I little expected to meet [such] ungrateful returns." (The injuries to Arnold's leg had shortened it by two inches, and he was now forced to wear a special boot.)

He also fell in love. During this time Arnold renewed his acquaintance with Peggy Shippen, the now eighteen-year-old daughter of Judge Edward Shippen. They were married on April 8, 1779. Peggy's previous suitor, the English major John André, had left the city when the British withdrew. About a year later, Arnold sought and was given command of the fort at West Point, perched above the Hudson River in New York just north of New York City. The fort controlled Hudson River traffic.

In September 1780, while George Washington was traveling to visit Arnold and Peggy at their home in what is now Westchester County, New York, Major André was captured in civilian clothes. Stripped by the Americans who were planning to rob him, André was found carrying the plans for Arnold's surrender of West Point to the British. With possession of the fort, the British could once again control the length of the Hudson River, reopening the possibility of an assault from Canada, which Arnold had fought so hard to prevent. For his betrayal, Arnold had been promised £20,000 and a brigadier's commission. Knowing the plan was undone, Arnold raced off to safety aboard a waiting British ship, leaving behind Peggy and their infant son to contend with a shaken but enraged Washington.

When George Washington went to see Peggy Arnold, she flew into a fit of hysterics at the news, claiming that men were trying to kill her and her baby, even allowing her dressing gown to fall open, offering a glimpse of "her charms," as genteel historians like to put it. Washington's aide Alexander Hamilton and the Marquis de Lafayette, the young French nobleman whom Washington had practically adopted as a son, were both asked by Peggy to intercede with the general. She was clearly a talented actress and duped them all. Convincing Washington that she knew nothing of the plot, Peggy Shippen was allowed to return to Philadelphia with her six-month-old infant. On the ride back to her family's home, she was unable to purchase food from anyone who knew who she was. It would be centuries before British military documents revealed the extent of her complete complicity in the plot.

On October 9, Arnold appeared in his new uniform, that of a British general. That same day, a letter appeared in a New York Tory newspaper, the *Royal Gazette*, addressed "to the Inhabitants of America." In it, the turncoat attempted to explain his actions. Once again, anti-Catholic sentiment moved to center stage. Arnold claimed that he had been loyal to the American cause as long as it was a "defensive" war. But when France joined the American side, that had changed, claimed Arnold. It was, wrote Arnold, "infinitely wiser and safer to cast my confidence upon [British] justice and generosity than to trust a monarchy too feeble to establish your independency . . . the enemy of the Protestant faith, and fraudulently avowing an affection for the liberties of mankind while she holds her native sons in vassalage and chains."[18]

Setting aside this sudden and convenient burst of anti-Catholic fervor, perhaps Arnold thought that he, like King Lear, was "a man more sinn'd against than sinning." More simply, Arnold's motives seem fairly clear: an ambition to rise in society born of his father's dramatic fall; bitterness at being constantly slighted and passed over; and greed—his own and that of his young wife, who had a taste for the finer things. In the end, Arnold's treachery did not affect the war's outcome. Major André was hanged as a spy after Washington unsuccessfully attempted to negotiate an exchange for Arnold with General Cornwallis. Arnold was given a command, calling it the "American Legion." He led this collection of loyalists and Continental army deserters against Richmond, Virginia, which they captured. Later, he moved north to attack New London, in his home state of Connecticut, burning it to the ground, in the hope it would divert Washington from Cornwallis at Yorktown, Virginia. During the attack, surrendering patriot defenders were massacred by Arnold's men. But the ploy failed as a diversion and Cornwallis surrendered his army to Washington, bolstered by French troops and a French fleet, in October 1781, essentially ending the Revolutionary War in America.

After the British surrender, the Arnolds lived in New York, still very much a loyalist stronghold, until 1783, when the treaty ending the war was signed. When some thirty-five thousand New York Tories evacuated the city, Arnold moved to New Brunswick, Canada, where he returned to his life as a merchant and shipper before finally moving to London in 1791. His son, Benedict VI, joined the British army against his father's wishes and died in the Napoleonic Wars.

Benedict Arnold V, hero and traitor, died in London in 1801, at age sixty. There were four state carriages and seven mourning coaches at his funeral, and he was buried at the Church of St. Mary's in Battersea. When the church was renovated a century later, his body was mistakenly disinterred and buried with a jumble of others in an unmarked grave.

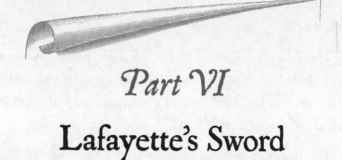

Part VI

Lafayette's Sword

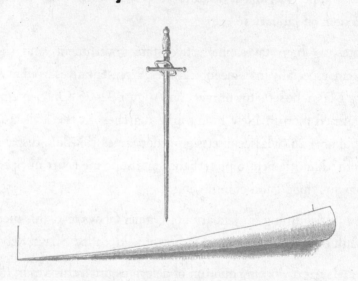

1784 James Madison publishes his *Memorial and Remonstrance Against Religious Assessments*, an argument for the separation of church and state.

1785 The Mount Vernon Conference. Meeting at Washington's home, delegates from Virginia and Delaware agree to a pact that deals with uniform currency. They invite Pennsylvania to join, an indication of the need for cooperation between the individual states.

1786 The Virginia legislature adopts an Ordinance of Religious Freedom on January 16.

Protesting high taxes, ineffective state government, and the legal system, especially in home foreclosures, representatives from more than fifty Massachusetts towns meet on August 22–25. On September 20, an armed mob in New Hampshire marches on the legislature. On September 26, Massachusetts governor James Bowdoin dispatches six hundred militiamen to protect the state supreme court in Springfield from an armed band of insurgents.

1787 Beginning on January 26, Daniel Shays leads his men in an assault on the federal arsenal at Springfield, called Shays' Rebellion.

On May 25 a working quorum of delegates finally arrives in Philadelphia, and George Washington is named president of the convention. On September 17, thirty-nine delegates to the constitutional convention vote to endorse the final form of the Constitution, which must be ratified by nine states. In October, advocates of the new Constitution begin to publish articles supporting ratification. Written by James Madison, Alexander Hamilton, and John Jay, the essays are compiled as *The Federalist Papers*.

December 7: Delaware is the first state to ratify the Constitution.

December 12:   Pennsylvania ratifies, the second state to do so.

December 18:   New Jersey ratifies.

1788   January 2: Georgia ratifies.

January 9: Connecticut ratifies.

February 6: Massachusetts ratifies after anti-Federalist forces led by Samuel Adams and John Hancock support the document with the promise of amendments guaranteeing certain civil liberties.

March 24: Rhode Island, which refused to send a delegation to Philadelphia, rejects the Constitution.

April 28: Maryland ratifies.

May 23: South Carolina ratifies.

June 21: New Hampshire ratifies. The federal Constitution is formally adopted.

June 25: Virginia ratifies with a call for the addition of a Bill of Rights.

July 26: New York ratifies, also with a recommendation for a Bill of Rights.

In New York, the temporary seat of government, the Congress, under the Articles of Confederation, adjourns on November 1. The United States has no central government until the first week of April 1789, when the new Congress meets.

1789   In the first presidential election, on February 4, newly chosen electors cast their ballots. The election of senators and representatives also proceeds.

George Washington is unanimously elected president on April 6; John Adams is vice president. On April 30, George Washington is inaugurated on the balcony of Federal Hall in New York.

November 21: North Carolina ratifies.

The first national Thanksgiving Day, established by congressional resolution and presidential proclamation, takes place on November 26. Intended to offer thanks for the Constitution, it is opposed by Antifederalists, who maintain that the proclamation violates states' rights.

Governments are instituted among Men, deriving their just powers from the Consent of the Governed, that whenever any Form of Government becomes destructive of these Ends, it is the Right of the People to alter or abolish it.

–The Declaration of Independence (July 4, 1776)

In monarchies, the crime of treason and rebellion may admit of being pardoned or lightly punished, but the man who dares rebel against the laws of a republic ought to suffer death.

–Samuel Adams (September 1786)

Are your people mad?

–George Washington,
to a friend in Massachusetts (October 1786)

What signify a few lives lost in a century or two? The tree of liberty must be refreshed from time to time with the blood of patriots and tyrants. It is its natural manure.

–Thomas Jefferson (November 1787)

Our new Constitution is now established, and has an appearance that promises permanency; but in this world nothing can be said to be certain, except death and taxes.

–Benjamin Franklin (November 13, 1789)

❧ *Springfield, Massachusetts–January* 1787

THE FRESHLY MINTED UNITED STATES was under attack. A small army was on the march near Springfield in western Massachusetts. Two thousand strong, and gaining strength and numbers by the day, this insurgent force was threatening to topple the government of Massachusetts, seedbed of the Revolution. It was little more than four years after the British surrender at Yorktown, and a few months shy of the tenth anniversary of the Declaration's adoption. But to more than a few worried observers around the country, among them a retired George Washington, the fate of the young nation hung in the balance.

If Massachusetts fell, wider war and chaos might quickly engulf the rest of the country. Everything Washington thought he had fought for was coming undone before his eyes. Along with many others, he even saw the hand of Great Britain pulling the strings: "There are surely men of consequences and abilities behind the curtains who move the puppets," Washington wrote to one of his former aides in Massachusetts.[1]

The attackers planned to strike on January 25, after a fierce storm blanketed western Massachusetts, leaving snow piled four feet deep in the state's hilly hinterlands. Three coordinated forces, most of them battle-tested veterans, were on the move. Their target was the federal armory in Springfield, just north of the Connecticut border, and its valuable store of weapons. In a three-pronged attack, they expected to easily overrun the armory, strengthen their hand with captured artillery, and continue east toward Boston from Springfield.

Since Springfield's founding in 1636 on the floodplain of the Connecticut River, the surrounding region, known as the Pioneer Valley, had seen its share of war and fighting. During the Revolution, weapons to fight the British had been collected and stored there. In 1777, when Springfield was still a small, struggling farming village, George Washington chose it as the site of a national arsenal. With access to the long, navigable Connecticut River, flowing more than four hundred miles from the New Hampshire–Canada border to Long Island Sound, and located along a key highway linking Boston with Albany, Springfield was well situated. But it was also sufficiently distant from any major British military outposts to be out of harm's way.

Now the arsenal in rural Massachusetts remained one of the new nation's two major arms depots, holding most of the guns and artillery pieces in New England. Still stockpiled in the Springfield armory in January 1787 were thousands of muskets and bayonets, artillery pieces and carriages, along with powder and tons of shot and shells, all technically the property of the federal government. At the moment, that government was a rather toothless Congress, formed under the Articles of Confederation. Ratified in 1781, the Articles of Confederation and Perpetual Union was essentially a thirteen-state mutual-defense pact that provided for a Congress operating with a "one-state, one-vote" rule, and lacking the ability to levy taxes to raise funds. Although Congress had the power to wage war, not a man in its standing army of about seven hundred soldiers was within a rifle shot of Springfield. Among its many other shortcomings, America's national government was essentially impotent in the face of its first genuine threat.

The plotters who had come to capture the Springfield arsenal needed those weapons for their army, just as New England militiamen had once confiscated guns and powder from British storehouses such as Fort Ticonderoga. According to the alarming, hysterical reports circulating in the Massachusetts press, these rebels—or "insurgents," as they were called—aimed at nothing short of marching on Boston with the captured artillery, plundering the town, and laying waste to it.

The insurgent army knew Boston well. Despite Washington's suspicions, they were not mercenaries, a proxy army playing out a British attempt to retake America. Mostly veterans of the American Revolution, some of them had stood on Breed's Hill back in June 1775. They were the soldiers George Washington had heaped derision upon when he had arrived to take command of the Continental army in Cambridge that same year. But Washington came to depend upon their ragtag, undisciplined, and overly democratic kind to win the war. Some of them had been at the capture of Fort Ticonderoga or made the bitter march to Quebec with Benedict Arnold. They had fought in many of the Revolution's major battles—the devastating routs and the crucial victories that turned the tide. And they had suffered through the worst of Valley Forge's winter. Now these same men of the "Massachusetts Line" were ready to make war on the state and the country they had helped create. In their minds, perhaps, this was to be "the American Revolution's last battle," as historian Leonard L. Richards called it.

Like the minutemen of Revolutionary legend and lore, most of these soldiers were local farmers, village merchants, or tradesman, some armed with ancient muskets, others with their Continental army issue. Some wielded swords—old family heirlooms—while many carried nothing more than pitchforks. Although some of the men had donned their old Continental uniforms, others wore their everyday clothes. Many of the men also sported a sprig of hemlock in their hats, symbol of the Revolutionary spirit they had once fought for.

Opposing them were some eleven hundred state militiamen, well equipped with cannons and howitzers taken from the Springfield arsenal, which they had managed to reach before the insurgent army could. Technically, as a state militia, they had no right to take the weapons, either, but the state's survival hung in the balance. Polite legalities were pushed aside. The state's first line of defense, this militia was led by Major General William Shepard. A fifty-year-old farmer from Westfield, Massachusetts, Shepard had served eight years in the Revolutionary War. As commander of the Fourth Massachusetts Regiment, he had been wounded at the disastrous battle of Long Island on August 27, 1776, when the British had routed the patriot army and chased George Washington from New York City. More than likely, Shepard had commanded or served with some of the men now readying to assault his troops. With Massachusetts men filling the ranks on each side of the battle, this was an American civil war.

What William Shepard knew and the attackers moving toward the armory did not was that one key component of the insurgents' battle plan was missing. In West Springfield, on the far side of the Connecticut River, commander Luke Day had decided not to attack and was holding back his four hundred men. Instead of joining the assault, as planned, Day had decided to send Shepard an ultimatum, allowing him twenty-four hours to lay down his arms in the hopes of avoiding a bloodbath. Luke Day's wisdom might be questioned—and it would be—but not his courage or patriotism. Like General Shepard, he had spent eight years in service to the American cause. Born into a prominent West Springfield family, he had been among the first men to answer the call after Lexington and Concord. Day had manned the lines during the siege that chased the British from Boston. He was also among the Massachusetts volunteers who had accompanied

Benedict Arnold on the deadly march to Quebec and the disastrous assault on that city. Promoted to captain of the Seventh Regiment of the Massachusetts Line, he served until the end of the war, and Day was part of the regiment that led the charge at Yorktown, helping to force Cornwallis to surrender.[2]

But on the eve of the attack on Springfield, Luke Day's message to his two fellow commanders, conveying his change in plans and counseling a delay in the attack, had been intercepted by General Shepard. Nearly one-third of the expected assault force, which was supposed to swoop in on one flank of Shepard's militia, never left for the armory. Knowing this, Shepard was able to concentrate his forces on a single frontal attack.

Preparing to lead that assault on the Springfield armory was an advance guard of about four hundred "old soldiers," as the Revolutionary veterans were called. They marched shoulder to shoulder, eight deep. As the first ranks moved toward the armory through the deep, fresh snow, General Shepard ordered a warning shot. The first volley was fired over the advancing regiment's heads. But instead of slowing their progress, the cannon fire spurred on the men in the front ranks, and they broke into a trot. Meanwhile, the horses of the mounted men behind them were thrown into confusion; mostly farm animals, they were unaccustomed to the crash of artillery. A dozen men fell from their mounts, adding to the general mayhem of the moment.

A second volley was ordered by Shepard, this time at "waistband height." Finally, the ranks of the oncoming insurgents were sprayed with grapeshot, loosely packed metal balls fired from a hidden howitzer. Three men died instantly, and a fourth was mortally wounded. Seeing the many wounded men fall, and facing overpowering artillery, the rear ranks of attackers broke and ran off in a panicky, confused retreat. And like that, the assault on the federal arsenal was over.

Soon after the brief but deadly face-off, another detachment of three thousand militiamen arrived on the scene. Sanctioned by War Secretary Henry Knox and Congress, they were ostensibly organized to defend against an Indian threat, a flimsy cover that was widely mocked in Massachusetts, where their real purpose was all too clear. They were there to put down an armed insurrection by American citizens.

Paid with funds raised by private subscriptions from some of the wealthiest men in Massachusetts, including Governor James Bowdoin, this "federal" force was commanded by an overweight, fifty-three-year-old Benjamin Lincoln. A veteran of the Revolution, Lincoln had performed heroically at the crucial battle of Saratoga. But after surrendering an entire army to Henry Clinton at Charleston, South Carolina, in 1780, in one of the Continental army's worst debacles, Lincoln had been captured. Later exchanged for a British officer—and in spite of his visible and costly failure—Lincoln remained in Washington's good graces and had actually been given the honor of accepting Cornwallis' sword at the Yorktown surrender.

Benjamin Lincoln's militia arrived too late to help repel the assault on the Springfield armory, but they soon joined Shepard's troops to give chase to the disintegrating rebel army as it retreated from Springfield. Lincoln pursued the men north through the Connecticut River valley, while Shepard moved his men up the frozen river. Marching his troops through a blinding snowstorm, Lincoln caught the rebel army by surprise at Petersham, about fifty miles north of Springfield, early on February 4. In a bloodless battle, a boastful Lincoln reported that about 150 of the insurgents were captured, a claim unsupported by evidence; the rest, including their leader, escaped. There were a few small follow-up incidents, but the insurgency that had seemed to threaten America's very existence was shattered. The "horrid and unnatural Rebellion and War," as the Massachusetts legislature called the uprising, ended with a few small bangs and a whimper.

The "little rebellion," as Thomas Jefferson would describe it—famously writing from Paris that the "Tree of Liberty should be refreshed from time to time with the blood of patriots and Tyrants"—came to be known throughout New England and the rest of America as Shays' Rebellion. It was named for its putative and somewhat reluctant leader, a forty-year-old farmer from Pelham, Massachusetts, Daniel Shays. Back in 1775, Daniel Shays had been among the thousands who eagerly joined the patriot army gathering outside Boston right after Lexington and Concord. Becoming a member of what was known as Woodbridge's Regiment, Shays fought at Bunker Hill, earning a promotion to sergeant. Rounding out his relatively distinguished five years in George Washington's army, Shays had, as Alden T. Vaughan once recorded, "served under Ethan Allen at Ticonderoga, helped thwart Gentleman Johnny Burgoyne at Saratoga and stormed Stony Point with Mad Anthony Wayne. For recruiting a company of volunteers in Massachusetts, Shays ultimately received a commission as their captain, a position he seems to have filled adequately. And before leaving service, Shays suffered at least one wound in battle."[3]

But why was Daniel Shays leading thousands of men, many of whom had served America loyally and often at great sacrifice, against the rightfully elected government of Massachusetts? And by attacking a federal arsenal, why were they fighting against the new American republic they had helped birth?

꒰•꒱

THE COMMONLY ACCEPTED wisdom back then was that these were disgruntled backwoods farmers or rootless "mobbers," lawless men overburdened by debt and faced with foreclosures on their homes. The debt part was certainly true. Taxes were high, hard cash was unavailable. The Continental currency they were given had been made worthless by inflation, and Congress was reneging on promised pensions to veterans. Like many others, a strapped Daniel Shays had been forced into giving up prized possessions. Shays had paid off a twelve-dollar debt by selling the famous gold-handled ceremonial sword that had been presented to him by the Marquis de Lafayette in honor of the victory at Saratoga. His detractors would later point to this act of necessity as a comment on his low character—only an ill-bred money-grubber would part with such a patriotic icon.

But to Daniel Shays and thousands of other Massachusetts men who joined his cause, it may have seemed that nothing had changed since they swapped an arrogant, distant Parliament for a Massachusetts legislature filled with Boston's elitist merchants and lawyers—men derided as "thieves, knaves, and robbers" by the average people in Massachusetts. The trouble had begun as early as 1782 when angry crowds closed the courts in the Berkshire Mountains town of Pittsfield to prevent any more foreclosures or confiscated property. In Northampton, Massachusetts, not far from Springfield, a former clergyman named Samuel Ely led a mob that attacked the state courts. Arrested and jailed, Ely was later freed by a large crowd and escaped to that last refuge of the lawless to the north, Vermont. These were people who had fresh memories of the days before the Revolution when western Massachusetts mobs had shut down the colonial courts in reaction to Parliament's Government Act. To them, the new state courts were just old wine in new bottles.

Although a few seasons of better crops and some halting reforms made by the legislature provided some temporary relief, by late 1786 the situation in Massachusetts had grown even worse. That year, the state legislature issued a new tax that fell most heavily on the poor, pushing the situation over the brink. In one county in August 1786, a crowd of more than fifteen hundred men with clubs, swords, and guns forced the closure of court sessions. Similar outbreaks occurred around Massachusetts, and there were growing reports of the contagion spreading, with outbursts in neighboring New Hampshire and Vermont. Some of these mobs were met effectively by state militia forces. The "Cradle of the Revolution" was rocking madly.

But it was about more than just unfair taxes and keeping out of debtor's prison. While the insurgent army included many dirt-poor farmers, straining under the threat of bankruptcy, its ranks were not filled with the dregs of Massachusetts society, as opponents and critics claimed then and for centuries after. Men such as Luke Day, whose decision to delay the attack was blamed for the defeat of the Shaysites at the Springfield armory, were established members of prominent old families. For his insightful account of Shays' Rebellion, historian Leonard L. Richards unearthed the tax rolls of old Massachusetts to reveal that many of those who joined Daniel Shays at Springfield were pillars of their communities, landed families at the top of their town's list of taxpayers. They included Moses Dickinson and four other members of his immediate family, one of the most respected and prominent in Amherst; a total of thirty Shaysites were Dickinsons by blood or marriage, among them the great-grandfather of poet Emily Dickinson.[4]

To many of these protesters, the system itself was rotten, and they were as angry at who was passing the taxes as at the taxes themselves. One of the "muster forms" signed by some of the insurgents read, "We do Each one of us acknowledge our Selves to be Inlisted . . . in Colo

Hazleton's Regiment of Regulators . . . for the Suppressing of tyranni-cal government in the Massachusetts State."⁵

Across the state, unauthorized town conventions petitioned for drastic reforms aimed at taking power out of the hands of the Boston merchants and professional men who were gaming the tax system to their advantage. Boston's attorneys were especially singled out for abuse.⁶ They were seen as crafting laws and tax codes that helped mostly themselves. Indeed, history does repeat itself.

During the run-up to the actual fighting in Springfield, the retired George Washington waited anxiously for news from Massachusetts. It was only a few years before, in November 1783, that he had addressed a farewell to the army: "Who, that was not a witness, could imagine that the most violent local prejudices would cease so soon, and that Men who came from the different parts of the Continent, strongly disposed, by the habits of education, to despise and quarrel with each other, would instantly become but one patriotic band of Brothers . . . ? And shall not the brave men, who have contributed so essentially to these inestimable acquisitions, retiring victorious from the field of War to the field of agriculture, participate in all the blessings which have been obtained; in such a republic, who will exclude them from the rights of Citizens, and the fruits of their labour."⁷

Washington had asked, "Who will exclude them?" and the Massachusetts legislature had answered by its deeds. Regressive taxes were sapping the people who tilled Washington's "field of agriculture." Poll taxes and restrictive rules kept them from voting. Legislative rules tipped the scales in favor of merchants and bankers in the eastern part of the state.

But to men such as Samuel Adams, who had finally made some money and now owned property in the West Indies, the rules had changed. So had his revolutionary tune. "In monarchies, the crime of treason and rebellion may admit of being pardoned or lightly punished," Adams said in September 1786, as the insurgency was building toward its climax. "But the man who dares rebel against the laws of a republic ought to suffer death." Adams, always a conservative Puritan at heart, helped push through the legislature a Riot Act that made sheriffs and other officials blameless for killing rioters and threatened rioters with forfeiture of homes and property and with public whippings—"39 stripes on the naked back."

Henry Knox, Washington's trusted old friend who now served as war secretary, saw the insurgents as a danger to the republic. Knox, whose wife had inherited an enormous parcel of Maine land, making the former bookseller a wealthy man, was sending Washington regular dispatches. His letters to Mount Vernon were not reassuring and included alarming accounts of "twelve to fifteen thousand desperate and unprincipled men" scattered throughout New England. He claimed—inaccurately—they were "determined to annihilate all debts public and private."

"This was an exaggeration of the rebels' number and their intentions," Richard Brookhiser notes in his admiring biography of Washington, *Founding Father*. "The principle of self-government, which he had fought a war to secure, seemed to be threatened, for the rulers Shays and his followers were rebelling against were their own representatives. . . . Washington felt he knew what the government should do. 'Know precisely what the insurgents aim at. If they have *real* grievances, redress them if possible. . . . If they have not, employ the force of government against them at once.'"[8]

The fears of mayhem and chaos that Shays' Rebellion had provoked among many of America's "great men" was far from unique in post-Revolutionary America. The idealized image of the heroic min-uteman valiantly joining in solidarity with political geniuses and pa-triotic icons such as Washington and the Adamses to overthrow a tyrannical English monarch is tidy and convenient. But its simplicity masks the complexity of the American Revolution and the motives of the men who fought it.

The sort of popular, grassroots rebellion represented by Daniel Shays is an excellent reminder that *E pluribus unum,* the national motto later chosen by the Framers, means "Out of the many, one." There was no one America before the Revolution, but many. And there were many Americans with very different agendas fighting for indepen-dence. Among them were the colonial-era have-nots, some of whom called themselves "Regulators," just as the men who enlisted in Daniel Shays' revolt would.

The first Americans to call themselves Regulators were a group of North Carolina's backcountry farmers distressed at the way the east-ern coastal aristocracy was abusing them. Often members of the Bap-tists, Quakers, or other sects, they were all opposed to paying taxes to support the Anglican Church, as was the practice in North Carolina, Virginia, and other southern states. (The Congregational Church en-joyed similar support in Massachusetts.) As Gary Nash explains in *The Unknown American Revolution,* "They called themselves Regula-tors, a term borrowed from England, where it had been used for gen-erations to describe those who reformed 'publick grievances and abuses of power.'"[9]

The movement got its start in the late 1760s and exploded in open revolt in North Carolina in 1771. Claiming that corrupt local officials "continually Squez'd and oppressed poor . . . families through taxa-tion and extortion," the Regulators vowed not to pay any more taxes until their grievances were addressed. As in the Shays' Rebellion years later, they disrupted the courts and freed their leaders from jail. But the movement was doomed. As Ray Raphael notes, "Although the Regulator movement in the North Carolina backcountry involved an overwhelming 80 percent of the white male residents, in 1771 the Regulators were defeated in a full-scale military confrontation with the colonial government that left more than 25 killed and 160 wounded. Forced to disband, over 6,000 former Regulators repudiated their past misdeeds by signing oaths of allegiance to the Crown. In this trial run at Revolution—featuring an oppressive government accused by ordinary citizens of unfair taxation and abuses of power—the rebels lost."[10]

A similar mood had struck in New York a few years before. In 1766, ten years before the Declaration, land disputes—not tea and taxes—had sparked a major rebellion, not against England but against American landowners. Inspired by the Stamp Act riots in New York City, tenants on some of New York's vast estates—a holdover from the Dutch era when wealthy patroons were granted enormous parcels of land—refused to pay their rents. These properties were owned by the most powerful families of New York, who ruled more like medieval feudal lords than modern landlords. In April 1766, an angry crowd from Van Cortlandt Manor, complaining of rising rents, short leases, and frequent evictions, decided to march to New York City, liberate prisoners from debtor's jail, and tell John Van Cortlandt they would "pull down his house in Town" if he did not give them "a grant forever of his Lands."

"The 1766 uprisings in New York foreshadowed the greater conflict that followed," historian Ray Raphael has argued. "Angry farmers, apparently powerless, stood tall in the face of their rulers, who had to be bailed out by the British Army. The tenant rebellions of the middle colonies, along with the Regulator movements in the South, contributed indirectly to the coming Revolution by chipping away at the notion that a few men of prestige and privilege could exploit those beneath them with impunity."[11]

Although the concept of socialism wouldn't appear until the early nineteenth century, this was a sort of class warfare that carried over into America's Revolutionary years. In 1779, Philadelphia had just changed hands once again after the British had evacuated in May 1778. The city was also sharply divided among rich and poor. Its wealthiest families and merchants, such as Robert Morris—known as the "financier of the Revolution"—were accused of price gouging, profiteering by hoarding goods to drive up prices on all basic necessities, including flour. Morris and other merchants argued that this was free trade and they had the right to charge whatever prices the market would bear. Although a city committee recommended price controls in Philadelphia, they were difficult to enforce in a city fighting for independence. But by the fall of 1779, the working class of Philadelphia was ready to go to the barricades against the city's merchants and power brokers, some of whom had cozied up to the British while they were occupying the city.

Making hostages of four Philadelphia merchants singled out as particularly onerous for their practice of hoarding to force prices higher, an armed militia marched to the house of James Wilson, an attorney who had argued against the price controls. Wilson and thirty-five other Philadelphia gentlemen, including Robert Morris, barricaded themselves inside the house at Third and Walnut Streets. The angry militiamen wheeled artillery pieces in front of Wilson's home; the Revolution was threatening to eat its own. After a brief skirmish, a detachment of Pennsylvania soldiers, led by the state's governor, Joseph

Reed, one of George Washington's most trusted aides, rescued Wilson and the others. But in what came to be known as the Fort Wilson Riot, five men died and fourteen others were wounded in the heart of Franklin's City of Brotherly Love.

"Poor Pennsylvania has become the most miserable spot under the surface of the globe. Our streets have been stained already with fraternal blood—a sad prelude we fear of the future mischiefs our constitution will bring upon us," worried the enlightened Philadelphia physician Dr. Benjamin Rush, a signer of the Declaration.[12]

The spilling of fraternal blood was assuredly not what James Wilson envisioned when he had signed the Declaration of Independence. Born in Carskerdy, Scotland, he sailed to America in 1765, where he became a tutor at the College of Philadelphia (later the University of Pennsylvania). Wilson then worked as a legal assistant in the office of John Dickinson, one of the wealthiest men in the colonies. Dickinson won his greatest fame and patriot's stripes when he penned the influential *Letters from a Farmer in Pennsylvania*. An argument for American liberty written in response to the Townshend Acts in 1767, this series of essays had appeared in a Pennsylvania journal, but the modest title somewhat belied Dickinson's status as the largest slaveholder in Delaware, where his family had long owned a tobacco farm and other properties.

After training for the bar in Dickinson's office, James Wilson became an attorney in Carlisle, Pennsylvania, in an area largely settled by Ulster Scots like himself in the 1750s. Wilson had great success arranging land deals for his Scots-Irish clients. Although he was prospering, he also began to borrow funds with which to aggressively speculate on land.

Nearly from the time of his arrival in Pennsylvania, Wilson was involved in patriot politics, and he chaired the Carlisle Committee of Correspondence. In 1774, the erudite Wilson published a pamphlet called Considerations on the Nature and Extent of the Legislative Authority of the British Parliament. Actually written as early as 1768, the essay denied Parliament's authority over the Colonies. In it, Wilson had written, "All men are by nature, equal and free. No one has a right to any authority over another without his consent. . . . The consequence is, that the happiness of the society is the first law of every government."

Small wonder that Wilson was among the signers of the Declaration of Independence two years later. In fact, his vote had broken a deadlock within the Pennsylvania delegation, where the influential John Dickinson opposed the Declaration, preferring to reconcile with Great Britain by sending off the ill-fated Olive Branch Petition. When the hostilities broke out, Wilson was made colonel of a militia battalion and fought under Washington in the New Jersey campaign of 1776.

Once independence was achieved, Wilson, like many other Founders, aligned himself with more aristocratic and conservative views. His experience in the Fort Wilson Riot no doubt cemented those views. And they were shared by more than a few of his fellow Founders, particularly in the aftermath of the Shays uprising in Massachusetts. James Wilson, like Washington, Samuel Adams, and Benjamin Franklin, all shuddered at the prospect of more unrest at the hands of a "mobocracy." As Franklin biographer H. W. Brands once wrote, "From classical times the argument against republicanism was that it degenerated into democracy—government not simply in the name of the people but by the people themselves. And democracy degenerated into anarchy, because the people were not fit to govern themselves. In Massachusetts the name of anarchy was Daniel Shays, and the lesson

Shays taught was that if America's republicanism did not take preventive measures soon, it might be lost."[13]

The brief moment known as Shays' Rebellion had tremendous repercussions for the young nation. In the big picture, it was a relatively minor incident in a far-flung corner of the New England frontier, quickly subdued as cooler heads—and better-armed militias—prevailed. But many people viewed the event as a dangerous storm warning.

Following the collapse of Shays' Rebellion, which produced a series of minor tax and voting reforms in Massachusetts, there remained a sense that America under the Articles of Confederation was a dog without much bite. Undoubtedly, the uprising set the table for the constitutional convention that met in Philadelphia in the spring of that year. A movement to throw out the Articles of Confederation and start afresh had been gathering momentum. Shays' Rebellion provided the added urgency that prompted Congress to call for the convention. As economic historian John Steel Gordon noted, "Referring to the changes in the debtors' law brought about by Shays' Rebellion, a Boston newspaper snootily noted in May 1787 that 'sedition itself will sometimes make laws.' In a very real sense, Shays' Rebellion helped make a constitution."[14]

꘠

WORKING FROM MAY 25, when a quorum was established, until September 17, 1787, when the convention voted to endorse the final form of the Constitution, the delegates gathered in the Pennsylvania state-house in Philadelphia were actually obligated only to revise or amend the Articles of Confederation. Under those articles, however, the government was plagued by weaknesses, such as its inability to raise revenues to pay its foreign debts or maintain an army. From the outset, most of the convention's organizers, James Madison and Alexander Hamilton chief among them, knew that splints and bandages wouldn't do the trick. The government was broke—literally and figuratively— and they were going to fix it by inventing an entirely new one. James Madison had been studying more than two hundred books on con- stitutions and republican history sent to him by Thomas Jefferson in preparation for the convention. The moving force behind the conven- tion, Madison came prepared with the outline of a new constitution.

A reluctant George Washington, whose name was placed at the head of list of Virginia's delegates without his knowledge, was unques- tionably spurred by the events in Massachusetts. Elected president of the convention, he wrote from Philadelphia in June to his close war- time confidant and ally, the Marquis de Lafayette, who had presented that now-infamous sword to Daniel Shays after Saratoga, ten years earlier: "I could not resist the call to a convention of the States which is to determine whether we are to have a government of respectability under which life, liberty, and property will be secured to us, or are to submit to one which may be the result of chance or the moment, springing perhaps from anarchy and Confusion, and dictated perhaps by some aspiring demagogue."[15]

Washington rarely spoke at the convention, preferring as the pre- siding officer not to influence the debates. He conveyed his views in private, and others noted his occasional expressions of disgust or plea- sure as the debate proceeded. The fifty-five delegates slowly trickled in from twelve states. With a legislature that didn't want a central govern- ment to force it to pay its debts, Rhode Island sent no delegates, which George Washington deemed "scandalous" and inspired the name "Rogue Island." Those present—in varying degrees of attendance—

included some of the most prominent men in America. Thomas Jefferson, ambassador to France, and John Adams, in London, were notably absent, but not by choice; Patrick Henry, on the other hand, declined and famously said he "smelt a rat in Philadelphia, tending toward monarchy." But it was Washington's presence, along with that of Benjamin Franklin, that was required to give the meeting its legitimacy in the public eye.

With windows closed and guards posted to preserve secrecy, the delegates hammered out the details of the future American government in excruciating debates that carried through Philadelphia's summer heat and humidity. The broad outlines of the debates and positions have been well documented. There were disagreements between large states and small over representation in the legislature. There was tremendous disagreement over the role, title, duties, and selection of the executive, finally called the president. Eventually, two main plans emerged. Largely James Madison's work, the Virginia Plan proposed a bicameral legislature, an executive, a judiciary, and proportional representation, and became the unofficial agenda for the convention. Fearful of large-state power and overly strong central government that would overwhelm smaller states, the second plan was offered by William Patterson and became known as the New Jersey plan. Among its chief differences was a single legislative chamber.

New York's brilliant and ambitious Alexander Hamilton presented his own plan. Best known as Washington's aide-de-camp during the Revolution, Hamilton was the illegitimate son of a Scotsman and a woman from the tiny West Indies island of Nevis, and had become a successful and influential New York attorney, connected by marriage to one of the state's most powerful families. Hamilton's proposal, modeled on Rome's republic, outlined a presidency and senate elected for life—continuing to serve on condition of "good behavior"—and a lower house elected for shorter terms. To many of the delegates, the plan reeked of monarchy and was not seriously considered.

Another plan that has generated considerable historical controversy was proposed by South Carolina's Charles Pinckney, a rather colorful character who lied about his age so he could present himself as the youngest delegate (in fact, Jonathan Dayton of New Jersey was). According to scholarly accounts of papers not discovered until the twentieth century, Pinckney suggested more than thirty of the provisions that ended up in the Constitution. Madison apparently loathed him, and as the unofficial note taker of the Convention, the future fourth president later diminished Pinckney's role. (Madison's notes were published in 1840 and are widely viewed as highly definitive but not entirely objective.) In their book on the constitutional convention, *Decision in Philadelphia*, Christopher Collier and James Lincoln Collier give the flamboyant, womanizing Pinckney his due, while serving up a reminder that the "demigods" gathered in Philadelphia were still flesh-and-blood people with ample humanity: "Whatever character flaws he may have had—the egotism, the political instincts that so many of the other gentlemen around him abhorred—he was an intelligent, experienced, and clear-sighted man whose ideas and opinions should not be discounted. The Father of the Constitution he was not; but he must be seen as one of the group whose influence was significant."[16]

James Wilson's name is not usually mentioned in the same breath with some of the more "marbleized" of the Constitution's Framers. But the six-foot-tall, bespectacled Scotsman ranks only behind Madison, and perhaps Hamilton, in his contribution to its creation. Certainly one of the most learned lawyers at the meeting, he spoke more than anyone else, including Madison. Wilson also read aloud the written statements of eighty-one-year-old Benjamin Franklin, too gout-ridden to stand. Franklin was carried to the sessions on a sedan chair conveyed by prisoners from a nearby jail.

As a member of the Committee of Detail, Wilson has been credited by some as the man behind the document's opening words—"We the People"—which became a source of consternation, because some delegates argued that the nation was the creation of the states. Although more closely linked to the new American aristocracy, Wilson was a champion of democracy, not a popular notion among men who viewed an excess of democracy as one short step removed from rebellion by men like Daniel Shays. Another signer of the Declaration, Massachusetts delegate Elbridge Gerry, told the convention he had been "too republican heretofore: he was still however republican, but had been taught by experience the danger of the levelling spirit."[17] Wilson preferred popular election of the president and senators, and was crucial in crafting the compromise that called for "electors," in essence inventing the electoral college, a term that does not appear in the Constitution but emerged in the nineteenth century before officially entering the United States Code.

It was also James Wilson who proposed the compromise that untied the most difficult of the convention's knots—the question of slavery and how slaves would be counted in the new nation. "James Wilson of Pennsylvania proposed that the new constitution adopt the expedient devised by the Confederation Congress in 1783, when the legislature allowed the states to count three-fifths of the total number of their slaves," according to Franklin's biographer, H. W. Brands. "This compromise made no one happy but none so upset as to bolt the convention, and it was accepted."[18]

Support for the Constitution was not unanimous, however. Several delegates left before signing, and others, most notably Virginia's George

Mason, refused to sign the finished document. In Mason's case, it was over the absence of a Bill of Rights. Another Virginian, Edmund Randolph, also balked. Calling for state conventions to propose amendments and a second national convention, Randolph believed failing to do so would "produce anarchy and civil convulsions which were apprehended from the refusal of individuals to sign it." (He later rallied behind ratification and became the nation's first attorney general.)

Washington signed the parchment copy first, as president of the convention. He was followed by the remaining delegates from the states in geographical order, from north to south, beginning with New Hampshire. When the last of the signatures was added—that of Abraham Baldwin of Georgia—Benjamin Franklin gazed at Washington's chair, on which was painted a bright yellow sun, then spoke. As James Madison recorded it: "I have . . . often in the course of a session, and the vicissitudes of my hopes and fears as to its issue, looked at that behind the President without being able to tell if it was rising or setting: But now at length I have the happiness to know that it is a rising and not a setting sun."

In another, perhaps more apocryphal tale, Franklin left the building and was confronted by a lady who asked, "Well, Doctor, do we have a monarchy or a republic?"

The witty sage of Philadelphia replied, "A republic, madam, if you can keep it."

❦ Aftermath ❧

Leaving no doubt as to the connection between the "little rebellion" in Massachusetts and the convention in Philadelphia, the pro-Constitution

Pennsylvania Gazette voiced what many were thinking: "Every state has its SHAYS who, either with their pens—or tongues—or offices—are endeavoring to effect what *Shays* attempted in vain with his sword." As the debate over ratification continued, the paper had gone beyond simply viewing men such as Shays as a danger to the nation, but also linked Shays to anyone who opposed the Constitution. To its supporters—called Federalists—the people who opposed the Constitution would be made to appear as dangerous anarchists.

In the end, the federal Constitution squeaked through the ratification process after an agonizing few months. Late in 1787 and early 1788, the Constitution's supporters won relatively comfortable victories in Delaware, New Jersey, Georgia, and Pennsylvania, though James Wilson might have disputed that Pennsylvania's decision came easily. After the state ratified, he was again assaulted by a mob during a post-vote celebration. This time his attackers were "Antifeds" who opposed the Constitution. According to Catherine Drinker Bowen in *Miracle at Philadelphia,* her landmark history of the convention, "When Wilson fought back they knocked him down and began to beat him as he lay. He would have been killed, it was said, had not an old soldier thrown himself on Wilson's body and taken the blows."[19]

Massachusetts came along after an initially reluctant Samuel Adams was convinced to endorse the Constitution with a guarantee that a Bill of Rights would be added. On June 21, 1788, New Hampshire ratified, becoming the ninth and final state needed to put the Constitution in effect. Tiny Rhode Island voted no. But more worrisome were Virginia and New York, two of the largest, most powerful, and most influential states. Without them, the Constitution was in effect but not very meaningful. By the end of July, both states had fallen into the "yes" category. North Carolina, along with Rhode Island, both voted in favor after Washington's inauguration.

In his "biography" of the Constitution, Yale scholar Akhil Reed Amar summarized:

All this was breathtakingly novel. In 1787, democratic self-government existed almost nowhere on earth. Kings, emperors, czars, princes, sultans, moguls, feudal lords, and tribal chiefs held sway across the globe. Even England featured a limited monarchy and an entrenched aristocracy alongside a House of Commons that rested on a restricted and uneven electoral base. The vaunted English Constitution that American colonists had grown up admiring prior to the struggle for independence was an imprecise hodgepodge of institutions, enactments, cases, usages, maxims, procedures, and principles that had accreted and evolved over many centuries. This Constitution had never been reduced to a single composite writing and voted on by the British people or even by Parliament. . . . Before the American Revolution, no people had ever explicitly voted on their own written Constitution.[20]

On April 30. 1789, George Washington stood on the balcony of Federal Hall in New York City, the temporary national capital. He took the oath of office on a Masonic Bible, ad-libbing the words "So help me God," which the oath of office as specified in the Constitution does not require.

It was not long before Washington was besieged by office seekers. Among them was James Wilson, who saw himself as an ideal candidate for chief justice of the Supreme Court. Calling Wilson perhaps the "best lawyer on the first Supreme Court," historian and member of the Supreme Court bar Peter Irons goes on to write: "Wilson sought the office of Chief Justice through shameless flattery and self-promotion. He wrote to President Washington that 'I commit myself to your Excellency without reserve and inform you that my aim rises to the important office of Chief Justice of the United States. But how shall I proceed? Shall I enumerate reasons in justification of my high pretensions? I have not yet employed my pen in my own praise.' Washington answered with an implied rebuke. . . . Nonetheless, Washington admired Wilson's legal skills and prevailed on him to accept the post of associate justice under John Jay."[21]

One reason that Wilson's name is less frequently cited among the "demigods," as Jefferson called the men in Philadelphia, might be his less-than-godlike demise. Long a speculator in land and finance, Wilson had borrowed heavily to invest in bank stock and land grants well before he joined the Supreme Court. Part of his plan was a utopian scheme to populate the empty western lands with European settlers.

But in a fall that mirrored the fates of Daniel Shays and thousands of other Americans pressed by hard times and high taxes, Wilson and his fellow Philadelphian Robert Morris were unable to pay mounting debts and were both hounded by creditors. Morris—financier of the Revolution—was sent to debtor's prison and was reduced to poverty at the end of his life, a fate shared by James Wilson. "He became the first—and, so far, the only—justice to be jailed while serving on the Court, not once, but twice," notes Supreme Court historian Irons. "Humiliated by his first term in debtors' prison, Wilson traded circuit-riding duties with Justice Iredell in 1798 and took refuge in North Carolina, where another creditor had him jailed for two months. Wilson died shortly after his release, penniless and stripped of the power he had once wielded on the Supreme Court."[22]

In August 1789, following a bout with malaria and suffering a stroke, Wilson died at fifty-six, and was buried on his friend's estate. As the Colliers sadly summarize, "James Wilson died an embarrassment to his friends, and in particular to his Federalist party, led by President John Adams. He was a stench, misshapen, and he was hustled offstage as quickly as possible, and allowed to disappear from history."[23]

Daniel Shays also died poor, although he outlived James Wilson by a considerable time. Sentenced to death in Massachusetts, he and other rebels were ultimately pardoned by the state. Shays was even granted a veteran's pension, and he moved to western New York, where he lived out the rest of his life as a struggling farmer. Daniel Shays died in 1825, at age seventy-eight.

Acknowledgments

Leaving the safety of familiar terrain and venturing into the unknown can be a daunting business. But as many stories in this book demonstrate, setting out for new territory has been an essential ingredient of the American experience for centuries. And as those stories also proved, the results can be disastrous. So it is vastly reassuring to know that you have good guides and companions alongside you on the expedition.

For me, leaving the comfortable landscape of the Don't Know Much About series to write about American history in a different style and format has been both exhilarating and scary. But I could not have ventured forth without the encouragement, support, and assistance of a great many people who have helped me out at every step of the journey.

That large group of people begins with David Black, my dear friend and literary agent, who always sees the possibilities, and propelled me on this new path. His excellent team at the David Black Agency has also been stalwart in their help over the years and I am very happy and grateful to have Dave Larabell, Leigh Ann Eliseo, Susan Raihofer, Gary Morris, Joy Tutela, and Antonella Iannarino behind me.

Acknowledgments

Over the years that the Don't Know Much About series has been published at Harper, I have also been very lucky to have the support of a dedicated publishing group behind me as well. For their continued support, I heartily thank Jane Friedman, Carrie Kania, Diane Burrowes, Leslie Cohen, Elizabeth Harper, Jen Hart, Hope Inelli, Carl Lennertz, Nicole Reardon, Michael Signorelli, and Virginia Stanley. I am also indebted to my tireless publicist, Laura Reynolds. Two early supporters of my pursuit of a new way in which to tell important stories were Don Fehr and Phil Friedman, and I will always value their encouragement.

It has also been my privilege to meet and work with an editor of great skill, intelligence, and enthusiasm. Elisabeth Dyssegaard of Smithsonian Books played a crucial role in shaping and recasting this work. I value her judgment and friendship. I am also grateful to the other members of the Collins and Smithsonian team: Steve Ross, Kate Antony, Larry Hughes, Jean Marie Kelly, Susan Warga, Diane Aronson, Nicola Ferguson, Shubhani Sarkar, and Richard Ljoenes.

My children, Colin Davis and Jenny Davis, have always provided me with joy and inspiration. I treasure their wonderful spirits. In this case, my daughter, Jenny, also added immeasurably to this book with her editorial skills and deep insights into colonial American history.

And finally, this new venture really started many years ago, when my wife, Joann, said to me, "You love American history. Why don't you write about it?" That's how it all began. And in this and every other journey we have shared, she has been "constant as a northern star." No explorer or adventurer could ever ask for a better companion.

Notes

Part 1: Isabella's Pigs

1. Charles E. Bennet, *Laudonnière and Fort Caroline*, p. 41.
2. Cited in Jerald T. Milanich, *Florida Indians and the Invasion From Europe*, p. 148.
3. Cited in David J. Weber, *The Spanish Frontier in North America*, p. 62.
4. Bennett, *Laudonnière and Fort Caroline*, pp. 42–43.
5. Ibid.
6. Hugh Thomas, *Rivers of Gold*, p. 25 (emphasis added).
7. Henry Kamen, *The Spanish Inquisition: A Historical Revision*.
8. James Reston Jr., *Dogs of God*, pp. 60–61.
9. Christopher Columbus, *The Four Voyages of Christopher Columbus*, p. 120.
10. Charles Hudson, *Knights of Spain, Warriors of the Sun*, pp. 77–78.
11. Charles C. Mann, *1491*, p. 107.
12. Alvar Núñez Cabeza de Vaca, *Castaways*, p. 110.
13. Michael Wood, *Conquistadors*, p. 25.
14. Paul Schneider, *Brutal Journey*, pp. 98–99.
15. Cited in Bennet, *Laudonnière and Fort Caroline*, p. 16.
16. Milanich, *Florida Indians and the Invasion from Europe*, pp. 153–54.
17. Neil Hanson, *The Confident Hope of a Miracle*.

Part II: Hannah's Escape

1. Cited in Mary Beth Norton, *In the Devil's Snare*, p. 15.

2. Cotton Mather, "A Notable Exploit," in Kathryn Zabelle Derounian-Stodola, ed., *Women's Indian Captivity Narratives*, p. 58. Hannah Dustin's name is also variously spelled Dustan or Duston.

3. Cited in Colin G. Calloway, *Dawnland Encounters: Indians and Europeans in Northern New England*, p. 144.

4. Mather, "A Notable Exploit," p. 60.

5. Kathryn Zabelle Derounian-Stodola, ed., *Women's Indian Captivity Narratives*, p. 344.

6. Henry David Thoreau, *A Week on the Concord and Merrimack Rivers* (1849).

7. Writing more than 150 years after the fact, Henry David Thoreau recorded his version of what had become local legend in *A Week on the Concord and Merrimack Rivers* (1849). According to Thoreau's account, "The family of Hannah Dustan all assembled alive once more, except for the infant whose brains were dashed out against the apple-tree, and there have been many who in later times have lived to say that they had eaten of the fruit of that apple tree." Other prominent American writers, including Nathaniel Hawthorne and Haverhill native John Greenleaf Whittier, also wrote about the incident, with Hawthorne striking a very unsympathetic note, calling the much-lionized Hannah Dustin "an old hag."

8. David Hackett Fischer, *Albion's Seed: Four British Folkways in America*, pp. 88–89.

9. Laurel Thatcher Ulrich, *Good Wives: Image and Reality in the Lives of Women in Northern New England, 1650–1750*, pp. 184–185.

10. Derounian-Stodola, ed., *Women's Indian Captivity Narratives*, p. 56.

11. Alden T. Vaughan and Daniel K. Richter. "Crossing the Cultural Divide: Indians and New Englanders, 1605-1763." Cited in Derounian-Stodola, ed., *Women's Indian Captivity Narratives*, p. xv.

12. Carol Berkin, *First Generations: Women in Colonial America*, p. 44.

13. Hutchinson's Bible was the Geneva Bible, one of the first complete

English translations of the Bible, completed in 1560. It was the first Bible to include both Testaments and also divided the books into chapters and verses. This was Shakespeare's Bible as well as the Bible carried on the *Mayflower*. The more famous King James Version was completed in 1611 but was not widely accepted until the 1640s.

14. Berkin, *First Generations*, p. 24.

15. Nathaniel Philbrick, *Mayflower*, pp. 173–74.

16. In 1692, after James II had appointed a royal governor to rule over New England, Plymouth became a part of Massachusetts.

17. Morgan, *The Puritan Dilemma*, p. 186.

18. Ibid., p. 197.

19. Reverend Peter J. Gomes, *Harvard Magazine*, November-December 2002. http://harvardmagazine.com/2002/11/anne-hutchinson.html.

20. Eve LaPlante, *American Jezebel: The Uncommon Life of Anne Hutchinson*, pp. 238–39. Hutchinson's many generations of descendants include Thomas Hutchinson, who later became governor of Massachusetts during the pre-Revolutionary days and whose policies incited the Boston Tea Party (see Chapter 4). In the twentieth century, her descendants included Franklin D. Roosevelt, George H. W. Bush, and George W. Bush, making this rather extraordinary woman the ancestor of three American presidents.

21. Ibid., pp. 240–41.

22. Richard Francis, *Judge Sewall's Apology: A Biography*, p. 17.

23. Jill Lepore, *The Name of War: King Philip's War and the Origins of American Identity*, p. 9.

24. Colin G. Calloway, *The World Turned Upside Down*, p. 78.

25. David Hackett Fischer, *Albion's Seed: Four British Folkways in America*, p. 17 (emphasis added).

26. Cited in Francis J. Bremer, *John Winthrop: America's Forgotten Founding Father*, p. 191.

27. William Bradford, *Of Plymouth Plantation*, p. 227.

28. Bremer, *John Winthrop*, p. 238.

29. Bradford, *Of Plymouth Plantation*, p. 331.

30. If Uncas and Mohegan sound vaguely familiar, you are probably thinking of James Fenimore Cooper's epic 1826 novel, *The Last of the Mohicans*, one of the most popular novels of its time and a school reading list staple for centuries. Cooper's "Mohicans" were actually an Algonquian-speaking tribe called Mahicans, based in New York's Hudson River valley. Although Uncas is a character in the novel, he had nothing to do with the historical Uncas of the Mohegans, a different Algonquian tribe based in eastern Connecticut.

31. From *Collections of the Massachusetts Historical Society*, cited in Calloway, *The World Turned Upside Down*, p. 80. The Pequot were not entirely wiped out, and a Pequot reservation was established in Connecticut in 1667. More than three hundred years later, in 1983, the tribe received federal recognition and eventually went on to open the Foxwoods Resort Casino. Their traditional rivals, the Mohegans of Connecticut, remained allies of the English during the seventeenth century. In 1994, they too received federal recognition and now operate the Mohegan Sun casino in Connecticut.

32. Ibid.

33. Cited in Calloway, *The World Turned Upside Down*, p. 20.

34. Philbrick, *Mayflower*, p. 332.

35. Salisbury, "Introduction," in Mary Rowlandson, *The Sovereignty and Goodness of God*, p. 1.

36. Lepore, *The Name of War*, pp. 173–75.

37. Rowlandson, *The Sovereignty and Goodness of God*, p. 70.

38. An extraordinary coincidental connection existed between the Rowlandson and Hannah Dustin captivity stories. The Indian who had provided young Samuel Lennardson with such excellent instructions on the use of a tomahawk and the precise methods of scalp taking had learned English while he was a servant in the Rowlandson household in Lancaster.

39. Known in Europe as the War of the Spanish Succession.

40. Tony Horwitz, "Apalachee Tribe, Missing for Centuries, Comes Out of Hiding," *Wall Street Journal*, March 9, 2005. According to Hor-

witz, the Apalachee Tribe's bleak history continued for centuries. Eighty survivors of the original tribe settled along the Red River in Louisiana. In 1803, American settlers burned the Apalachee's cabins and seized their land. Later, their land was sold to a cotton planter who used his slaves to drive the Indians out. Struggling in bayou country, their descendants were later set upon by Klansmen in the early 1900s. The Apalachee are still fighting to win federal recognition.

Part III: Washington's Confession

1. Fred Anderson, *Crucible of War,* p. 6.
2. Washington, *Writings,* p. 43.
3. Ibid., pp. 47-48.
4. Cited in James Thomas Flexner, *The Forge of Experience,* p. 92.
5. Robert Jenkins was a British privateer. He claimed that the Spanish had boarded his ship and severed his ear. When Jenkins' pickled ear was eventually exhibited in the House of Commons, England was whipped into a war frenzy. In 1739, the British declared war on Spain.
6. David Hackett Fischer, *Albion's Seed: Four British Folkways in America,* p. 212.
7. Over the centuries, it has been suggested that this bout with small-pox may have rendered George Washington, the "Father of His Country," sterile. He fathered no children with his wife, Martha, a widow who had given birth to two children of her own in her first marriage. The suggestion that Washington fathered children by slaves is treated in Henry Wiencek's *An Imperfect God: George Washington, His Slaves and the Creation of America,* but in spite of oral histories suggesting otherwise, Wiencek offers that no definitive answer to the question is possible.
8. David L. Holmes, *The Faiths of the Founding Fathers,* p. 106.
9. H. Paul Jeffers, *Freemasons: Inside the World's Oldest Secret Society,* pp. 46–47.
10. James Thomas Flexner, *Washington: The Indispensable Man,* p. 15.

11. Ibid., p. 16.
12. Anderson, *Crucible of War,* p. 86.
13. Ibid., pp. 292–93.
14. Washington, "Reward for Runaway Slaves," *Writings,* pp. 102–03.
15. Washington, *Writings,* pp. 162–63.

Part IV: Warren's Toga

1. Cited in David Hackett Fischer, *Paul Revere's Ride,* p. 70.
2. Mark Puls, *Samuel Adams: Father of the American Revolution,* p. 167.
3. Cited in Richard M. Ketchum, *Decisive Day: The Battle for Bunker Hill,* p. 57.
4. Gordon S. Wood, *The Radicalism of the American Revolution,* p. 104.
5. Fred Anderson, *A People's Army: Massachusetts Soldiers and Society in the Seven Years' War,* p. 22.
6. Colin G. Calloway, *The Scratch of a Pen: 1763 and the Transformation of North America,* p. 98.
7. Ray Raphael, *A People's History of the American Revolution,* pp. 49–50.
8. Cited in Puls, *Samuel Adams,* pp. 163–64.
9. Elizabeth A. Fenn, *Pox Americana: The Great Smallpox Epidemic of 1775–82,* pp. 46, 88.
10. Cited in Lynne Withey, *Dearest Friend: A Life of Abigail Adams,* pp. 44–45.
11. Cited in Fischer, *Paul Revere's Ride,* p. 67.
12. Ibid., p. 66.
13. Thomas Fleming, *Liberty: The American Revolution,* p. 106.
14. Puls, *Samuel Adams,* pp. 155–56.
15. Cited in Raphael, *A People's History of the American Revolution,* pp. 3–4.
16. Fleming, *Liberty,* p. 106.
17. Cited in Puls, *Samuel Adams,* p. 129.
18. Cited in Puls, *Samuel Adams,* p. 129.

19. Cited in *Paul Revere's Ride,* p. 26.

20. Ibid., p. 19.

21. William H. Hallahan, *The Day the American Revolution Began,* pp. 49–50.

22. Cited in Fischer, *Paul Revere's Ride,* p. 269.

23. Puls, *Samuel Adams,* p. 173.

24. Cited in Ketchum, *Decisive Day,* p. 195.

25. Fischer, *Paul Revere's Ride,* p. 97.

26. Simon Schama, *Rough Crossings: The Slaves, the British, and the American Revolution,* p. 7.

27. Ibid., p. 8.

Part V: Arnold's Boot

1. A veteran of the wars with France, Skene had acquired the property that he named Skenesborough. More than fifty-six thousand acres of Skene property were later confiscated when Major Skene and his family were declared "enemies of the state" during the Revolution by New York. Today it is known as Whitehall, New York.

2. Willard Sterne Randall, *Benedict Arnold: Patriot and Traitor,* p. 94.

3. Ian K. Steele, *Betrayals: Fort William Henry and the "Massacre,"* p. 144.

4. Cited in Randall, *Benedict Arnold,* p. 92.

5. Michael A. Bellesiles, *Revolutionary Outlaws: Ethan Allen and the Struggle for Independence on the Early American Frontier,* p. 4.

6. Cited in Randall, *Benedict Arnold,* p. 97.

7. Cited in Bellesiles, *Revolutionary Outlaws,* p. 121.

8. It is worth noting that to this day some histories of the attack on Ticonderoga still either fail to mention Benedict Arnold or seriously underplay his role in events.

9. James Thomas Flexner, *Washington: The Indispensable Man,* p. 141.

10. Randall, *Benedict Arnold: Patriot and Traitor,* p. 39.

11. Dave R. Palmer, *George Washington and Benedict Arnold: A Tale of Two Patriots*, p. 4.

12. Randall, *Benedict Arnold*, p. 136.

13. Boston's large and notable Irish-Catholic populace did not arrive until the mass immigration of the nineteenth century, when millions of Irish Catholics came to America and endured bias and bigotry for generations.

14. Randall, *Benedict Arnold*, p. 151.

15. Richard M. Ketchum, *Saratoga: Turning Point of America's Revolutionary War*, p. 14.

16. Elizabeth Fenn, *Pox Americana: The Great Smallpox Epidemic of 1775–82*, p. 63.

17. Cited in Randall, *Benedict Arnold*, p. 560.

18. Cited in ibid., p. 574.

Part VI: Lafayette's Sword

1. Cited in Leonard L. Richards, *Shays's Rebellion: The American Revolution's Final Battle*, p. 130.

2. Ibid., pp. 45–46.

3. Alden T. Vaughan, "The 'Horrid and Unnatural Rebellion' of Daniel Shays." http://www.american heritage.com/articles/magazine/ah/1966/4/1966_4_50_prints.html.

4. Richards, *Shays's Rebellion*, p. 92.

5. Leonard L. Richards, *Shays's Rebellion: The American Revolution's Final Battle*, p. 63.

6. Cited in ibid., p. 63.

7. George Washington, *Writings*, p. 544.

8. Richard Brookhiser, *Founding Father: Rediscovering George Washington*, pp. 53–54.

9. Gary B. Nash, *The Unknown American Revolution*, p. 76.

10. Ray Raphael, *A People's History of the American Revolution*, p. 31.

11. Ibid., p. 33.

12. Cited in Nash, *The Unknown American Revolution*, p. 319.

13. H. W. Brands, *The First American: The Life and Times of Benjamin Franklin*, p. 671.

14. John Steele Gordon, *An Empire of Wealth*, p. 65.

15. Washington, *Writings*, p. 652.

16. Christopher Collier and James Lincoln Collier, *Decision in Philadelphia*, pp. 100–1.

17. Peter Irons, *A People's History of the Supreme Court*, p. 24.

18. Brands, *The First American*, p. 689.

19. Catherine Drinker Bowen, *Miracle at Philadelphia*, p. 277.

20. Akhil Reed Amar, *America's Constitution: A Biography*, p. 8.

21. Peter Irons, *A People's History of the Supreme Court*, pp. 89–90.

22. Ibid., p. 90.

23. Collier and Collier, *Decision in Philadelphia*, p. 288.

Bibliography

This list of readings is organized by chapter. Many of the books are referenced in more than one chapter, but are listed here only under the chapter in which they are first cited.

Part I: Isabella's Pigs

Bennet, Charles E. *Laudonnière and Fort Caroline: History and Documents.* Tuscaloosa: University of Alabama Press, 2001.

Bolton, Herbert Eugene, editor. *Spanish Exploration in the Southwest, 1542–1706.* New York: Barnes and Noble, 1908.

Bradford, Sarah. *Lucrezia Borgia: Life, Love and Death in Renaissance Italy.* New York: Viking, 2004.

Castañeda, Pedro de, et al. *The Journey of Coronado.* Translated and edited by George Parker Winship. Mineola, N.Y.: Dover, 1990.

Clayton, Lawrence A., Vernon James Knight Jr., and Edward C. Moore, editors. *The De Soto Chronicles: The Expedition of Hernando De Soto to North America in 1539–1543.* 2 vols. Tuscaloosa: University of Alabama Press, 1993.

Colbert, David, editor. *Eyewitness to America: 500 Years of American History in the Worlds of Those Who Saw It Happen.* New York: Pantheon, 1997.

Columbus, Christopher. *The Four Voyages of Christopher Columbus.* Edited and translated by J. M. Cohen. New York: Penguin Books, 1969.

Diamond, Jared. *Collapse: How Societies Choose to Fail or Succeed.* New York: Viking, 2005.

———. *Guns, Germs and Steel: The Fates of Human Societies.* New York: Norton, 1998.

Díaz, Bernal. *The Conquest of New Spain.* Edited and translated by J. M. Cohen. New York: Penguin Books, 1963.

Duncan, David Ewing. *Hernando de Soto: A Savage Quest in the Americas.* New York: Crown, 1995.

Earle, Peter. *The Pirate Wars.* New York: St. Martin's Press, 2003.

Eltis, David. *The Rise of Slavery in the Americas.* New York: Cambridge University Press, 2000.

Flint, Richard. *Great Cruelties Have Been Reported: The 1544 Investigation of the Coronado Expedition.* Dallas, Tex.: Southern Methodist University Press, 2002.

Galloway, Patricia, editor. *The Hernando De Soto Expedition: History, Historiography, and "Discovery."* Lincoln: University of Nebraska Press, 1997.

Hanson, Neil. *The Confident Hope of a Miracle: The True History of the Spanish Armada.* New York: Knopf, 2005.

Hudson, Charles. *Knights of Spain, Warriors of the Sun: Hernando de Soto and the South's Ancient Chiefdoms.* Athens: University of Georgia Press, 1997.

Kamen, Henry. *Empire: How Spain Became a World Power, 1492–1763.* New York: HarperCollins, 2003.

———. *Philip of Spain.* New Haven, Conn.: Yale University Press, 1997.

———. *The Spanish Inquisition: A Historical Revision.* New Haven, Conn.: Yale University Press, 1997.

Kessell, John L. *Spain in the Southwest: A Narrative History of Colonial New Mexico, Arizona, Texas, and California.* Norman: University of Oklahoma Press, 2002.

Klein, Herbert S. *The Atlantic Slave Trade.* New York: Cambridge University Press, 1999.

Kolchin, Peter. *American Slavery, 1619–1877.* New York: Hill and Wang, 1993.

Liss, Peggy K. *Isabel the Queen: Life and Times.* New York: Oxford University Press, 1992.

Lockhart, James, and Stuart B. Schwartz, editors. *Early Latin America: A History of Colonial Spanish America and Brazil.* New York: Cambridge University Press, 1983.

Mancall, Peter, and James H. Merrell, editors. *American Encounters: Natives and Newcomers from European Contact to Indian Removal, 1500–1850.* New York: Routledge, 2000.

Mann, Charles C. *1491: New Revelations of the Americas Before Columbus.* New York: Knopf, 2005.

Milanich, Jerald T. *Florida Indians and the Invasion from Europe.* Gainesville: University Press of Florida, 1998.

Núñez Cabeza de Vaca, Alvar. *Castaways: The Narrative of Alvar Núñez Cabeza de Vaca.* Edited by Enrique Pupo-Walker, translated by Frances M. Lopez-Morillas. Berkeley: University of California Press, 1993.

———. *The Account: Alvar Núñez Cabeza de Vaca's Relación.* Translated and annotated by Martin A. Favata and José B. Fernández. Houston, Tex.: Arte Público Press, 1993.

Price, David A. *Love and Hate in Jamestown: John Smith, Pocahontas, and the Heart of a New Nation.* New York: Knopf, 2003.

Restall, Matthew. *Seven Myths of the Spanish Conquest.* New York: Oxford University Press, 2003.

Reston, James, Jr. *Dogs of God: Columbus, the Inquisition, and the Defeat of the Moors.* New York: Doubleday, 2005.

Rubin, Nancy. *Isabella of Castile: The First Renaissance Queen.* New York: St. Martin's Press, 1991.

Schneider, Paul. *Brutal Journey: The Epic Story of the First Crossing of North America.* New York: Henry Holt, 2006.

Stannard, David E. *American Holocaust: The Conquest of the New World.* New York: Oxford University Press, 1992.

Thomas, Hugh. *Conquest: Montezuma, Cortes, and the Fall of Old Mexico.* New York: Simon and Schuster, 1993.

————. *Rivers of Gold: The Rise of the Spanish Empire, from Columbus to Magellan.* New York: Random House, 2003.

Thoreau, Henry David. *A Week on the Concord and Merrimack Rivers/ Walden; Or, Life in the Woods/Cape Cod.* New York: Library of America, 1985.

Weber, David J. *The Spanish Frontier in North America.* New Haven, Conn.: Yale University Press, 1992.

Wood, Michael. *Conquistadors.* Berkeley: University of California Press, 2000.

Wright, Ronald. *Stolen Continents: The Americas Through Indian Eyes Since 1492.* Boston: Houghton Mifflin, 1992.

Part II: Hannah's Escape

Berkin, Carol. *First Generations: Women in Colonial America.* New York: Hill and Wang, 1996.

Boorstin, Daniel J. *The Americans: The Colonial Experience.* New York: Random House, 1958.

————, editor. *An American Primer.* New York: Mentor Books, 1966.

Bradford, William. *Of Plymouth Plantation: 1620–1647.* New York: Modern Library, 1981.

Bremer, Francis J. *John Winthrop: America's Forgotten Founding Father.* New York: Oxford University Press, 2003.

Calloway, Colin G., editor. *Dawnland Encounters: Indians and Europeans in Northern New England.* Hanover, N.H.: University Press of New England, 1991.

————. *The World Turned Upside Down: Indian Voices from Early America.* Boston: Bedford/St. Martin's, 1994.

Calloway, Colin G., and Neal Salisbury, editors. *Reinterpreting New England Indians and the Colonial Experience.* Boston: Colonial Society of Massachusetts, 2003.

Carroll, Andrew, editor. *Letters of a Nation: A Collection of Extraordinary American Letters.* New York: Broadway Books, 1997.

Church, Benjamin. *Diary of King Philip's War: 1675–1676.* Introduction by Alan Simpson and Mary Simpson. Little Compton, R.I.: Lockwood Publishing, 1996.

Cronon, William. *Changes in the Land: Indians, Colonists, and the Ecology of New England.* New York: Hill and Wang, 1983.

Demos, John. *A Little Commonwealth: Family Life in Plymouth Colony.* 2nd edition. New York: Oxford University Press, 2000.

———. *The Unredeemed Captive: A Family Story from Early America.* New York: Knopf, 1994.

Derounian-Stodola, Kathryn Zabelle, editor. *Women's Indian Captivity Narratives.* New York: Penguin Books, 1998.

Eliot, John. *The Indian Grammar Begun: Or, an Essay to Bring the Indian Language into Rules.* Bedford, Mass.: Applewood Books, 2001.

Fischer, David Hackett. *Albion's Seed: Four British Folkways in America.* New York: Oxford University Press, 1989.

Francis, Richard. *Judge Sewall's Apology: The Salem Witch Trials and the Forming of an American Conscience.* New York: HarperCollins, 2005.

Gunn, Giles, editor. *Early American Writing.* New York: Penguin Books, 1994.

Hawthorne, Nathaniel. *Tales and Sketches.* New York: Library of America, 1982.

LaPlante, Eve. *American Jezebel: The Uncommon Life of Anne Hutchinson, the Woman Who Defied the Puritans.* San Francisco: HarperSanFrancisco, 2004.

Lepore, Jill. *The Name of War: King Philip's War and the Origins of American Identity.* New York: Knopf, 1998.

Mather, Cotton. *On Witchcraft.* Mineola, N.Y.: Dover, 2005.

Morgan, Edmund S. *The Puritan Dilemma: The Story of John Winthrop.* New York: Pearson Longman, 2006.

———. *The Puritan Family: Religion and Domestic Relations in Seventeenth-Century New England.* New York: Harper and Row, 1966.

Morone, James A. *Hellfire Nation: The Politics of Sin in American History.* New Haven, Conn.: Yale University Press, 2003.

Norton, Mary Beth. *Founding Mothers and Fathers: Gendered Power and the Forming of American Society.* New York: Random House, 1996.

———. *In the Devil's Snare: The Salem Witch Crisis of 1692.* New York: Vintage, 2002.

Philbrick, Nathaniel. *Mayflower: A Story of Courage, Community, and War.* New York: Viking, 2006.

Richter, Daniel K. *Facing East from Indian Country: A Native History of Early America.* Cambridge, Mass.: Harvard University Press, 2001.

Rowlandson, Mary. *The Sovereignty and Goodness of God.* Edited with an introduction by Neal Salisbury. Boston: Bedford/St. Martin's, 1997.

Schultz, Eric B., and Michael J. Tougias. *King Philip's War: The History and Legacy of America's Forgotten Conflict.* Woodstock, Vt.: Countryman Press, 1999.

Shorto, Russell. *The Island at the Center of the World: The Epic Story of Dutch Manhattan and the Forgotten Colony That Shaped America.* New York: Doubleday, 2004.

Ulrich, Laurel Thatcher. *Good Wives: Image and Reality in the Lives of Women in Northern New England, 1650–1750.* New York: Knopf, 1980.

Vaughan, Alden T., editor. *New England Encounters: Indians and Euroamericans, ca. 1600–1850.* Boston: Northeastern University Press, 1999.

Part III: Washington's Confession

Anderson, Fred. *Crucible of War: The Seven Years' War and the Fate of the Empire in British North America, 1754–1766.* New York: Random House, 2000.

————. *A People's Army: Massachusetts Soldiers and Society in the Seven Years' War.* Chapel Hill: University of North Carolina Press, 1984.

Bennett, Lerone, Jr. *The Shaping of Black America: The Struggles and Triumphs of African-Americans, 1619 to the 1990s.* New York: Penguin Books, 1975.

Brookhiser, Richard. *Founding Father: Rediscovering George Washington.* New York: Free Press, 1996.

Brumwell, Stephen. *White Devil: A True Story of War, Savagery, and Vengeance in Colonial America.* Cambridge, Mass.: Da Capo Press, 2004.

Calloway, Colin. *The Scratch of a Pen: 1763 and the Transformation of North America.* New York: Oxford University Press, 2006.

Chartrand, René. *Monongahela, 1754–1755: Washington's Defeat, Braddock's Disaster.* New York: Osprey Publishing, 2004.

Cooper, James Fenimore. *The Last of the Mohicans.* New York: Bantam Books, 1981.

Ellis, Joseph J. *His Excellency George Washington.* New York: Knopf, 2004.

Flexner, James Thomas. *George Washington: The Forge of Experience (1732–1775).* Boston: Little. Brown, 1965.

————. *Washington: The Indispensable Man.* New York: Little, Brown, 1974.

Hofstadter, Richard. *America at 1750: A Social Portrait.* New York: Random House, 1973.

Isaacson, Walter. *Benjamin Franklin: An American Life.* New York: Simon and Schuster, 2003.

Parkman, Francis. *France and England in North America.* 2 volumes. New York: Library of America, 1983.

Sheppard, Ruth, editor. *Empires Collide: The French and Indian War, 1754–63.* New York: Osprey Publishing, 2006.

Steele, Ian K. *Betrayals: Fort William Henry and the "Massacre."* New York: Oxford University Press, 1990.

Washington, George. *Major George Washington's Journal to the River Ohio.* Whitefish, Montana: Kessinger Publishing, n.d.

Wiencek, Henry. *An Imperfect God: George Washington, His Slaves and the Creation of America.* New York: Farrar, Straus and Giroux, 2003.

Part IV: Warren's Toga

Berkin, Carol. *Revolutionary Mothers: Women in the Struggle for America's Independence.* New York: Knopf, 2005.

Brands, H. W. *The First American: The Life and Times of Benjamin Franklin.* New York: Doubleday, 2000.

Commager, Henry Steele. *The Empire of Reason: How Europe Imagined and American Realized the Enlightenment.* London: Weidenfeld and Nicolson, 1978.

Fenn, Elizabeth. *Pox Americana: The Great Smallpox Epidemic of 1775–82.* New York: Hill and Wang, 2001.

Fischer, David Hackett. *Paul Revere's Ride.* New York: Oxford University Press, 1994.

Fleming, Thomas. *Liberty! The American Revolution.* New York: Viking, 1997.

Flexner, James Thomas. *George Washington in the American Revolution (1775–1783).* Boston: Little, Brown, 1967.

———. *Washington: The Indispensable Man.* New York: Little, Brown, 1974.

Hallahan, William H. *The Day the American Revolution Began: 19 April 1775.* New York: William Morrow, 2000.

Hawke, David Freeman. *Everyday Life in Early America.* New York: Harper and Row, 1988.

Herman, Arthur. *How the Scots Invented the Modern World: The True Story of How Western Europe's Poorest Nation Created Our World and Everything in It.* New York: Crown, 2001.

Hibbert, Christopher. *Redcoats and Rebels: The American Revolution Through British Eyes.* New York: Norton, 1990.

Jacoby, Susan. *Freethinkers: A History of American Secularism*. New York: Henry Holt, 2004.

Ketchum, Richard M. *Decisive Day: The Battle for Bunker Hill*. Garden City, N.Y.: Doubleday, 1974.

Miller, John C. *Sam Adams: Pioneer in Propaganda*. Stanford, Calif.: Stanford University Press, 1936.

Nash, Gary B. *The Unknown American Revolution: The Unruly Birth of Democracy and the Struggle to Create America*. New York: Penguin Books, 2005.

Norton, Mary Beth. *Liberty's Daughters: The Revolutionary Experience of American Women, 1750–1800*. Ithaca, N.Y.: Cornell University Press, 1980.

Puls, Mark. *Samuel Adams: Father of the American Revolution*. New York: Palgrave Macmillan, 2006.

Quarles, Benjamin. *The Negro in the Making of America*. New York: Macmillan, 1987.

Raphael, Ray. *A People's History of the American Revolution: How Common People Shaped the Fight for Independence*. New York: Perennial, 2002.

Royster, Charles. *A Revolutionary People at War: The Continental Army and American Character, 1775–1783*. Chapel Hill: University of North Carolina Press, 1979.

Schama, Simon. *Rough Crossing: The Slaves, the British, and the American Revolution*. New York: HarperCollins, 2006.

Unger, Harlow Giles. *John Hancock: Merchant King and American Patriot*. New York: John Wiley and Sons, 2000.

Withey, Lynne. *Dearest Friend: A Life of Abigail Adams*. New York: Simon and Schuster, 2002.

Part V: Arnold's Boot

Bellesiles, Michael A. *Revolutionary Outlaws: Ethan Allen and the Struggle for Independence on the Early American Frontier*. Charlottesville: University of Virginia Press, 1995.

Cohen, I. Bernard. *Science and the Founding Fathers: Science in the Political Thought of Jefferson, Franklin, Adams, and Madison.* New York: Norton, 1995.

Edgar, Walter. *Partisans and Redcoats: The Southern Conflict That Turned the Tide of the American Revolution.* New York: William Morrow, 2001.

Fischer, David Hackett. *Washington's Crossing.* New York: Oxford University Press, 2004.

Fleming, Thomas. *Duel: Alexander Hamilton, Aaron Burr and the Future of America.* New York: Basic Books, 1999.

———. *Washington's Secret War: The Hidden History of Valley Forge.* New York: Smithsonian Books, 2005.

Gay, Peter. *The Enlightenment: An Interpretation, the Rise of Modern Paganism.* New York: Knopf, 1966.

Holmes, David L. *The Faiths of the Founding Fathers.* New York: Oxford University Press, 2006.

Isenberg, Nancy. *Fallen Founder: The Life of Aaron Burr.* New York: Viking, 2007.

Jefferson, Thomas. *Writings.* New York: Library of America, 1984.

Ketchum, Richard. *Saratoga: Turning Point of America's Revolutionary War.* New York: Henry Holt, 1997.

———. *The Winter Soldiers.* New York: Doubleday, 1973.

McCullough, David. *John Adams.* New York: Simon and Schuster, 2001.

———. *1776.* New York: Simon and Schuster, 2005.

Nelson, James L. *Benedict Arnold's Navy: The Ragtag Fleet That Lost the Battle for Lake Champlain but Won the American Revolution.* New York: McGraw-Hill, 2006.

Paine, Thomas. *Rights of Man.* Introduction by Eric Foner. New York: Penguin Books, 1984.

Palmer, Dave R. *George Washington and Benedict Arnold: A Tale of Two Patriots.* Washington, D.C.: Regnery, 2006.

Randall, Willard Sterne. *Benedict Arnold: Patriot and Traitor.* New York: Morrow, 1990.

Royster, Charles. *A Revolutionary People at War: The Continental Army and American Character, 1775–1783.* Chapel Hill: University of North Carolina Press, 1979.

Schecter, Barnet. *The Battle for New York: The City at the Heart of the American Revolution.* New York: Walker and Company, 2002.

Stephenson, Michael. *Patriot Battles: How the War of Independence Was Fought.* New York: HarperCollins, 2007.

Wood, Gordon S. *The Creation of the American Republic: 1776–1787.* Chapel Hill: University of North Carolina Press, 1998.

———. *The Radicalism of the American Revolution.* New York: Vintage Books, 1991.

———. *Revolutionary Characters: What Made the Founders Different.* New York: Penguin Books, 2006.

Part VI: Lafayette's Sword

Amar, Akhil Reed. *America's Constitution: A Biography.* New York: Random House, 2005

Bailyn, Bernard. *To Begin the World Anew: The Genius and Ambiguities of the American Founders.* New York: Knopf, 2003.

Beard, Charles A. *An Economic Interpretation of the Constitution of the United States.* Mineola, N.Y.: Dover, 2004.

Bowen, Catherine Drinker. *Miracle at Philadelphia: The Story of the Constitutional Convention, May to September 1787.* New York: Little. Brown, 1966.

Brookhiser, Richard. *Gentleman Revolutionary: Gouverneur Morris—The Rake Who Wrote the Constitution.* New York: Free Press, 2003.

Chernow, Ron. *Alexander Hamilton.* New York, Penguin, 2004

Collier, Christopher, and James Lincoln Collier. *Decision in Philadelphia:*

The Constitutional Convention of 1787. New York: Ballantine Books, 1986.

Dahl, Robert A. *How Democratic Is the American Constitution?* 2nd edition. New Haven, Conn.: Yale University Press, 2003.

Ellis, Joseph J. *American Sphinx: The Character of Thomas Jefferson.* New York: Knopf, 1997.

————. *Founding Brothers: The Revolutionary Generation.* New York: Knopf, 2001.

Flexner, James Thomas. *George Washington and the New Nation (1783–1793).* Boston: Little, Brown, 1970.

Holmes, David L. *The Faiths of the Founding Fathers.* New York: Oxford University Press, 2006.

Ketcham, Ralph, editor. *The Anti-Federalist Papers and the Constitutional Convention Debates.* New York: Mentor Books, 1996.

Larson, Edward J., and Michael P. Winship. *The Constitutional Convention: A Narrative History from the History of James Madison.* New York: Modern Library, 2005.

Levy, Leonard W. *Original Intent and the Framers' Constitution.* Chicago: Ivan R. Dee, 1988.

————. *Origins of the Bill of Rights.* New Haven, Conn.: Yale University Press, 2001.

Madison, James. *Notes of Debates in the Federal Convention of 1787.* New York: Norton, 1987.

————. *Writings.* New York: Library of America, 1999.

Rakove, Jack N. *James Madison and the Creation of the American Republic.* 2nd edition. New York: Longman, 2002.

————. *Original Meanings: Politics and Ideas in the Making of the Constitution.* New York: Knopf, 1996.

Richards, Leonard L. *Shays's Rebellion: The American Revolution's Final Battle.* Philadelphia: University of Pennsylvania Press, 2002.

Rossiter, Clinton, editor. *The Federalist Papers.* New York: Mentor Books, 1999.

Weisberger, Bernard A. *America Afire: Jefferson, Adams, and the First Contested Election.* New York: William Morrow, 2000.

Wills, Garry. *James Madison.* The American Presidents Series. New York: Henry Holt/ Times Books, 2002.

Wood, Gordon S. *The Creation of the American Republic: 1776–1787.* Chapel Hill: University of North Carolina Press, 1998.

Index

Index